UNCOVERING FOOD POVERTY IN IRELAND
A Hidden Deprivation

Michael Drew

First published in Great Britain in 2022 by

Policy Press, an imprint of
Bristol University Press
University of Bristol
1–9 Old Park Hill
Bristol
BS2 8BB
UK
t: +44 (0)117 374 6645
e: bup-info@bristol.ac.uk

Details of international sales and distribution partners are available at
policy.bristoluniversitypress.co.uk

British Library Cataloguing in Publication Data
A catalogue record for this book is available from the British Library

ISBN 978-1-4473-6153-4 hardcover
ISBN 978-1-4473-6154-1 ePub
ISBN 978-1-4473-6155-8 ePdf

Cover design: Clifford Hayes
Front cover image: Delicious bread on the table © Freepik and Euro coins
© Freepik
Bristol University Press and Policy Press use environmentally
responsible print partners.
Printed and bound in Great Britain by CPI Group (UK) Ltd,
Croydon, CR0 4YY

To those for whom life is a daily struggle

Contents

List of figures and tables

Figures

Tables

List of abbreviations

AROP	at-risk-of-poverty
AROPE	At Risk of Poverty or Social Exclusion
DCCAE	Department of Communications, Climate Action and Environment (renamed DoECC in 2020)
DoECC	Department of the Environment, Climate and Communications
DOEASP*	Department of Employment Affairs and Social Protection
DSP*	Department of Social Protection
ESRI	Economic and Social Research Institute
EU-SILC	European Union – Survey of Income and Living Conditions
FEAD	Fund for European Aid to the most Deprived
FEBA	European Food Banks Federation
HAP	Housing Assistance Payment
HRP	Household Reference Person
HSE	Health Service Executive
MESL	Minimum Essential Standard of Living
NAPinclusion	National Action Plan for Social Inclusion
OECD	Organisation for Economic Co-operation and Development
PRSI	Pay Related Social Insurance
RS	Rent Supplement
SDG	Sustainable Development Goals
SSM	social supermarket
SVP	The Society of Saint Vincent de Paul
UN FAO	United Nations Food and Agriculture Organization
VLWI	very low work intensity
WFP	Working Family Payment

*The DSP was renamed DOEASP in 2017 and subsequently reverted to DSP in 2020

Acknowledgements

I would like to thank the members and staff of the Society of Saint Vincent de Paul, who inspired this investigation. The insights provided by Liam Casey, in particular, were invaluable. Crosscare generously facilitated my study and I am grateful for the support and cooperation of their staff and volunteers. FoodCloud and other charities responded to all my queries and impressed with their dedication and progressive approach.

I acknowledge the support of UCD School of Social Policy, Social Work and Social Justice, particularly Nessa Winston and Stephan Köppe. The team at Policy Press were very encouraging and helpful throughout.

It would not have been possible to complete this work without the unfailing encouragement of my family. Thank you all!

Most importantly, no words would be adequate to thank all the recipients of food aid interviewed for this book. They selflessly told their stories, some through tears, but nonetheless stoical and determined to provide for their families. Invariably, their experiences were heart-breaking and I am humbled that they shared them with me.

1

Introduction

Background

Ireland's history of catastrophic famines is seared into the nation's collective memory. The disaster of crop failures that resulted in the Great Famine of 1845–52 is now scarcely imaginable. However, food poverty in 21st-century Ireland remains largely overlooked, reflecting a paucity of research and only occasional media coverage. In contrast to other developed Western countries, such as the United States and the United Kingdom, there has been limited discussion on food poverty, which can be understood in simple terms as the inability to afford or access a healthy diet. This book aims to address this gap, raise awareness of food poverty and consider the actions needed to address the issue effectively.

For many years, developed countries such as Ireland have had sufficient food supplies in aggregate terms, in addition to well-developed social safety nets (Riches, 1997a: 63). It therefore seems contradictory that food poverty remains a health and social issue, alongside problems of over-consumption and obesity. Despite economic progress, it is argued that the issue has re-emerged as a growing social policy concern. Food poverty affects over 300,000 people in Ireland (Department of Social Protection [DSP], 2020c) and there is evidence that the situation has been exacerbated by COVID-19. The financial impact of the pandemic has disproportionally affected groups that are already at high risk of food poverty, such as low-income families with children, lone parents, people with disabilities and renters (Society of St Vincent de Paul [SVP], 2021a).

While the profile of food poverty in Ireland remains low, the problem of global hunger and food nutrition has received considerable recognition over recent decades, from the United Nations and other international bodies with which Ireland is affiliated. The World Food Summit of 1996, organised by the UN Food and Agriculture Organization (UN FAO), declared that it was a universal right to have access to safe and nutritious food (UN FAO, 1996: 4). According to Riches (1997: 63), food security is a fundamental human right, which should be afforded 'the highest priority' by the state and civil society. Despite this international affirmation and concern, Dowler and O'Connor (2012) argue that neither Ireland nor the UK 'accepts or fulfils its obligations' (2012: 49). However, in research sponsored by the UK's Department for Environment, Food and Rural Affairs, over three quarters of survey respondents agreed that it was the responsibility of the British

Government to ensure 'basic food items are affordable for all UK residents' (Kneafsey et al, 2013: 109).

The UN Agenda for Sustainable Development was launched in 2015 and includes a target of zero hunger by 2030 (United Nations [UN], 2021a). This focus on food poverty follows other international initiatives, which have involved commitments by Ireland. The 'right to food', as set out in Article 11 of the International Covenant on Economic, Social and Cultural Rights (ICESCR), came into force in 1976 (UN, 2021b). Ireland signed and ratified the ICESCR in 1989, confirming its obligations under international law. In 1999, the right to adequate food was subsequently clarified by the UN in General Comment No. 12 as being: 'when every man, woman and child, alone or in community with others, has physical and economic access at all times to adequate food or means for its procurement' (UN, 2021c). Against this background, it is argued that addressing food poverty should be a key goal of public policy (Riches, 1997a: 66). This has not been the case in Ireland, prompting Friel and Conlon (2004: 10) and O'Connor et al (2008: 102) to question why such a fundamental issue has a low priority and profile in policy discussions on poverty. O'Connor has described the policy response to food poverty in Ireland as characterised by 'inaction, incoherence and ineffectiveness' (2018: 195). While the Government included a high-level goal of tackling energy poverty in its 'National Action Plan for Social Inclusion 2015–2017' (DOESP, 2016b), it was silent on the issue of food poverty.

The lack of visibility in Ireland is in sharp contrast to the UK, where experts have warned that food poverty should not be allowed to be the 'next public health emergency' (Taylor-Robinson et al, 2013: 7157). Recognising the seriousness of the problem, a representative body for public health professionals published an open letter to the British Prime Minister on food poverty (Ashton et al, 2014: 1631). Following these interventions, a Parliamentary Group on Hunger and Food Poverty was established to investigate 'the root causes of hunger and food poverty' (Downing et al, 2014: 1). This led to the publication of 'Feeding Britain', a report which set out several recommendations for further action (All-Party Parliamentary Inquiry, 2014). Meanwhile, food bank networks such as The Trussell Trust have undertaken campaigns advocating for policy measures to address food poverty. In addition, the activism of high-profile personalities such as Marcus Rashford, the English professional footballer, has had a significant impact in increasing awareness of the issue.

Given these developments, this book is timely and represents an important step towards raising the profile of food poverty in Ireland and enhancing understanding of the issue. It investigates the meaning of food poverty and the related concept of food insecurity. A quantitative analysis is undertaken to assess its prevalence in Ireland in a comparative European context. This is complemented by a qualitative strand, comprising interviews with food bank users in Dublin, a sub-group of those experiencing food poverty. Both approaches inform an examination of risk factors and structural barriers affecting pathways into and through food poverty, with a focus on core social policies that influence these trajectories. This leads to a review of the key factors driving the level and pattern of food charity in Ireland, together with the limitations of these responses and emerging trends in support models.

Literature on poverty and food poverty

Poverty

Understandings of poverty in the developed world have shifted over time from absolute to relative deprivation. Early interpretations of poverty focused on physical subsistence, reflecting the minimum needs to stay alive, with food regarded as one of the basic necessities (Smeeding, 2016). The modern literature was influenced in the 1960s and 1970s by academics, most notably Townsend, who argued that these basic needs had changed. In his interpretation, poverty meant that people were not able to purchase goods or be involved in activities expected of someone as part of normal day-to-day living, which resulted in them being excluded from society. Townsend defined poverty as relative deprivation, pointing out that lack of income results in people being excluded 'from ordinary living patterns, customs and activities' (1979: 31). This definition was subsequently adopted by the European Union (EU) in the mid-1980s (Nolan and Whelan, 2011: 4). Another strand of research explored the multifaceted aspects of poverty, illustrating that it is not only a question of financial resources, but also of a complex range of deprivations in areas such as food, health and housing (Alkire, 2007). This led to the development of non-monetary deprivation indicators to measure the experience of poverty, and these included different aspects of food poverty. The relevance of food poverty declined in importance as a factor in measuring deprivation, as poverty became interpreted by an increasing number of dimensions. This is illustrated by the range of non-monetary indicators which were developed for the Survey of Income and Living Conditions (EU-SILC), carried out across the EU from the mid-1990s. By 2016, out of a total of 24 principal items used as indicators of non-monetary deprivation, only four related to food poverty (Central Statistics Office [CSO], 2018a).

In contrast to Europe, food expenditure remains at the heart of poverty assessment in the United States (US). It was the foundation for official poverty measures developed in the 1960s, as part of the 'War on Poverty'. An absolute income threshold, the Orshansky scale, was introduced as the standard poverty measure in 1969 by the Federal Government (Fisher, 1992: 4). The budget standard was developed from the cost of basic but nutritionally adequate food plans, which were multiplied by a set factor to produce a poverty threshold. This US approach to measuring poverty in absolute terms has not changed significantly in recent decades.

Definitions

While poverty manifests itself in many ways, research on food poverty conveys that it is also complex and multi-faceted. Food poverty is 'central to the experience of poverty' (Friel and Conlon, 2004: 10) and the lack of food 'represents the very essence of poverty' (McIntosh, 1996: 133), while it usually arises from social exclusion (Purdy et al, 2007: 11). In the literature, food poverty is generally the term used in Europe, whereas the term food insecurity is prevalent in North America and Australia. However, both terms are sometimes used interchangeably. In Ireland, there is currently no official definition of food poverty, while Lambie-Mumford (2017: 20) points out that there is no agreed definition in the UK.

Food poverty has been described in the literature as 'the inability to access a nutritionally adequate diet and the related impacts on health, culture and social participation' (Friel and Conlon, 2004: 120). It has also been defined as 'the inability to have an adequate and nutritious diet, due to issues of affordability or accessibility' (Dowler, 1998). Both definitions convey that food poverty concerns the need to have sufficient quality and quantity of food. However, there are also references to impacts on social participation and being able to physically access suitable food. As in the case of food poverty, there is a lack of consensus on the definition and measurement of food insecurity (Radimer, 2002). A definition widely used in the US is that food insecurity exists 'whenever the availability of nutritionally adequate and safe foods or the ability to acquire acceptable food in socially acceptable ways is limited or uncertain' (Anderson, 1990: 1576). In order to investigate these terms, this book will review and seek to advance these concepts of food poverty.

Food poverty research

A review of the literature in Ireland indicates that food poverty is relatively under-researched. Studies have tended to focus on nutritional aspects and healthy eating, such as Friel et al (2006) and Friel and Conlon (2004). Purdy et al (2007) investigated the nutritional consumption patterns of low-income and deprived groups and how this negatively impacted on their health. Broader studies on how living on a low income affects different household types have provided evidence that some social groups are at higher risk of food poverty. For example, MacMahon et al (2017) found that for all household types in the year to March 2017, apart from pensioners, social welfare support was insufficient to support a Minimum Essential Standard of Living (MESL). Households with teenage children and single parents with teenagers were worst affected, with the basic cost of food and utilities representing a high proportion of household income. Some studies have addressed other facets, such as rights-based approaches (Dowler and O'Connor, 2012) and the physical availability of food outlets (Layte et al, 2011). Carney and Maître (2012) developed a food poverty indicator and subsequently carried out quantitative assessments of food poverty in Ireland using EU-SILC (discussed in Chapter 4). They estimated that food poverty peaked at 13.2 per cent of the population in 2013, with a reduction to 7 per cent in 2018. In relation to particularly vulnerable groups, a study was undertaken during 2002 and 2003 on food poverty and homelessness in Dublin (Hickey and Downey, 2003).

In comparison with Ireland, there has been significantly more research on food poverty in some other European countries, most particularly in the UK. Examples of the diversity of research focus include discussion on food poverty and politics (Livingstone, 2015) and consideration of a food poverty definition (Beacom et al, 2020). Other studies, such as Sosenko et al (2019), have sought to improve the evidence base and recommend areas for consideration by policymakers to address food poverty. Research on food poverty in Europe has been stimulated by the growth of food aid in the aftermath of the 2008 global financial crisis (Davis and Baumberg Geiger, 2017). Food banks have expanded their networks and other responses to food poverty have emerged, which have helped to increase awareness of the problem in many countries. Members of the European Food Banks Federation (FEBA), which represents food banks in 24 countries, provide over 700,000 tons of food products (the equivalent of 4.2 million daily meals) to 9.5 million people, through 40,000 charity partner organisations (FEBA, 2021). Country-specific research has revealed many different challenges faced across Europe. Caraher and Furey (2018) have reviewed the causes of food poverty in the UK, against the background of significant growth of food aid. Garthwaite (2016) investigated the experience of food bank users, while Loopstra et al (2015) examined the growth of food banks, including their locations and the implications of increased levels of food aid.

In Germany, Pfeiffer et al (2011) argue that there is a denial of the problem of food poverty by the political and social welfare systems. Their study provided quantitative and qualitative evidence to challenge this position, which is supported by the expanding network of community food banks across Germany. In Finland, the need for food aid was stimulated by a deep recession in the early 1990s, which put Nordic ideals of universalism under strain. Although food aid was envisaged as temporary relief during a difficult period, Silvasti and Karjalainen (2014: 72) reported that food poverty has been an issue since that time, reflecting the shortfall of welfare support in meeting basic household expenditure, including food. In Spain, the catalyst for the strong expansion of food banks was the international financial crisis of 2008, which resulted in a series of austerity measures that impacted on food poverty, particularly for vulnerable groups (Pérez de Armiño, 2014). Generous family solidarity, which has traditionally provided help to those experiencing food poverty, has recently shown signs of exhaustion, while Spain's income guarantee system has struggled to address the issue (Inza-Bartolomé and San-Epifanio, 2020). Reflecting the diverse landscape of food poverty across Europe, with many different structural issues influencing the problem, Ireland has its own set of policy drivers which are explored in detail in this book. These include challenges regarding social protection, housing, illness/disability, caring, low-pay and precarious employment.

In the US, awareness of food insecurity first re-emerged in the 1960s with the 'rediscovery' of hunger. The issue has sustained a relatively high public profile over several decades, with extensive literature on the topic. Recognising the importance of gathering regular data to assess its prevalence, national food security surveys have been carried out in the US since 1995. In 2019, 10.5 per cent of adults (13.7 million households) were reported as food insecure (Coleman-Jensen et al, 2020). Australia's National Health Survey 2011–12 found 5 per cent of the population were food insecure, but this is likely to be an underestimate (McKechnie et al, 2018). As pointed out by McKay et al (2019), measurement has been infrequent and food insecurity was not assessed during the National Health Survey in 2014–15 (Australian Bureau of Statistics, 2017). However, the problem was expected to increase in subsequent years, with groups such as single parents, refugees and children in socially disadvantaged households continuing to be most at risk (Lockie and Pietsch, 2012). The situation has been exacerbated with expenditure cuts by federal governments, including measures that restrict eligibility for welfare payments. It is important to acknowledge that food poverty and food security are often found to be linked to other aspects of poverty. For example, research on the experiences of low-income residents of Vancouver's Downtown Eastside highlighted the relationship between food security and difficulty obtaining adequate housing (Miewald and Ostry, 2014: 709). Another study found that low-income inner-city households with inadequate kitchens had a rate of food insecurity three times higher than those with better food storage and preparation facilities (Broughton et al, 2006).

Why a book on food poverty?

A review of the literature shows that there has been limited research on contemporary food poverty in Ireland. The research database Scopus indicates an increase of publications on the issue of food poverty internationally since

2007. While the UK and the US feature strongly in these publications, only eight articles concern food poverty in Ireland. This book aims to consider some questions that have yet to be addressed, given limitations in previous research on food poverty. The literature focuses on either food poverty or food insecurity and no study has been identified that compares these related concepts. This book takes a close look at what is meant by the term food poverty and compares this with food insecurity. It considers the prevalence of food poverty and locates Ireland's experience in an international context, reviewing how it compares with levels in other, similar jurisdictions. Analysis of secondary data sources on Ireland, using the latest deprivation indicators relating to food, facilitates a detailed assessment of the demographic and socio-economic characteristics associated with food poverty. Following investigation of the characteristics of those experiencing food poverty in Ireland, it explores the main pathways into and through food poverty and how it is experienced. This is undertaken through interviews with food bank users, seeking to determine the reasons why food aid was needed and their lived experience of food poverty. The book then analyses the key policy drivers of food poverty in Ireland, as a major aim is to understand the policy context of food poverty and its role in contributing to the problem. Policy lessons are then drawn from the evidence, complementing existing qualitative studies in Ireland, which have focused on health and nutritional aspects (Safefood, 2011). Responses to food poverty by the state and the voluntary sector are also considered in an EU15 context. The focus is on the key factors that are shaping developments and how these will impact the likely future evolution of responses.

Structural outline

Chapter 2 draws on the international poverty literature in order to provide context for the investigation, including a historical overview on how interpretations of poverty have changed and how it has been defined and measured. This is followed by a more detailed review of both food poverty and food insecurity, including definitions, measurement and empirical findings. The chapter considers research on food bank use, which provides an indirect indication of food poverty. This leads to an investigation of risk factors associated with food poverty and the growth of food aid. An overview of core areas of social policy that potentially influence food poverty is also provided.

Chapter 3 provides an overview of poverty research in Ireland from a food perspective and factors that influence food poverty. It includes an overview of the literature on core areas of social policy relevant to contemporary food poverty in Ireland. Risk factors include demographic and socio-economic characteristics, the cost of food, household and accommodation type, as well as location-based food poverty. The review of policy areas includes social protection, the minimum/living wage, precarious work, in-work poverty and caring responsibilities.

Chapter 4 provides a comparative quantitative analysis of Ireland with the largest economies in Europe (EU15), drawing on EU and Organisation for Economic Co-operation and Development (OECD) surveys for food poverty and UN for food insecurity. The chapter also builds on existing quantitative research to provide an updated analysis of food poverty in Ireland, using the latest secondary data available. This analysis explores the characteristics of those experiencing food poverty in Ireland and considers factors that may predict food poverty.

Chapter 5 and Chapter 6 present the results of interviews with food bank users in Dublin. The overarching framework of these chapters is a pathways approach, which assesses the different trajectories into (Chapter 5) and through (Chapter 6) food poverty for participants in the research study. These two chapters set out a thematic analysis of the data generated from interviews, involving more than 40 participants. The discussion identifies important social policy issues that impact on these pathways.

Chapter 6 presents the results of the interviews with respondents regarding their pathways through and lived experience of food poverty. These include the emotional experience of obtaining food aid and living in food poverty. The work uncovers the impacts of these experiences, including hunger and social exclusion. The discussion also reveals multidimensional aspects of life on a low income, including fuel poverty, and how respondents use multiple strategies to cope with these challenges.

Chapter 7 considers key social policy areas influencing food poverty in Ireland. It reflects back on the themes introduced in the literature review and assesses each area in the light of the results of analysing the research data. The discussion is informed by both the literature, the secondary analysis and the evidence from the interviews with food bank users.

Chapter 8 explores responses to food poverty in Ireland from both the state and the voluntary sector, in a comparative EU15 context. This includes the key role of the EU-wide Fund for European Aid to the most Deprived (FEAD), facilitated in Ireland by FoodCloud. It investigates the landscape of food charity in Ireland, which has been influenced by the rising importance of food surpluses, linked to sustainable development. The impact of the COVID-19 pandemic and emerging developments in support models are also considered.

Chapter 9 draws together the main findings of the work. It summarises what has been learned about the prevalence of food poverty in Ireland. It brings together the complex picture emerging from interviews with food bank users, through an analysis of their pathways into and through food poverty. These pathways are impacted by a range of policies and practices of government, employers and other relevant stakeholders, which have wide-ranging implications. The work reflects on experiences in Ireland and responses to food poverty in a comparative European context. It concludes by considering how these results contribute to an understanding of the problem and what action needs to be taken.

2

An international perspective

Introduction

The international literature on poverty is extensive and this chapter seeks to focus on the importance of food in this discourse. It reviews the literature relating to both food poverty and food insecurity, which examines definitions, measurement and the results of recent empirical research. An overview of food bank research and the growth of charitable responses leads to consideration of the explanations for food poverty.

Poverty is a contested concept, characterised by continuous change (Coakley, 2004: 112). Understandings of poverty and how to deal with the problem tend to vary across countries, as well as over time, and there is no politically neutral perspective (Menton, 2007: 149). Perspectives have shifted from absolute to relative, while Sen (1984) offers an alternative capabilities approach. As pointed out by Ravaillon (1992: v), the measurement of poverty is often 'clouded in conceptual and methodological uncertainties', with approaches ranging from unidimensional to multidimensional (Walker, 2014: 15). In developed countries, absolute measures of poverty were used until the second half of the last century, normally based on physical subsistence needs, such as food (Spicker et al, 2007: 7). Reflecting economic progress and the emergence of welfare states, these measures suggested that poverty was no longer a serious problem (Walker, 2014: 17). In the second half of the 20th century, the measurement of poverty shifted to a relative approach in many countries, with measures set in comparison to income or consumption levels across society (Smeeding, 2016). Since the 1970s, approaches to poverty measurement have also been framed in terms of non-monetary deprivation measures, often combined with income (Menton, 2007: 7). No one method or set of measures is commonly agreed, as 'in attempting to understand the changing nature of poverty, it is unwise to rely on any single measure' (Layte et al, 2000: 571).

As is the case for poverty in general, the specific concept of food poverty is contested and the theoretical debate conveys complex and multi-faceted conceptualisations. In Europe, the terms food poverty and food insecurity are sometimes used interchangeably, although the latter term predominates in the US. As researchers have adopted different approaches to both defining and measuring these concepts, their findings tend to vary. The main approaches have been surveys of individuals/households asking about the topic or investigations of the use of food banks/food aid.

Poverty: a food perspective

In the poverty literature, food has been regarded as a key aspect of poverty, given that 'a family is poor if it cannot afford to eat' (Joseph and Sumption, 1979: 27). Historical definitions of poverty reflect a time when it was seen in subsistence terms (Cantillon, 2000). 'Absolute poverty' is the term used to describe people who lack the basic physical requirements of food, water, clothing and shelter (Williamson and Reutter, 1999). Absolute poverty definitions were used in Western Europe up until the mid-1980s, but are now mainly used in the context of developing countries.

Early work on poverty, which followed a subsistence approach, focused on the nutrition required to undertake paid work (production) and rear children (Lister, 2004: 21). In some cases, this research was instigated as a result of social unrest among the poor, due to lack of food. For example, studies of family budgets undertaken in Europe during the 19th century reflected concern about the increasing unrest among the working classes that led to the revolutions of 1848 (Stigler, 1954: 96). One of the most prominent 19th-century statisticians, Ernst Engel, Director of the Statistical Bureau of Saxony, investigated the social condition of the poor and established food as a key aspect of poverty: 'The poorer is a family, the greater is the proportion of the total outgo which must be used for food.... The proportion of the outgo used for food, other things being equal, is the best measure of the material standard of living of a population' (Engel quoted in Zimmerman, 1932: 80). Engel's studies influenced later research on budget standards, both in Europe and in North America, where Engel's Law was used by Orshansky in establishing poverty thresholds based on food plans (Wayand, 1970).

The motives of pioneering poverty researchers were mostly driven by philanthropic concerns. Social reformer and early pioneer, Charles Booth (1840–1916), carried out innovative work in London identifying and describing the conditions of the poor. He was indignant about how many people were 'ill-fed, ill-clad and ill-housed' (Spicker, 1990: 22). Inspired by the work of Booth, Rowntree (1836–1925) surveyed poverty in York at the turn of the 20th century and took into account the 'minimum necessaries for the maintenance of merely physical efficiency' (1901: 87). He found that food accounted for the largest share of subsistence, although there was a small allowance for other necessary household items such as clothing, light and fuel.

Following increases in living standards, understandings of poverty in the developed world evolved over time from the concept of subsistence. This was a gradual paradigm shift, with an emerging recognition that poverty should be described in terms of relative, rather than absolute, deprivation. Lister (2004: 27) argues that, while Booth and Rowntree put forward subsistence definitions of poverty, they were conscious that the basic needs of the poor were social and not merely for 'physical efficiency'. Booth referred to poverty as a relative concept, arguing that the 'very poor' were those whose resources were less than required 'according to the normal standards of life in this country' (1892: 33). Rowntree acknowledged that some poor people used their scarce resources on social pursuits, rather than food:

> The explanation is that working people are just as human as those with more money. They cannot live just on a 'fodder basis'. They crave for relaxation and recreation just as the rest of us do. But … they can only get these things by going short of something which is essential to physical fitness, and so they go short, and the national standard of health is correspondingly lowered. (1937: 126)

Townsend developed the highly influential concept of relative deprivation. He argued that the subsistence approach represented a narrow conception of human needs and that, if individuals experience a sharp fall in resources, they may choose to meet their social obligations before their basic physical requirements (1993: 47). In his seminal study, 'Poverty in the United Kingdom', Townsend defined relative poverty:

> Individuals, families and groups in the population can be said to be in poverty when they lack the resources to obtain the types of diet, participate in the activities and have the living conditions and amenities which are customary, or at least are widely encouraged or approved, in the societies to which they belong. Their resources are so seriously below those commanded by the average individual or family that they are, in effect, excluded from ordinary living patterns, customs and activities. (1979: 31)

In this definition, Townsend highlighted the importance of food, referring to being unable to have a normal diet and being excluded from social aspects of participation in society, which can often relate to food. Reflecting that people are 'social as well as physical beings' (Lister, 2004: 24), Mack and Lansley describe poverty as an 'enforced lack of socially perceived necessities' (1985: 39). Physiological needs, such as the nutrients required for physical functioning, will vary according to an individual's work and dietary customs. They are thus inextricably linked to the social and cultural situation, reflecting social responsibilities and expectations. As people eat 'food, not nutrients' (Dowler and Leather, 2000: 208), consumption of food has been described as 'an expression of who a person is, what they are worth, and of their ability to provide for basic needs' (2000: 200). In 1985, the European Commission adopted a definition of poverty that was broadly aligned with Townsend's approach, which suggests that it was a critical juncture in the interpretation of poverty (European Commission, 1985).

In offering an alternative lens to the narrow focus of poverty analysis in terms of low income, Sen contributed to the conceptualisation of poverty by focusing on individual capabilities. Sen acknowledged that there is 'an irreducible absolutist core in the idea of poverty' (1983: 159), citing the need 'to meet nutritional requirements, to be sheltered, to be clothed … to live without shame' (1983: 162–3). While economists have conventionally approached poverty measurement from an income and expenditure (consumption) perspective, Sen's approach used broader criteria, including the 'capabilities to be and to do things of intrinsic worth' (Kingdon and Knight, 2006: 1199). Sen introduced the concept of a person's 'capabilities', where poverty is understood as deprivation in the capability to live a good life (to be nourished, healthy and so on). His interpretation of poverty is that it is 'not ultimately a matter of incomes at all', but is a 'failure to achieve certain minimum capabilities' (1983: 670). Capability is the 'freedom to achieve valuable functionings' (Coates et al, 2013: 164). Functionings range from basic achievements, such as adequate food, good health and shelter to more complex states, such as being safe, being happy and having self-respect. A person's total opportunities depend on the set of all functionings from which they can choose, given the set of resources at their command.

Townsend challenged this approach, contending in a rejoinder to Sen that his conceptualisation did not adequately take into account 'the social nature of peoples' lives and needs' (1985: 667). Townsend argued that human needs, such as food and shelter, are relative to society and this has to be at the core of any poverty analysis. This was on the basis that food requirements depend on activity, such as work roles, and vary across time and cultures. Gordon regarded much of this debate as a matter of semantic definitions (2006: 34), referring to Sen's comment that 'there is no conflict between the irreducible absolutist element of the notion of poverty … and the thoroughgoing relativity to which Townsend refers' (1985: 674).

According to Lister (2004: 15), Sen's ideas are 'percolating through' and this is supported by Hick (2012), who argues that the capabilities approach has become more established, despite differences arising from the debates with Townsend. Sen's capabilities approach highlighted that conventional economic measures (such as individuals' income levels) do not reflect 'the reality of people's lives' (Kennedy, 2013: 20). Money is a means to an end, as the goods and services obtained are pathways to achieve outcomes. Sen's work has contributed to a more multidimensional approach to the examination of poverty (Jenkins and Micklewright, 2007: 9), reflecting how multiple disadvantages can be experienced, rather than just low income. Further evidence of the influence of Sen's capabilities approach was provided when it was adopted by the United Nations Development Programme.

Some research has been carried out to progress a human development and capability approach to food security in the context of developing countries (Burchi and De Muro, 2012). Using this approach, hunger and food insecurity is considered as a capability deprivation, which can impact on human development, including health, nutrition, education and security.

Measurement of poverty

Absolute poverty

In the early 20th century, Rowntree (1901) took an absolutist approach, constructing a poverty line which was based on the cost of sufficient food to meet basic nutritional requirements and essential clothing, household and fuel needs. Using this budget standard method, it was deemed that anyone below this level would experience 'primary poverty'. This method has the advantage that basic needs are, at least at a superficial level, being assessed scientifically and can be indexed to prices. However, needs may be determined by social criteria and are therefore open to debate, while Atkinson (1983: 226) has pointed out that nutritional estimates for physical efficiency cannot be precise. In addition, actual data on household expenditure are often used to determine needs for those on low incomes, which is a further weakness in the methodology, as these may not be judged as necessities (Maître et al, 2006: 15). Despite these limitations, the measurement of household income using a subsistence 'poverty line' standard heavily influenced much early work on poverty, which Townsend argued reflected 'an out-dated conception of needs in modern society' (Townsend, 1979: 160).

The food ratio method, an alternative approach to poverty measurement, establishes a poverty line by multiplying the cost of a basic diet by an agreed factor (Fisher, 2008). For example, a US household food survey in the mid-1950s established that a typical household spent about one third of its income on food and this was used as a multiplier to calculate a poverty threshold (Poppendieck, 1998). This method is relatively simple, as it avoids the need to specify what is needed for subsistence (Callan and Nolan, 1991). However, it also has limitations, as the amount spent on necessities can vary significantly for each income level and problems arise in adjusting these lines over time, in light of changes in both consumer prices and spending patterns (Nolan and Whelan, 1996: 16). Rein (1970: 61) points out that a definition of poverty based on nutritional requirements depends on an expert definition and on living patterns, a procedure which lacks scientific precision and requires value judgements. By way of example, McKenzie (1970: 71) described a study where the recommended allowance of Vitamin C for adults from the United States National Research Council at 70 milligrams per day was over three times the British Medical Association recommendation of 20 milligrams per day. Where poverty lines were based on dietary requirements, they have often been the bare minimum. For example, Rowntree created a diet that was 'more austere than that provided in workhouses and prisons', explaining that this was 'because I didn't want people to say, "Rowntree's crying for the moon"' (Englander and O'Day, 1995: 216, quoting a letter to Caradog Jones from 1952). This defensive stance is perhaps understandable given criticisms of his work, including from those who viewed poverty as a moral failure of individuals not providing for self and family (Bowpitt, 2000: 25).

Measurement of poverty in the United States

In the US, food has played a core role in the definition and measurement of poverty. The official poverty line still in use today, the Orshansky Scale, was designated in 1969 as the standard poverty measure used by the Federal Government (Fisher, 1992: 4). The US has a long tradition of reporting poverty statistics based on thresholds, which are based on applying a multiplier to a budget standard which was developed using low-cost food plans (Spicker et al, 2007: 212). Orshansky carried out a number of family income studies during the 1960s, based on Bureau of Census data. She found that one in seven of families of two (or more) people and nearly half of those living alone (or with non-relatives) had incomes below the required level to afford even a basic diet required to provide sufficient nutrients and pay for other basic necessities (1965: 4). Orshansky developed a range of poverty thresholds and it was decided to use the lowest 'economy' level as a working definition of poverty. Food plans were the only area of expenditure costed and the chosen food plan was a subsistence diet intended for short-term use (Poppendieck, 1998: 51). It was found that across families of three or more individuals at all income levels, food expenditure accounted for approximately one third of their income after taxes (Fisher, 1992: 4). Using the food ratio method, it was therefore decided to use a multiplier of three to calculate poverty thresholds for such families (with adjustments for smaller families to reflect relatively higher fixed costs). Orshansky referred to these poverty thresholds, which were based on the dollar cost of food, as effectively an absolute measure of poverty (1959: 10). As Orshansky observed, managing economically within the constraints of a low-cost food plan requires restrictions on food quality and variety, together with food preparation skills, to ensure adequate and acceptable meals (1965: 5).

Nolan and Whelan (1996) argue that the US view of poverty has not broadened out beyond the relatively narrow focus of the 1960s, indicating a high level of path dependency in redistributive and poverty policymaking. The methodology behind the poverty thresholds developed by Orshansky has remained in use but, although adjusted annually for changes in the cost of living, it has not been updated to reflect changes in dietary customs or needs. According to Hutto et al (2011), there is widespread agreement that the measure is no longer effective at determining the needs of families in the US. The methodology has a number of shortcomings, such as using the same poverty line across the US, which assumes that the cost of living is similar in each state. Over 20 years ago, Townsend expressed 'astonishment' (1993: 34) that the US was still implementing a poverty line based on household surveys carried out as long ago as 1955 and 1961. The Orshansky poverty thresholds are still used for poverty estimates, but are complemented by poverty guidelines, which determine eligibility for poverty relief programmes (Fisher, 2008).

Relative poverty

In Europe, most government and research studies measure poverty levels by assessing household income relative to an income poverty line, set as the average or median level for the particular country. The poverty threshold as a percentage of the median is normally set on an arbitrary basis, as 40 per cent, 50 per cent or 60 per cent of the national median (Walker, 2014: 17). However, the official at-risk-of-poverty (AROP) rate in Ireland uses the benchmark of 60 per cent of median income and this is the main threshold used for the EU Common Indicators of Social Protection and Social Inclusion (Watson et al, 2012).

The literature conveys that there are limitations on the sole use of income measures in poverty measurement. In considering the conceptualisation of poverty in relative terms, Watson et al (2012: 9) argue that low income 'does not identify those who are excluded from a customary standard of living due to a lack of resources'. Atkinson et al (2002) point out the limitations of using income measurements exclusively, as an assessment of poverty, while Layte et al (2004: 4) opine that the use of such measures alone 'can potentially be seriously misleading as to the level and causes of poverty'. Ringen (1988) argues that, if poverty is assessed in terms of a low standard of living, income only provides an indirect measure, while deprivation indicators provide a direct measure. As a result of these limitations, further studies were undertaken that combined income-based measures and non-monetary indicators to improve poverty assessment. Ireland was one of the first countries to set national targets based on a multidimensional approach using deprivation indicators (Callan et al, 1993), which are discussed later.

Material deprivation

In parallel with shifting understandings of poverty over time, it became clear that poverty cannot be measured adequately using a single measure. When Townsend set out a relative definition of poverty in 1979, he carried out pioneering studies using non-monetary indicators, which helped to highlight the prevailing deprivation experienced by the poor in Britain (Nolan and Whelan, 2011: 2). Non-monetary indicators provide insights into what people have or are able to do, as well as what they cannot have, such as a meal with meat, chicken, fish (or vegetarian equivalent) every second day. Subsequently, 'Breadline Britain' studies carried out by Mack and Lansley (1985: 294) took a new perspective and sought to improve Townsend's methodology by asking a sample of respondents to identify a list of necessities. The use of these indicators was subsequently taken up by the EU, initially through the European Community Household Panel Survey (ECHP), which ran from 1994 to 2001. In order to assess material deprivation, the survey included questions as to whether the household possessed items such as a car or telephone and, if not, was this because they could not be afforded. There were approximately 24 items (some of which were drawn from Townsend's 1979 study), of which only two related to food poverty. While the inclusion of a wide range of everyday items and activities helped to highlight the multidimensionality of poverty, it resulted in the dilution of food poverty in overall poverty measurement.

The approach of seeking to measure poverty using more than one dimension of well-being was influenced by research indicating that the population of people on low income may be different from that of the most materially deprived (Cappellari and Jenkins, 2007). Increasing efforts were made to capture useful supplementary data from non-monetary indicators to help identify the poor and to capture the multidimensionality of poverty (Nolan and Whelan, 2007: N162). Given the difficulty of measuring material poverty, it is not surprising that Townsend's attempts to measure relative poverty proved controversial. Townsend undertook empirical work to calculate an objective measure of poverty, but encountered criticism from Mack and Lansley (2015: 15) that the measures he used as a standard of necessity in creating a 'deprivation index' were arbitrary. Mack and Lansley found that one of the top three necessities was having two meals per day, which 3 per cent of households were unable to afford (2015: 19). This represented a level of food poverty that had not been reached for 30 years (2015: 38). In relation to quality of food, their survey reported that affording fresh fruit and vegetables was regarded as a necessity by 83 per cent of respondents. However, adults had to go without these products in an increasing number of households, up from 5 per cent in 1999 to 7 per cent in 2012 (2015: 38).

Assessments of deprivation have been incorporated into national anti-poverty strategies, and deprivation indicators are now included in major social surveys at EU level. These include the EU-SILC, which is now established as a key reference source in relation to statistics on poverty across the EU (Nolan and Whelan, 2011: 23).

Food poverty and food insecurity: definitions, measurement and empirical findings

Definitions of food poverty

The term 'food poverty' locates the concept as an aspect of the experience of being poor, while poverty and deprivation have 'contributed synergistically to food poverty' (Dowler, 2003: 572). Issues that drive social exclusion, such as low educational attainment, lack of employment, health inequalities and poor-quality environments (Bradshaw et al, 2004), may also create or exacerbate existing problems of food poverty in disadvantaged areas. Purdy et al (2007: 11) argue that food poverty is 'caused by more than an infrequent occurrence that results in a poor diet and usually arises from a range of associated problems'. They, like many researchers, locate it in a social exclusion framework, which reveals its multidimensional aspects. No commonly accepted definition of food poverty has been located in the literature. Dowler and O'Connor (2012) regard food poverty as synonymous with food insecurity, which Lambie-Mumford points out has no agreed definition, at least in the UK (2017: 20). In Ireland, the first National Anti-Poverty Strategy (Government of Ireland, 1997) set out a definition of poverty, but there is no corresponding official definition of food poverty (Hickey and Downey, 2003: 7). This may reflect the evolution over time of our understanding of this concept, an ongoing process influenced by changes in society and prevailing attitudes. Although there is currently a lack of an officially endorsed indicator, a qualitative study in Northern Ireland with policymakers, food bank representatives and other stakeholders concluded that an agreed definition of food poverty would aid understanding and awareness of the problem (Beacom et al, 2020).

In the absence of an official definition, the following four conceptualisations prominent in the literature are reviewed.

1. 'The inability to access a nutritionally adequate diet and the related impacts on health, culture and social participation' (Friel and Conlon, 2004: 120).
2. 'The inability to have an adequate and nutritious diet due to issues of affordability or accessibility' (Dowler, 1998).
3. 'The inability to afford, or to have access to, food to make up a healthy diet' (Department of Health UK, 2005: 7).
4. 'The inability to afford, or have reasonable access to, food which provides a healthy diet. Whilst the link between nutritional status and low income is well established, food poverty extends beyond economic aspects to include issues such as access, ethnicity and education' (Food Standards Agency Wales, 2003: 7).

A comparison between these definitions is set out in Table 2.1. Each definition contains explicit reference to having sufficient quantity and quality of food. Research indicates a link between education and poor dietary habits, with studies showing that level of education can predict quality of diet (Harrington et al, 2011). Poor literacy and numeracy skills can also be a barrier to information in relation to healthy eating and managing a household budget (Mwatsama and Stewart, 2005: 3). Research has shown that those without educational qualifications are more likely to eat unbalanced diets (Robinson et al, 2004), while low educational attainment has been established as a risk factor for eating less fruit and vegetables (Barker et al, 2008).

Only two of the four definitions refer to the social implications of food poverty. The literature refers to many social aspects of food, such as food acquisition strategies and consumption types/levels, together with the risk of social exclusion for those experiencing food poverty (Pfeiffer et al, 2011: 418). For example, food acquisition may present difficulties for those experiencing food poverty. In this situation, people may be forced to implement food acquisition strategies and have food consumption patterns that diverge from social norms and contribute to social exclusion (Dowler and Leather, 2000). Riches argues that an inability to afford to shop at the local supermarket, thus having to rely on occasional food-bank supplies, is humiliating and 'personally undermining and stigmatising' (1997a: 65). Dowler and Dobson agree that people should be able to 'shop like everyone else', without being isolated and forced to purchase only low-cost options or resort to handouts (1997: 56).

According to Pfeiffer et al, food and nutrition are 'the most basic and central participation mechanism in every social system' (2011: 420). Food practices are both 'shaped by, and help to construct' social relationships (Wills, 2011: 3). This reflects the important function that food plays in everyday life, as set out by Feichtinger: 'Apart from its biological functions, food has many social, cultural and psychological functions. Food is an important vehicle for social relationships, communication and control. It not only conveys friendship, integration and acceptance, but social status, differences in social standing and exclusion as well' (Feichtinger, 1997: 47). Food is a 'focus for social exchange' (Dowler, 1998: 58), and cultural norms include social activities involving food (Carney and Maître, 2012: 5). Food provides an avenue for status to be expressed: in many societies people are able to demonstrate this through having guests for meals and eating out (McIntosh, 1996: 133). Given that food has significant social and cultural value, food poverty links with and exacerbates social exclusion, as people in need are effectively excluded from a method of participation in modern society (Pfeiffer et al, 2011). In addition to providing opportunity for hospitality, food helps to ensure individual and group identity, as it is regarded as a

Table 2.1: Definitions of food poverty and food insecurity/food security

Definitions of food poverty	Dimensions			
	Quantity of food	Quality of food	Social*	Psychological**
'The inability to access a nutritionally adequate diet and the related impacts on health, culture and social participation' (Friel and Conlon, 2004: 120).	✓	✓	✓	×
'The inability to afford, or to have access to, food to make up a healthy diet' (Department of Health UK, 2005: 7).	✓	✓	×	×
'The inability to have an adequate and nutritious diet due to issues of affordability or accessibility' (Dowler, 1998).	✓	✓	×	×
'The inability to afford, or have reasonable access to, food which provides a healthy diet. Whilst the link between nutritional status and low income is well established, food poverty extends beyond economic aspects to include issues such as access, ethnicity and education' (Food Standards Agency Wales, 2003: 7).	✓	✓	✓	×
Definitions of food insecurity/food security	**Dimensions**			
	Quantity of food	**Quality of food**	**Social***	**Psychological****
'Food insecurity is limited or uncertain availability of nutritionally adequate and safe foods or limited or uncertain ability to acquire acceptable foods in socially acceptable ways' (Anderson, 1990).	✓	✓	✓	✓
'Food insecurity – the inability to acquire or consume an adequate quality or sufficient quantity of food in socially acceptable ways, or the uncertainty that one will be able to do so' (Davis and Tarasuk, 1994).	✓	✓	✓	✓
'Food insecurity – lack of consistent, dependable access to enough food for active, healthy living' (Coleman-Jensen et al, 2014: v).	✓	✓	×	✓
'Food security – existing when all people at all times have access to sufficient, safe, nutritious food to maintain a healthy and active life' (World Food Summit, 1996).	✓	✓	×	✓

Notes: * Social aspects include social participation and being able to access food in socially acceptable ways. ** Psychological aspects include worry and anxiety about food access.

means to express who we are, who we are connected to and a sense of belonging (Wills, 2011). Some argue that food poverty refers to cultural or social elements, as available food needs to be 'culturally appropriate and acceptable, as well as affordable' (Bowyer et al, 2009: 6). A research study on low-income families in Ireland by MacMahon and McEvoy (2018) reported that birthdays, Christmas and other religious celebrations result in a severe strain on financial resources, causing stress and worry.

Definitions of food insecurity

Food insecurity, as for food poverty, is an elusive concept (Barrett, 2010: 825). In the US, following increasing public awareness and concern about the problem in the 1960s (Kotz, 1969: vii), it was argued that lack of agreement about definitions of food insecurity and hunger held back the development of public policies to deal with the problem (Radimer, 2002: 859). Hunger has been defined as 'a condition resulting from chronic under-consumption of food and/or nutritious food products' (Lenhart and Read, 1989: 1269). Recognised as a complex issue, it has been described as a 'many-headed monster', which is related to biological, economic and social deprivations (Drèze and Sen, 1989). A high-level panel set up by the US Department of Agriculture (USDA) expressed concern about the 'lack of conceptual clarity' regarding the use of terms such as hunger and food insecurity (National Research Council, 2005: 33). However, it was particularly concerned about the use of the term 'hunger', which was felt to be a 'very politically sensitive word' (2005: 33). Hunger is seen as an extreme form of food insecurity, which is the prevailing term generally used in the recent literature.

The definition of food insecurity used by the US Department of Health and Human Services was developed by the American Institute of Nutrition. It states that food insecurity exists 'whenever the availability of nutritionally adequate and safe foods or the ability to acquire acceptable food in socially acceptable ways is limited or uncertain' (Anderson, 1990: 1576). The reference to quality, quantity and socially acceptable access to food are key elements included in most food poverty definitions. However, the uncertainty arising from limited availability or ability to access appropriate food introduces an aspect absent from definitions of food poverty. This psychological dimension is experienced as worry or anxiety caused by uncertainty relating to aspects of food supply (Radimer, 2002: 860). Davis and Tarasuk (1994: 50) have put forward a definition that aligns closely with Anderson's and captures the uncertainty regarding food access. They define the term food insecurity as 'the inability to acquire or consume an adequate quality or sufficient quantity of food in socially acceptable ways, or the uncertainty that one will be able to do so'. The USDA, which operates a monitoring programme for state food and nutrition assistance programmes, defines food insecurity as the 'lack of consistent, dependable access to enough food for active, healthy living' (Coleman-Jensen et al, 2014: v). As in the aforementioned conceptualisation by Davis and Tarasuk, the uncertainty regarding access is clearly conveyed. It is apparent that, although definitions of food poverty and food insecurity are similar, not all include the same aspects. A comparison of definitions of food insecurity is included in Table 2.1, together with those of food poverty discussed earlier. Understanding these conceptual differences will guide the development of measures to assess food poverty, both comparatively and in Ireland. In the following paragraphs, the different measures of food poverty are reviewed, which will form the basis for the quantitative analysis in this work.

Measuring food poverty and food insecurity

Food poverty

A review of the literature indicates that food poverty is a global problem in advanced countries. Riches and Silvasti (2014: 193) argue that food poverty in advanced economies increased during and after the global recession of 2007–09. However, they point out that little official data are collected systematically on the prevalence of the problem, which makes empirical cross-national comparisons challenging (2014: 193). In many countries, food poverty is not measured at a household or individual level by surveys designed for this purpose (Lambie-Mumford and Dowler, 2014). As in other countries, researchers in Ireland use food-related measures from general surveys or proxy measures, such as the use of food banks, to assess food poverty. However, after years of campaigning from advocacy groups and parliamentarians, the UK now measures food insecurity annually, using questions designed for this purpose. This is described in the section on food insecurity further on, which also discusses the regular surveys undertaken in the US and Canada.

The OECD (2014b) has highlighted the growing problem of food poverty in many advanced countries. Their analysis is based on one question in a representative survey, which assesses the proportion of people who respond 'yes' to the question: 'Have there been times in the last 12 months when you did not have enough money to buy food that you or your family needed?' The percentage of people in Ireland who said that they cannot afford food increased to 9 per cent in the 2011–12 survey, from 4 per cent in 2006–07 (see Figure 2.1). This figure (9 per cent) is significantly below the US (21 per cent) and Canada (12 per cent), but slightly higher than the UK (8 per cent) and wealthy European countries such as Germany and Switzerland, which report the lowest levels. While more recent OECD 'Society at a Glance' reports on social indicators were published in 2016 and 2019, they did not cover food poverty.

Figure 2.1: Percentage of people who feel they cannot afford food, by country (2006–07 and 2011–12)

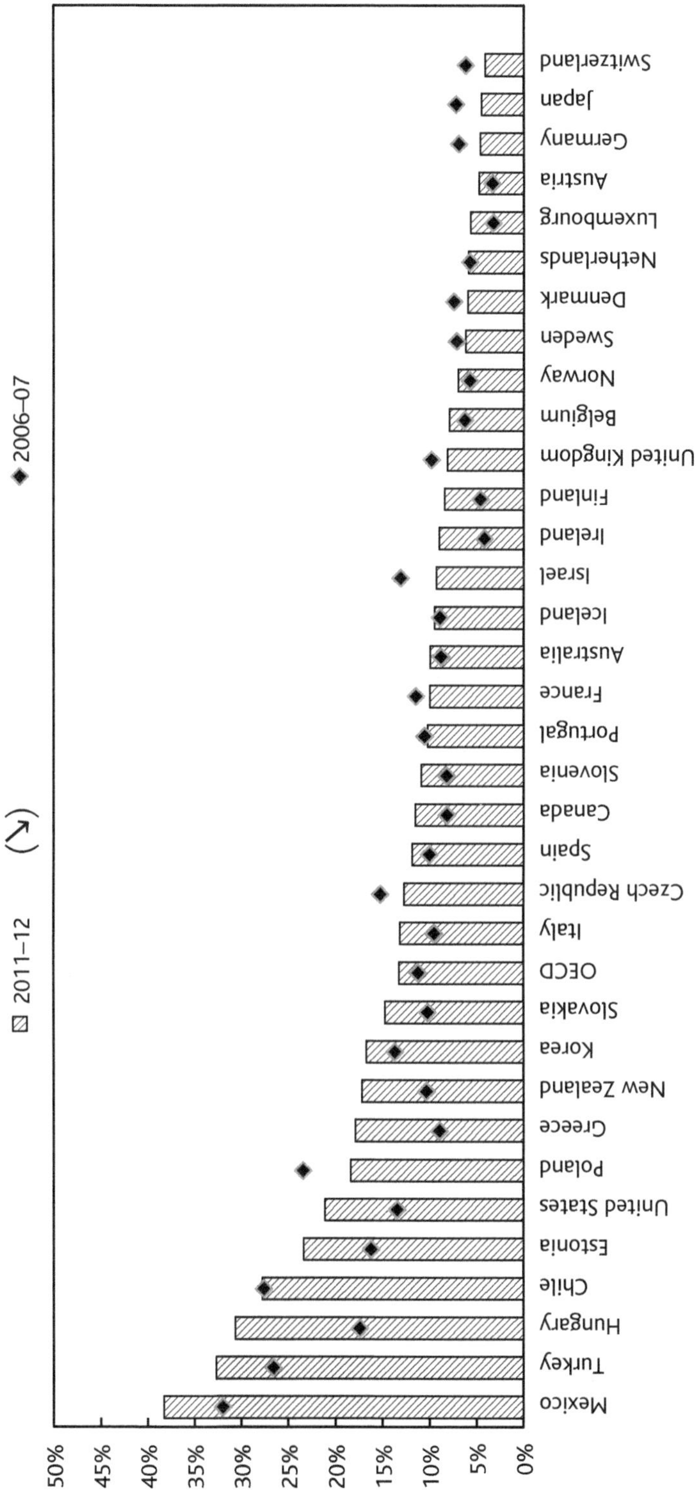

Source: (OECD, 2014b: 28)

Research on the measurement of food poverty has largely centred around two main areas. Some studies have collated and analysed information from different sources relating to food expenditure patterns, specifically focusing on health inequalities and poor dietary consumption (Friel and Conlon, 2004). Other work has sought to identify operational measures using food deprivation indicators, which are either part of broader surveys, such as the EU-SILC, or specifically used to assess food poverty at household level (Carney and Maître, 2012). In the European Union, the European Council has adopted outcome indicators to help monitor the progress of member states in achieving social inclusion (Marlier et al, 2007: 143). The first main harmonised data source was the European Community Household Panel survey (ECHP). In 2007, the ECHP was replaced by 'Community Statistics on Income and Living Conditions' (EU-SILC), in which Ireland is an active participant.

The official measure used to assess consistent poverty uses 11 items in a deprivation index, each of which is considered to be a social norm in Irish society (Carney and Maître, 2012: 10). The purpose is to measure the percentage of people who experience enforced deprivation, which means being deprived of an item (for example, could not afford it), rather than choosing not to have it. Measurement of these deprivation items provides key indicators of social exclusion, including the following food-related questions:

1. Does your household eat meals with meat, chicken, fish (or vegetarian equivalent) every second day? (If no, is it because the household cannot afford to, or is there another reason?)
2. Does your household have a roast joint (or its equivalent) once a week? (If no, is it because the household cannot afford to, or is there another reason?)
3. Does the household have family or friends for a drink or a meal once a month? (If no, is it because the household cannot afford to, or is there another reason?)

In addition, there is a further food-related question in the EU-SILC survey, asked of each household member aged 16 years or over:

4. During the last fortnight was there ever a day (that is, from getting up to going to bed) when you did not have a substantial meal due to lack of money?

Carney and Maître (2012) constructed a food poverty index, composed of those reporting any one of questions 1, 2 or 4. The item 'unable to afford family and friends for a meal or drink' was excluded, as they regarded it as incompatible with the others. The results indicated a decrease in food poverty from 2004 to 2007 and a subsequent increase from 2008 to 2010, at which time they concluded that 10 per cent of Irish households were experiencing food poverty. The authors highlighted the limitations of their methodology, particularly given that some vulnerable groups at risk of food poverty are excluded from the SILC survey, notably certain minority ethnic groups, asylum seekers and homeless people. In addition, the indicator does not address the issue of accessibility or quality of food that could be afforded. However, subsequent updates using this methodology reported a steady increase in food poverty from 10 per cent in 2010, to a peak of 13 per cent in 2013 and a fall to 7 per cent by 2018 (Government of Ireland, 2020b).

Food insecurity

As a response to the National Nutrition Monitoring Act 1990, measures were developed to regularly monitor food insecurity and hunger in American households. Anderson (1990) argues that food insecurity presents across a wide range of severity, from initial worry about supplies running out, through impacts on the quality and choice of food consumed, to the experience of hunger in case of food shortage. This highlights the need to develop a methodology to measure food-insecure conditions at different levels of severity. It is significant that the survey measures the frequency and duration of periods of food insecurity. If the situation exists for longer and more frequent periods, this is indicative of a more severe problem (Wunderlich and Norwood, 2006).

Since 1995, the US Census Bureau has carried out an annual survey, which is the largest and most comprehensive data gathering exercise in relation to food insecurity. The 2019 survey was completed by over 34,000 households, who responded to a series of questions designed to identify difficulties in meeting basic food needs (Coleman-Jensen et al, 2020). Each question asks whether a specific condition arose in the previous 12 months, due to a lack of money. There are three questions about the food situation in the household as a whole, seven questions relating to the food conditions of adults and, if relevant, a further eight questions which focus on the food conditions of children in the household. The questions used in the survey are set out in Table 2.2.

The food security status of the household is assessed by the number of food-insecure responses to the questions. If a household reports fewer than three food-insecure conditions, it is classified as food secure. If it reports greater than two food-insecure conditions, the household is further classified as either having *low food security* or the more severe category of *very low food security*. This sub-division attempts to distinguish between households with occasional problems in accessing food and adequate diet,

Table 2.2: Survey questions on food insecurity in the USDA Food Security Survey (Questions 11–18 asked only if the household included children aged 0–17.)

No.	Question
1	'We worried whether our food would run out before we got money to buy more.' Was that often, sometimes, or never true for you in the last 12 months?
2	'The food we bought just didn't last and we didn't have money to get more.' Was that often, sometimes, or never true for you in the last 12 months?
3	'We couldn't afford to eat balanced meals.' Was that often, sometimes, or never true for you in the last 12 months?
4	In the last 12 months, did you or other adults in the household ever cut the size of your meals or skip meals because there wasn't enough money for food? (Yes/No)
5	If yes to question 4, how often did this happen? – almost every month, some months but not every month, or in only 1 or 2 months?
6	In the last 12 months, did you ever eat less than you felt you should because there wasn't enough money for food? (Yes/No)
7	In the last 12 months, were you ever hungry, but didn't eat, because there wasn't enough money for food? (Yes/No)
8	In the last 12 months, did you lose weight because there wasn't enough money for food? (Yes/No)
9	In the last 12 months, did you or other adults in your household ever not eat for a whole day because there wasn't enough money for food? (Yes/No)
10	(If yes to question 9) How often did this happen – almost every month, some months but not every month, or in only 1 or 2 months?
11	'We relied on only a few types of low-cost food to feed our children because we were running out of money to buy food.' Was that often, sometimes, or never true for you in the last 12 months?
12	'We couldn't feed our children a balanced meal, because we couldn't afford that.' Was that often, sometimes, or never true for you in the last 12 months?
13	'The children were not eating enough because we just couldn't afford enough food.' Was that often, sometimes, or never true for you in the last 12 months?
14	In the last 12 months, did you ever cut the size of any of the children's meals because there wasn't enough money for food? (Yes/No)
15	In the last 12 months, were the children ever hungry, but you just couldn't afford more food? (Yes/No)
16	In the last 12 months, did any of the children ever skip a meal because there wasn't enough money for food? (Yes/No)
17	If yes to question 16, how often did this happen? – almost every month, some months but not every month, or in only 1 or 2 months?
18	In the last 12 months, did any of the children ever not eat for a whole day because there wasn't enough money for food? (Yes/No)

Source: Coleman-Jensen et al (2014: 3)

from multiple indications of disrupted eating patterns and reduced food consumption, due to insufficient money for food. In most households with *very low food security*, the respondent reported that he or she was hungry at some time during the year for this reason (Coleman-Jensen et al, 2014: 4).

There are limitations to the data arising from this methodology that may affect estimates of food insecurity. Household surveys do not access homeless individuals or families, which may bias food insecurity and very low food security estimates. Other very vulnerable groups, such as illegal migrants, may be less likely to take part in these surveys, although be exposed to food poverty. Within a household that is food insecure, household members may be affected in different ways. In relation to food insecurity among children, it is acknowledged that parents may not report food insecurity due to embarrassment (or fear), which may result in underreporting. No estimates have been made for bias arising from these factors. It is recognised that in a food-insecure household, some members (for example young children) may be less affected than adults, depending on food sharing priorities within the family (Coleman-Jensen et al, 2013: 8).

All ten questions in the survey either directly or indirectly address the quantity of food. Most of these questions are designed to assess the extent of the problem, including whether a situation (such as insufficient money to buy food) occurred 'often, sometimes, or never' for the respondent in the last 12 months. In relation to the qualitative component of food insecurity, there are no questions regarding the nutritional adequacy of food, but Question 3 refers specifically to balanced meals, which relates to the quality of dietary intake. However, responses to this question have to be treated with caution, as research suggests that the interpretation of the concept of a 'balanced meal' is not reliable as a measure of food insecurity (Derrickson et al, 2001). The survey includes a question designed to capture whether the respondent worried about the household running out of food, but there are no questions that cover the social aspects of food insecurity.

National food security surveys in the US have been carried out since 1995 (USDA, 2015). As illustrated in Figure 2.2, the percentage of US households experiencing food insecurity rose significantly with the Global Financial Crisis in 2007, peaking at 14.9 per cent in 2011 and subsequently reducing each year to 10.5 per cent in 2019 (Coleman-Jensen et al, 2020). This means that about 13.7 million households reported difficulty at some stage in the year in providing food for all their family members due to a lack of resources (2020: 4). The total of food-insecure households includes 4.1 per cent (5.3 million), who experienced very low food security in 2019. This level of food insecurity is experienced when the eating patterns of one or more household members are disrupted and they had less food than they needed at least some time during the year, due to a shortage of money

Figure 2.2: United States – trends in household food insecurity, 2001–19

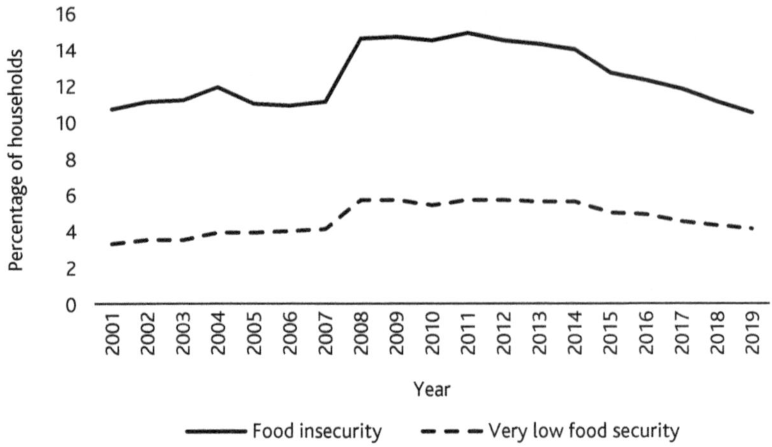

Source: Coleman-Jensen et al (2020: 12)

for food. This research has yet to be updated to reflect the impact of the COVID-19 pandemic.

Coleman-Jensen et al (2020) also reported that a typical food-secure household spent 24 per cent more on food than a similar sized household classified as food insecure. This takes into account food purchased with benefits from the Supplemental Nutrition Assistance Program (SNAP) (previously known as the Food Stamp Program), which is run by the Department of Agriculture and offers food assistance to eligible low-income individuals and families (USDA Food and Nutrition Service, 2021). The SNAP programme is a federal programme where low-income families, who have met means-testing requirements, are entitled to use a payment card at stores to purchase food. Over half of the households surveyed reported that they had used SNAP or another similar food assistance programme in the previous month. The minimum threshold to qualify is gross income below 130 per cent of the federal poverty line (approximately $28,000 per annum for a family of three persons) and a net income equal or below the poverty line (Center on Budget and Policy Priorities, 2021). This poverty line, which is used for determining eligibility for federal subsidies such as SNAP, is essentially the one originally developed by Orshansky (US Department of Health and Human Services, 2018). Despite welfare austerity, Nord argues that the Food Stamp/SNAP programmes are effective in alleviating very low food insecurity (2012: 811). However, Figure 2.2 indicates that the problem is persistent, with the percentage in this category at the same level of 4.1 per cent in 2019, as in 2007.

In 2013, the UN FAO established the 'Voices of the Hungry' project to assess comparable rates of household and individual food insecurity across over 140 countries on an annual basis. It was decided, based on ethnographic research, to develop a tool that would gather information to assess different levels of food insecurity (Radimer et al, 1990, 1992). As a result, the UN FAO developed the Food Insecurity Experience Scale (FIES) from experience-based food security scales, such as the USDA Food Security Survey (Saint Ville et al, 2019). A study of the FIES by Smith et al (2017) found that the five characteristics most likely to result in food insecurity were low household income, poor social networks, lower social capital, lack of education and being unemployed.

Figure 2.3 sets out the prevalence of moderate or severe food insecurity in the total population for OECD countries in 2017–19 (averaged). The percentage of people in Ireland reporting food insecurity was 7 per cent, higher than the UK (5 per cent), but lower than the US (8.5 per cent). The lowest levels were reported in Japan and wealthy European countries, such as Germany, Luxembourg and Switzerland, while the highest were in Mexico and Chile.

During the last couple of decades, several other measures of food insecurity have been developed, although there has been no consensus between the various agencies involved regarding the most appropriate indicators to use (Carletto et al, 2013). An example is the Global Food Security Index (GFSI), which is published annually by the Economist Intelligence Unit. It is a broad measure, constructed from 59 different indicators, and is regularly updated through consultation with an expert panel. The 2020 GFSI is the ninth edition of the index, which considers food affordability, availability, quality and safety, together with natural resources and resilience across 113 countries. In 2020, Ireland ranked second in the index after Finland, a position it has maintained since the first index was published in 2009 (Economist Intelligence Unit, 2021).

The UK Government, through the Department for Work and Pensions (DWP), began a national measurement of household food insecurity in 2019. This is carried out by incorporating a national index of food insecurity into the existing Family Resources Survey, which investigates household incomes and living standards. Ten additional questions relating to food insecurity are used from the US Government's survey, as described in Table 2.2 earlier. This UK-wide annual survey, which has a large sample size of 20,000 households, published its first results on food insecurity in March 2021. It found that 8 per cent of households were food insecure, with half of these households experiencing the more severe category of very low food security (DWP, 2021). It reported that households in the youngest age category (16 to 24 years old) were most likely to be food insecure (16 per cent), compared with older heads of household. In addition, there were higher levels of food insecurity where the head of household had lower educational attainment. In Northern Ireland, the 'Food and You

Figure 2.3: Food insecurity as a percentage of the total population for OECD countries, 2017–19 (average)

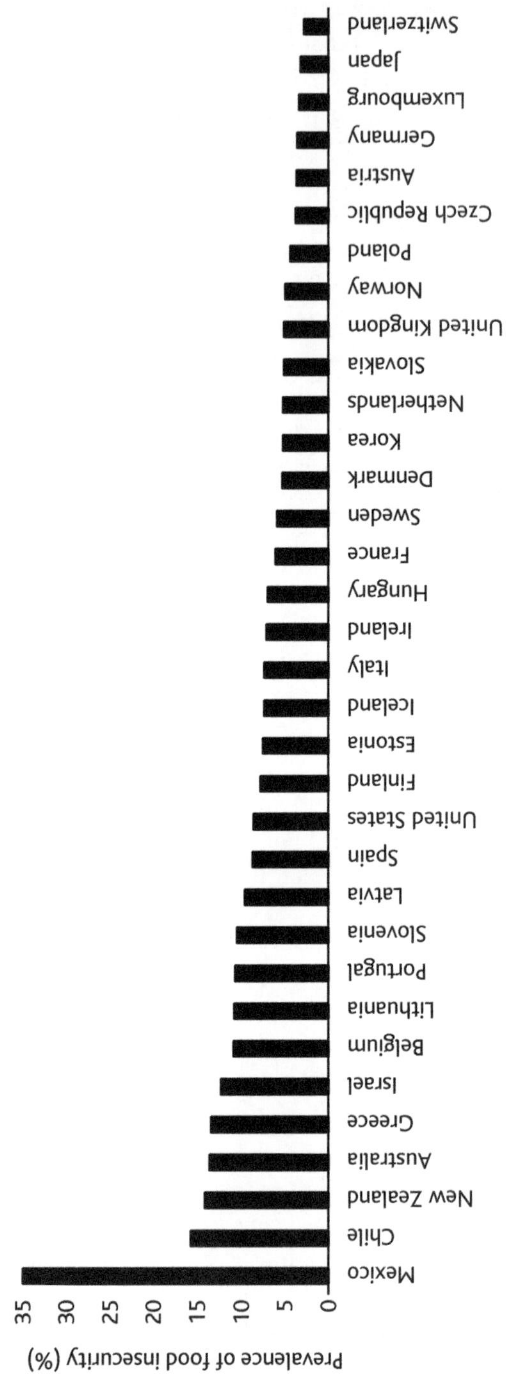

Note: Canada, Colombia and Turkey are excluded, as no data available

Source: Prepared by author based on UN FAO (2020: Table A1.1)

2' survey was commissioned by the Food Standards Agency (FSA), with fieldwork undertaken by Ipsos MORI (market research company) from July to October 2020. Approximately one in six of the 2,079 respondents (from 1,389 households) were classified as food insecure (9 per cent low, 6 per cent very low). The survey was undertaken during the COVID-19 outbreak and the results suggest that the pandemic had a significant impact on the reported level of food insecurity.

Food bank research

The use of food banks and food aid may provide an indication of food poverty. However, assessing the demand for, and scale of food aid is challenging, partly due to the informal nature of providers (Sosenko et al, 2013). Research in Canada concluded that food bank usage significantly underestimates the prevalence of food insecurity and those who use food banks are usually driven by extreme need (Loopstra and Tarasuk, 2015). Lord Freud, former Minister of State for Welfare Reform in the UK, suggested that growth in food aid charities was supply-driven, given that free food was distributed (Hansard, 2013). However, research carried out for the UK Department for the Environment, Food and Rural Affairs (Defra) reported that, although demand was rising, they could find no evidence that this was stimulated by the availability of free food (Lambie-Mumford et al, 2014). According to Davis and Baumberg Geiger (2017), the increase in demand for food aid since the 2008 economic crisis was a catalyst for academic research on food poverty and food banks across advanced economies. The growth of organisations, such as The Trussell Trust Foodbanks in the UK, has significantly increased the profile of food banks and also stimulated research interest (Lambie-Mumford, 2013). This interest is often from a public health and nutritional standpoint, rather than a social policy perspective. For example, in the UK increasing numbers of patients are requesting food bank referrals from their doctors (Loopstra et al, 2015).

Food banks have expanded in many countries. The European Food Banks Federation (FEBA, 2020) has 24 members, mainly national organisations across EU countries. In 2019, FEBA member organisations distributed the equivalent of 4.2 million meals per day. Food was sourced mainly from recovery of surplus food (70 per cent) and the Fund of European Aid to the Most Deprived (FEAD) (17 per cent). FEAD is an EU scheme designed to support Member States in addressing the basic needs of their most deprived people (Gov.ie, 2020a). In recent years, there has been an increasing level of debate, particularly in North America and the UK, about the underlying reasons for the growth in food aid and the role of food banks. For example, it is argued that food bank usage is driven by continuing welfare cutbacks in many countries (Caraher and Furey, 2018). However, a review of food banks in high-income countries found a lack of evidence that they help to reduce food poverty and concluded that, even if they do succeed in some cases, they do not reach sufficiently large numbers of people who need food aid (Loopstra, 2018).

A recent contribution to the debate on the growth of food banking is 'The Rise of Food Charity in Europe' (Lambie-Mumford and Silvasti, 2020), which includes seven national case studies. It takes a comparative social policy approach to study food charity responses in Finland, Germany, Italy, the Netherlands, Slovenia, Spain and the UK. The analysis indicates that, while food charities across Europe have certain common features, responses to food poverty vary widely between countries. In each of the countries studied, charities involved in providing food aid have increasingly found themselves filling the gap left by state-provided support. An important related issue is the increasing focus on food waste and surplus food redistribution by food aid providers. This has been described as a 'Band-Aid' solution to a much deeper problem (Caraher and Furey, 2017) and is discussed further in Chapter 8.

Since the mid-1990s, charity food aid has become more common in Finland, which has been described as disconnected from the Nordic welfare model (Silvasti, 2015: 471). In Germany, although there is a problem of food poverty, it is argued that the Government has overlooked the issue and left responses to charities, such as food banks, which is felt to be insufficient (Pfeiffer et al, 2015). Pfeiffer et al (2015) point out that in Germany the problem of food poverty does not have the same awareness as in the UK, where non-governmental organisations (for example food bank providers, church groups) have helped to highlight the issue (2015: 484). In the UK, it was estimated that in 2013 over 500,000 people (approximately 1 per cent of the population) were dependent on assistance from food banks and other forms of food aid, such as soup kitchens (Cooper and Dumpleton, 2013: 3). However, the growth of food bank networks has continued and The Trussell Trust reported 1.9 million referrals in 2019–20, with an average of two referrals for each person assisted (Trussell Trust, 2020a). In the six-month period from April to September 2020, the number of emergency food parcels distributed by the network exceeded 1.2 million, representing a 46 per cent increase on the comparable period in 2019 (Trussell Trust, 2020a). This significant expansion of its network of over 1,200 food banks in the UK has provided an effective platform for the charity's campaign for long-term change to address the problem of food poverty.

Food charities have maintained that the growth in demand reflects rising food poverty and a study based on 25 interviews, mainly with Trussell Trust food bank managers and staff, concluded that welfare reform in the UK had a significant impact on demand for food aid (Lambie-Mumford and Dowler, 2014: 1). This is supported by recent statistics from the Trussell

Trust (2020b), which indicated that the main reasons for referral to a Trussell Trust food bank in 2019–20 were low income (39 per cent), benefit delays (17 per cent) and benefit changes (15 per cent). Loopstra et al (2017) investigated the impact on food bank usage of welfare reforms by linking data from The Trussell Trust food bank with sanctioning records from over 200 local authorities across the UK during the period 2012–15. Welfare measures included reduced entitlements, benefit delays and restrictions on housing and child benefits, accompanied by stricter conditionality and sanctions for non-compliance (2017: 4). In 2013, over one million welfare sanctions were implemented, resulting in benefits being delayed for over four weeks. The research reported a close link between sanctioning and food bank usage.

The expansion of charitable food providers across Britain has spurred on large cities and local authorities to commission reports on the extent of food banks and usage. The Greater London Authority published 'A Zero Hunger City' (2013), while boroughs such as Lewisham also instigated studies (Green et al, 2014). Some of these studies are based on semi-structured qualitative interviews with users, managers and volunteers (Lewisham). Research commissioned by the Scotland Government focused only on the providers (Sosenko et al, 2013). Overall, the studies reported an increase in demand (Scotland, Lewisham), while the Greater London Authority identified a growing 'crisis' (2013: 3) of food poverty. The studies suggest that increasing demand was driven by welfare reform, benefit delays (Scotland, London), benefit sanctions (London), falling/low incomes (Scotland, London) and unemployment (London). This was supported by The Trussell Trust's own data, obtained by tracking referrals to their food banks, which reported that 49 per cent of their users need help due to problems with social security payments or refusal of a crisis loan (Cooper et al, 2014: 4).

As a result of the debate on the growth of food banks in the UK, an All-Party Parliamentary Inquiry into Hunger was set up in 2014 to investigate the causes and identify actions to address the problem. It published its final report, 'Feeding Britain', later that year, which concluded that hunger was 'here to stay in Britain until counteraction is taken' and set out several recommendations (All-Party Parliamentary Inquiry, 2014: 55). It recommended pilot projects in each UK region that would involve local organisations, such as charities and community groups, together with local authorities, working together on a joint programme. These initiatives would include matching fresh surplus food available in each area with food aid providers. In addition, the programme would involve linking with food retailers and manufacturers to make available food that would otherwise be wasted (perhaps unacceptable to retailers because of physical appearance). The food bank movement was given the main responsibility to establish the Feeding Britain initiative. Overall, the recommendations delayed national government action (for example local pilots) and shifted responsibility onto the third sector and private companies.

A further development in tackling food poverty has been the introduction of 'social supermarkets' (SSMs), which were founded in Austria in the 1990s (Holweg et al, 2010). These outlets have expanded across other European countries in recent years, selling basic food items significantly cheaper than normal supermarkets. Access is restricted to people who are deemed at risk of food poverty (for example, in receipt of means-tested welfare benefits) (Renobales et al, 2015). In the UK, the first of these outlets was set up in 2013 and, following a recommendation from the Belfast Food Network, five SSMs were opened in Northern Ireland during 2017. This pilot exercise was funded by the Northern Ireland Government's Welfare Reforms Mitigations package, which was made available to ease the impact of recent welfare reforms (Department for Communities NI, 2018). Stock is sourced from surpluses offered by mainstream food retailers and other suppliers. In order to gain access to these SSMs, customers are obliged to commit to a range of additional services, such as money management and cooking on a low budget.

Overall, there is an apparent rise of food banks across Europe since the 1990s, particularly since the global financial crisis. Yet, there is also an apparent lack of research on these providers and users, often only measured sporadically in qualitative studies. It would seem that most research has been published about the UK, but we know relatively little about the extent in other European nations. Lambie-Mumford and Silvasti (2020) point out the need for more systematic and reliable knowledge about food assistance across Europe, particularly given the apparent significant growth in charitable responses to food poverty in many countries.

Drivers of food poverty and food insecurity

Following a review of the definitions and measurement of food poverty and food insecurity, together with recent food bank research, it is now appropriate to consider possible explanations for the problem. These include the cost of food, the impact of social policies and food deserts, as discussed in the following sections.

Cost of food

World food prices have moved upwards and spiked several times in the last 15 years, although the recent trend has been downwards. Figure 2.4 tracks the rise in the UN FAO Food Price Index, a measure of the monthly change in international prices of a basket of food commodities (UN FAO, 2018).

Figure 2.4: UN FAO Food Price Index

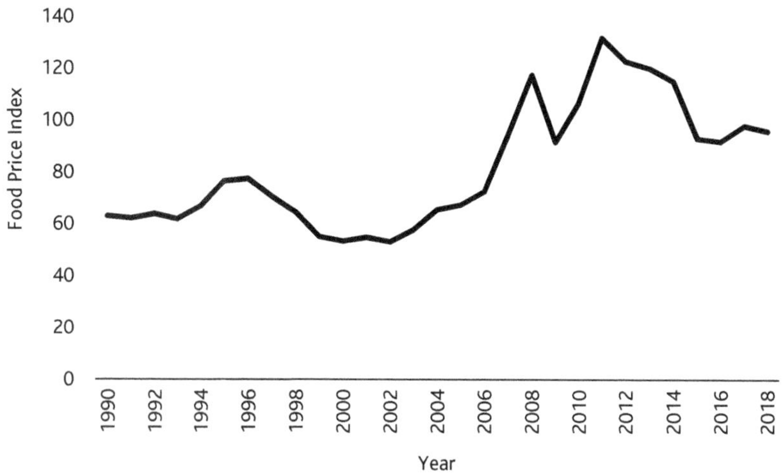

Source: Prepared by author based on data from UN FAO (2018)

There is evidence that price is the most significant factor of food choice for low-income groups (Steptoe et al, 1995). According to Loopstra et al (2015), the most recent epidemiological study of food poverty in the UK was the 2004 'Low Income Diet and Nutrition Survey', commissioned by the UK Food Standards Agency. They reported that 29 per cent of low-income households experienced food poverty within the previous month, defined as 'being without reliable access to a sufficient quantity of affordable, nutritious food' (Nelson et al, 2007). Just under two fifths (36 per cent) of the low-income population could not afford to eat balanced meals in the previous year. The study also revealed that 22 per cent of the nationally representative sample skipped meals, while 5 per cent reported not eating for a whole day, because they did not have enough money to buy food. Kneafsey et al (2013) reported that increases in food and fuel prices in 2010 had a serious impact on low-income households. In order to cope, families were forced through economic necessity to purchase food that was cheaper than normal and sometimes of poorer nutritional quality.

Impact of social policies

Social protection

In many European countries, the provision of food charity to support those experiencing food poverty expanded in parallel with the recent economic recession and related austerity measures (Lambie-Mumford, 2017). In the US and Canada, the emergence of food banking preceded these developments, but was against a similar background of welfare retrenchment and social security reforms that lessened welfare entitlements (Poppendieck, 1998; Riches, 2002). An analysis of data on food insecurity across 21 EU countries from 2004 to 2012 found a significant increase after 2009, but this varied significantly across countries (Loopstra et al, 2016). Their study demonstrated the effectiveness of high levels of social welfare in providing protection from this hardship during periods of high unemployment and lower wages. However, the impact of austerity measures involved reductions in social assistance entitlements in many European jurisdictions, such as Germany (Pfeiffer et al, 2011). In Spain, there has been 'progressive erosion' of the fledgling welfare state, which has been weakened by austerity programmes that have reduced social protection, with lower funding and increased conditionality requirements for social assistance (Pérez de Armiño, 2014: 133). In parallel with these European countries, the UK has also tightened entitlements and increased conditionality on social assistance. In this challenging environment, the international literature conveys the difficulty of meeting essential living costs while living on social welfare. For example, in Australia, a report on poverty provided evidence that welfare payments fell short of minimum income requirements, with two thirds of those living under the poverty line relying on social assistance (Australian Council of Social Service [ACOSS], 2012). According to Booth (2014), this reflected the policies of successive Australian governments, which introduced welfare reform, including tighter eligibility requirements, designed to promote welfare to work. In the UK, Hirsch (2015) reported that the adequacy of social welfare benefits fell from 2008 to 2015, although the impact of this fall in income varied across different household types. In addition to cuts and tighter eligibility requirements, the growth of food banks has occurred alongside activation policies and increased conditionality (Lambie-Mumford, 2017).

Low pay and precarious employment

Hirsch (2015: 17) found that, in recent years, families in the UK have experienced an increasing gap between income from working full-time on the National Minimum Wage (NMW) and the income required to meet essential living expenses. Income from low-wage and/or temporary employment, often precarious in nature, reflects a recommodification of labour and results in a more exposed environment for vulnerable workers (Darmon and Perez, 2010: 84). The term 'precarious work' is often used to describe insecure, low-wage and/or temporary work, although it is a relative concept and the line at which non-precarious employment becomes precarious is contested (Nugent, 2018). This global trend by employers to use temporary or casual work rather than permanent staff has resulted in weaker employment and social security protection (Schoukens and Barrio, 2017). According to the OECD, those undertaking precarious work are more likely to be women, tend to be employed in low-skilled roles, are predominantly young (under 25 years) and have low educational attainment (OECD, 2014c).

In-work poverty is an important and increasing problem, with the proportion of workers across the EU at risk of in-work poverty rising from 8 per cent (2007) to 9 per cent in 2014 (Eurofound, 2017b: 16). It is often linked to insecure and low-paid work in the services sector, such as hotels, restaurants and retail (Marx and Nolan, 2014: 132). A UK study found that low-paid workers in poverty are three times more likely than those in non-poor working households to become unemployed or lose their job for other reasons (Hick and Lanau, 2018). Research has shown that in-work poverty tends to arise more from lack of employment than low wages (Halleröd et al, 2015). Evidence suggests that part-time workers are more likely than those in full-time work to be poor, especially when their part-time status is involuntary (Horemans and Marx, 2013). The roots of in-work poverty were explored in a European Commission report (European Commission, 2011a), which identified a variety of individual and household factors. Low educational attainment is a key factor that increases the risk of earning low wages and, in turn, the risk of in-work poverty (Spannagel, 2013: 4). Household composition is also important, as the risk of poverty is relatively high when there is a low level of work intensity at household level, such as a single earner who has a family to support (Eurofound, 2017b: 7).

Research conveys that some household types have a greater risk of poverty than others. One study in the UK reported that the groups at the highest risk were those with no workers in the household, those with permanently sick or disabled members and lone parents (Mack and Lansley, 2015: 85). In addition, adults living in households with children are also more at risk of poverty, with the risk rising as family size increases. A study by Furey et al (2019) used an online survey of 944 UK respondents to assess what personal and household circumstances can predict food poverty. Respondents with poorer health status (self-reported) and with more children were in households at higher risk of food poverty. The main factors which predicted households with lower risk of food poverty were older respondents, those who owned their own property and those in higher-income categories.

Studies of low-income single mothers also convey their risk of food poverty. For example, in Australia, McKenzie and McKay (2017) investigated the impact of changes to the welfare system on food choices and strategies for lone parents. They found serious constraints on respondents' food choices and eating practices, including having to purchase low-cost food that would 'fill up' their children. Some respondents reported that they had to seek food assistance from charities, in order to be able to feed their families. Access problems, temporary shortages of funds and a myriad of other reasons can give rise to an insufficient diet and temporary hunger from shortages or skipping meals. On occasion, these reductions in food consumption or disruptions in eating patterns can differ within households. For example, it can be by choice, such as a mother foregoing food herself by giving preference to her child (Coleman-Jensen et al, 2014: 7).

Housing costs, accommodation type and homelessness

Rising housing costs may be part of the explanation for a rise in food poverty. In many countries, it is reported that housing benefits for those on social welfare have not kept up with increased accommodation costs. Silvasti and Karjalainen (2014: 84) reported this problem in Finland, while the UN Special Rapporteur recommended increased housing benefits to help address the food needs of Canadians on low incomes, or reliant on social welfare (Riches and Tarasuk, 2014: 56). Homelessness is often an extreme form of poverty, likely to involve food poverty (Kore, 2014). It was one of the main reasons for referral to a food bank in the UK in 2014/15, according to The Trussell Trust (Garthwaite, 2016: 83).

Food deserts: location-based food poverty

A UK Government Health Minister has defined food deserts as areas 'where people do not have easy access to healthy, fresh foods, particularly if they are poor and have limited mobility' (Elliott, 1997). Research indicates that, particularly in urban areas, accessing healthy foods can present a range of complex problems (Cummins et al, 2005). Factors impacting on food access range from the physical distance to shops to physical impairment (Dibsdall et al, 2003). There is also evidence that a 'healthy' basket of food can be more expensive in deprived areas and can also be much more difficult to source (Wrigley, 2002: 2031). This may arise due to a lack of retail stores in some local communities (House of Commons Environment, Food and Rural Affairs Committee, 2015: 21).

The UK Government acknowledged in 'Transport and Social Exclusion – Making the Connections' (Social Exclusion Unit, 2003) that problems accessing food shopping with poor transport were a contributory factor to social exclusion. Transportation difficulties can play a significant role in creating food deserts, as access to a car for shopping has become increasingly necessary. Car ownership can be a major drain on the household budget for those on low incomes, resulting in a reliance on buses or walking to food stores, which can create a range of challenges. A UK report into risk factors for social exclusion refers to the 'stranglehold' of supermarkets, which can impede access to affordable, healthy food (Bradshaw et al, 2004: 78). This situation arises because major supermarket groups have focused much of their development on locations outside town or city centres, which are designed for shoppers travelling by car (Bradshaw et al, 2004: 79). Research from 1990s Britain found that cars were used for 77 per cent of shopping trips, thereby disadvantaging predominantly low-income households in terms of physical access for shopping (Church et al, 2001). In countries such as the UK, the mapping of access to healthy food has helped to identify barriers for different sectors of the community, such as older people, those with specific cultural food requirements and those with reduced physical mobility. A mapping study in the city of Preston, UK, concluded that there needed to be controls on the number of fast-food outlets and improvements in their quality, which it was argued contributed to food poverty (Caraher et al, 2010: 200).

Food and convenience

Purdy et al (2007) refer to a contributory factor to food poverty in the UK, arising from an expansion in the supply and variety of convenience foods, combined with declining cooking skills (2007: 37). It was found that cooking facilities and cooking skills tend to be poor for those living in disadvantaged areas of the UK (Lawrence et al, 2012), while those from higher social class backgrounds have a higher confidence in their cooking abilities (Lang, 1997). In relation to convenience foods, Friel et al (2006) maintain that 'an excess availability' of processed foods represents a barrier to choosing healthy food (2006: 1013). Some of the aforementioned findings are disputed in the literature. For example, Dowler and Lambie-Mumford (2015: 424) are wary of arguments which maintain that food poverty arises from personal or household shortcomings, such as poor domestic budgeting or lack of cooking skills. They point out that such arguments may suit governments who are seeking to drive down public expenditure, rather than tackle problems of low wages and inadequate social security payments. Dowler and Dobson argue that people on low incomes are usually 'very good at budgeting for food and producing economical meals' (1997: 60).

Conclusions

The literature conveys that food poverty is both complex and multifaceted, while it is regarded as 'central to the experience of poverty' (Friel and Conlon, 2004: 10). Empirical evidence from the OECD reveals it has been an increasing problem in many advanced countries since the late 1990s and particularly since the global financial crisis in 2007 and its aftermath. While food poverty declined in research and policy attention after the post-war era, the topic has subsequently returned as an important social policy issue (O'Connor et al, 2008: 3).

An increasing body of literature on food poverty is emerging in developed countries. This can be illustrated by the growing debate in the UK, where there have been responses from government bodies, with the phenomenon investigated by charitable organisations, city councils, regional governments and the House of Commons (Downing et al, 2014). Despite this attention, there is still no officially agreed definition, although the challenges in formulating one that is both clear and all-encompassing have been highlighted (Beacom et al, 2020). As a result, the lack of systematic measurement of food poverty leaves much of the debate around proxy measures, such as food bank usage (Lambie-Mumford, 2017: 20). However, the commencement of a systematic measurement of food insecurity in the UK is a step forward to an improved understanding of the issue in this country.

In Europe, measurement of food poverty has generally been limited to deprivation indicators in wider surveys, such as food-related questions in EU-SILC. In contrast, the US carries out annual surveys of food insecurity, which are designed to measure the problem at different levels of severity. Although some assessments in Europe have been based on food bank usage, research indicates that this is not an accurate measure of the problem (Loopstra and Tarasuk, 2015). Qualitative studies in the UK which have investigated the use of food banks are often sponsored by charitable organisations, such as Oxfam, Child Poverty Action Group, church or food bank organisations. The focus is sometimes on the providers, rather than users of food aid (for example, Sosenko et al, 2013).

3

Poverty and food: the Irish context

Introduction

Discourse on poverty in Ireland has historically been closely associated with food poverty. Following an overview of poverty research in Ireland from a food perspective, this chapter draws on the limited published material available to examine the causes and policy drivers of contemporary food poverty. A variety of factors have emerged that may explain food poverty in Ireland, including inadequate social protection, low-pay/precarious employment, housing, household type, the cost of food and food deserts. Given that unemployment is a significant cause of poverty and increases the risk of food poverty (Carney and Maître, 2012), a review of Ireland's welfare typology and social protection system is provided. Employment is not necessarily a route out of poverty and there is likely to be a real risk of in-work and food poverty for many in low-paid jobs, particularly given the increasing prevalence of precarious work. Many of those with illness/disability and caring responsibilities also face higher risk of food poverty, exacerbated by lack of state support and barriers to employment. Following a review of these and other explanations for food poverty, including the availability of affordable housing, the cost of food and food deserts, the conclusion summarises the key messages.

Food and poverty research in Ireland

In the 19th century, frequent famines arose due to the failure of potato crops and public disturbances were triggered by food shortages and high prices. The most devastating of these was the Great Famine between 1845 and 1849. Ireland's fledgling welfare state emerged under British rule in the 19th and early 20th centuries. According to Kennedy (2001: 58), 'absolute poverty persisted for decades after independence'. Earner-Byrne (2017: 25) argues that 'semi-starvation' was common, including in Dublin city, until at least the mid-1940s. Reflecting the economic problems post-independence, successive Irish governments adopted a conservative, cautious approach to welfare expenditure and payments remained low. An important feature of the state's approach was to share its welfare responsibilities with non-state organisations, in particular the Catholic Church (Fahey, 1998). The voluntary sector became an increasingly important and enduring part of Ireland's mixed economy of welfare, as charitable groups grew and played a key role in seeking to address poverty. In 1927, one charity reported to the Commission on the Relief of the Sick that many were 'unable to properly … feed their children on the present rates of outdoor relief' (Commission on the Relief of the Sick and Destitute Poor, 1927). The charity expressed concern that it had to divert its resources to those whom it felt should be supported by state services. Miller argues (2013) that responses to food poverty in Ireland have historically been dependent on the voluntary sector, and this situation prevails in 21st-century Irish society.

It was not until Ireland's more recent history that the so-called rediscovery of poverty, which emerged during the 1960s in the United States (US) and the UK, percolated through to Ireland in the early 1970s. Research based on a relative interpretation of poverty was first presented at the Kilkenny Conference on Poverty (1972), which was held under the auspices of the Catholic Church's Council for Social Welfare (Dukelow and Considine, 2017: 47). At the opening of the Conference, Bishop Kavanagh interpreted being poor as 'deprived of something which one might *reasonably* hope to have' (1972: 372; original emphasis). He sought a widening of the concept of poverty and interpreted it in relative terms. He argued that this should include not only income, but the lack of 'the ordinary decencies of living', including sufficient food, housing, health, educational opportunity and recreational facilities, which were all basic human rights (1972: 372). Ó Cinnéide presented a Conference paper which stimulated awareness of the extent of poverty in Ireland, using a variety of data sources to conclude that over 20 per cent of people in Ireland were poor (1972: 397). He also drew attention to the problems arising from formulating a robust methodology and sourcing accurate information, even when focusing on a narrow definition of material poverty based on income levels (1972: 400). It took a further 25 years before Ireland adopted its official definition of poverty, as set out in the original National Anti-Poverty Strategy:

> People are living in poverty if their income and resources (material, cultural and social) are so inadequate as to preclude them from having a standard of living which is regarded as acceptable by Irish society generally. As a result of inadequate income and resources, people may be excluded and marginalised from participating in activities which are considered the norm for other people in society. (Government of Ireland, 1997: 3)

This relative poverty definition aligned with Townsend's perspective, which related poverty to prevailing living standards. However, there was no specific recognition of food poverty, although the strategy document referred to the problem of fuel poverty (1997: 15). The report was subsequently used in the Government's response to alleviating poverty, as set out in 'The National

Action Plan for Social Inclusion (NAPinclusion) 2007–2016' (Department of Social and Family Affairs, 2007).

In contemporary discourse, social exclusion has become increasingly associated with poverty, although the term is somewhat ambiguous (Coakley, 2004: 112). In Ireland, the term has been used in government documents since 1996 (Curry, 2011: 244), when 'Partnership 2000 for Inclusion, Employment and Competitiveness' was published. In this document, social exclusion was described as: 'Cumulative marginalisation: from production (unemployment), from consumption (income poverty), from social networks (community, family and neighbours), from decision making and from an adequate quality of life' (Government of Ireland, 1997: 12). The report recognised that reducing unemployment, the biggest contributor to social exclusion, and increasing adequately paid employment were the key focus to improve levels of participation (Government of Ireland, 1997: 14).

Measurement

Since the 1980s, the Economic and Social Research Institute (ESRI) of Ireland has been at the forefront in developing methods to measure poverty (Curry, 2011: 245), and Ireland was one of the first countries to adopt a combined approach, using both income and deprivation measures (Menton, 2007: 29). In official poverty measurement, two main categories are in use, with persons or households either AROP or in 'consistent poverty'. The category AROP is measured for persons or households using an income poverty line at 60 per cent of median disposable income. Households that cannot afford basic goods and services regarded as the norm in society are considered to be suffering deprivation. This is measured by reference to 11 'deprivation items', three of which are food-related. Individuals without two or more of the 11 items, because they cannot be afforded, are considered to be experiencing enforced deprivation. Consistent poverty is the official Government approved poverty measure (Department of Employment Affairs and Social Protection [DOEASP], 2018a) and is designed to measure the level of income, together with the inability to afford necessities and to be able to participate in society as a result of poverty. Individuals are categorised as living in consistent poverty if their income is below the 60 per cent threshold and they are living in a household that is deprived of two of the basic necessities (Central Statistics Office [CSO], 2018a).

Figure 3.1 illustrates recent trends in rates of consistent poverty, deprivation and 'at risk of poverty' (CSO, 2020a). The increase in consistent poverty, from 4.2 per cent in 2008 to a peak of 9 per cent in 2013, reflects the economic downturn and difficulties in the public finances, which impacted on social

Figure 3.1: Poverty and deprivation rates in the population, by year, 2006–19

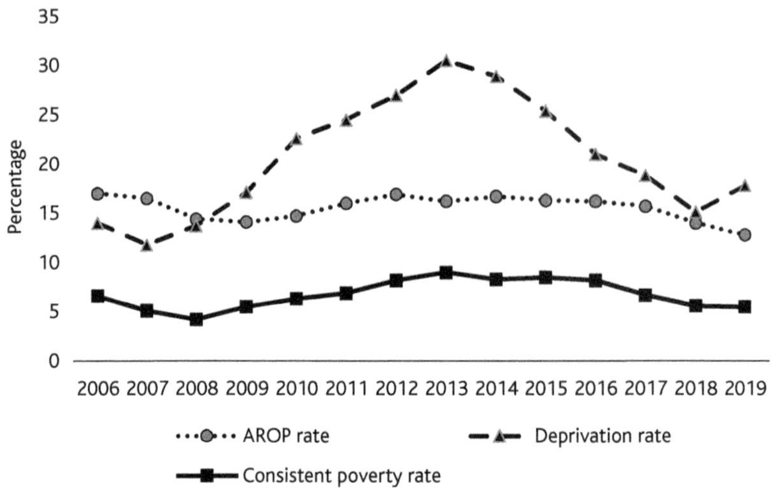

Source: Prepared by author based on data from EU-SILC (CSO, 2020a)

welfare and other programmes (Curry, 2011: 251). However, since 2014 the rate of consistent poverty has declined as the result of an improving economy. Enforced deprivation, based on respondents who lack two or more deprivation items, increased more sharply during the recession to a peak of 30.5 per cent in 2013, before improving to 17.8 per cent in 2019.

Qualitative research

Qualitative research on poverty in Ireland has focused on achieving an enhanced understanding of life on a low income, occasionally including aspects of food poverty. Some studies have focused on exploring the impact of poverty on families and children in particular, seeking to highlight policy areas requiring attention. Daly and Leonard (2002) investigated the experience of family life for 30 families living in poverty and social exclusion. In this study, parents and children from different family structures in three different locations across Ireland participated in interviews. The authors found that food expenditure accounted for over 30 per cent of household income and reported that some families needed regular help from charities, in order to have sufficient food to eat. A further study in Northern Ireland undertaken by Daly and Kelly (2015) was underpinned by interviews with 51 respondents (mostly mothers). The research, which focused on family life and poverty, revealed many problems in relation to food, although the study was not designed to investigate food poverty. For example, some respondents had difficulty affording sufficient food for their families and had to seek help from family support networks to feed their children (2015: 41). Mothers reported going without food, as children were prioritised (2015: 99). MacMahon and McEvoy (2018) carried out an in-depth investigation of 30 low-income households living in both urban and rural areas across Ireland. Respondents relayed experiences when their families had insufficient food or money to cover housing costs and essential household expenditure. While food was regarded as a basic priority, variety was limited and coping strategies included cutting back on a regular basis with cheaper alternatives. The study revealed that parents were aware of the need to have a healthy diet, but this was often not possible, as they tried to stretch their income to cover housing costs, household energy, education and other essentials. These studies on living on a low income revealed that many respondents experienced food poverty, pointing to the need for research with a specific focus on the problem.

Food poverty research in Ireland

Friel and Conlon's study concluded (2004: 120) that the data available in Ireland made it difficult to quantify the prevalence of food poverty. The research focused on how patterns of food consumption varied, depending on socio-economic status. It recommended that a strategy to address food poverty should be set out in the National Action Plan against Poverty and Social Inclusion (NAPSincl), although the latest NAPSincl (2015–17) lacks any reference to food poverty. In relation to high-risk groups, Coakley carried out a study of food and diet in low-income households (2001), which included interviews with 17 single mothers. Respondents reported a lack of choice in diet, although they endeavoured to provide food that met cultural norms. Coakley found that the purchase of fresh fruit and vegetables, luxuries for children and eating out was rarely possible. A qualitative study of food poverty and homelessness in Dublin found that the problem was viewed by many respondents as an 'unavoidable outcome' of homelessness (Hickey and Downey, 2003: 31). The study revealed that, while income inadequacy was a significant factor for respondents, there was a strong association between housing arrangements and food poverty. For example, respondents faced challenges accessing suitable facilities to store and prepare food and the availability of communal kitchen facilities was often problematic. A subsequent study on food poverty and homelessness was commissioned by the Food Standards Agency in Northern Ireland (FSA, 2007). It concluded that, although most homeless people have sufficient food, their dietary quality is poor. This reflects a shortage of money and lack of cooking skills, while alcohol and substance abuse are contributory factors.

Research by Carney and Maître (2012) used secondary data from the 2010 EU-Survey of Living Conditions (EU-SILC) to examine the profile of the population in Ireland experiencing food poverty. EU-SILC is a voluntary survey of the Household Reference Person (HRP), the family reference point in each private household. For the purpose of Carney and Maître's study, food poverty was measured as those reporting one or more out of three food-related deprivation indicators. In relation to demographic characteristics, the study found higher rates of food poverty where the HRP was single or divorced, under 40 years old, educated to intermediate level (or lower), in rented accommodation or in an urban location (2012: 28). Food poverty was higher where the family unit included two or more children, with the risk highest for households with a lone parent and children. The research also reported higher rates of food poverty where the respondent was categorised as AROP or in consistent poverty. Socio-economic categories at higher risk also included those unemployed or in lower grades of employment and those reporting as ill or disabled, or on home duties, such as caring roles. Following a series of national anti-poverty strategies from 1997 onwards, in 2020 the Irish Government published a 'Roadmap for Social Inclusion 2020–2025' (Gov.ie, 2020b). This report acknowledged the problem of food poverty in Ireland and noted that there was no official measurement. It included an update of the food poverty level in Ireland based on the methodology introduced by Carney and Maître (2012), which indicates a reduction from a peak of 13.2 per cent in 2013 to 7 per cent in 2018. This methodology is discussed further in Chapter 4, which reviews the prevalence of food poverty in Ireland using the latest data available.

Although research on food banking in Ireland has been very limited, Faughnan and Byrne (1998) examined the operation of the Dublin City Food Bank. This was the first food bank in Dublin run by Crosscare, the social support agency of the Catholic Archdiocese of Dublin. It identified four main issues: the supply-driven nature of its operation, which often did not match demand; lack of policy around member organisations who used the donated food; inadequate premises and staffing constraints which restricted the service; and challenges in local food distribution.

Explanations for poverty and food poverty in Ireland

Inadequate social protection

Welfare state typology

As a backdrop to a review of social protection, it is helpful to locate Ireland within welfare state typologies. Ireland does not often feature in the international literature of welfare states, reflecting either its relatively small size or the perceived similarities with Britain (Daly and Yeates, 2003: 86). Ireland's welfare typology reflects its history, as its modern welfare regime has its roots in pre-independence. Esping-Andersen (1990) identified Ireland as a liberal welfare state, alongside other English-speaking countries, including the UK. Subsequent studies have demonstrated that the results of comparing similarities and differences between countries depend on the methodological approach to analysis and the policy area being studied (Castles, 2010: 634). For example, although welfare services can be provided by the state, the market and the family, Esping-Andersen focused his analysis on the first two pillars. Daly and Lewis (2000) have argued that the additional pillars of care and family should be included, while other writers have proposed further welfare types. Castles and Ferrera (1996), followed by Bonoli (1997), put forward a Southern European type, pointing out the importance of the family over state and market provision in these Mediterranean countries. Minas et al (2014) concluded that Ireland fits into the Southern European cluster, describing it as a familialistic welfare regime, where the family is a significant welfare provider. The importance of the family as a provider of care reflects its history, when the Catholic Church had a strong influence on Irish society. Catholic social teaching promoted the principle of subsidiarity, whereby the state was encouraged not to take on functions that could be provided by the family (Curry, 2011: 10). The legacy of Catholic social teaching and impact on social policy has arguably continued to wane, reflecting increased secularisation in society, although it still has an important influence in areas such as social justice.

A mix of factors has led to Ireland being described in recent welfare state models as a hybrid (McCashin, 2015) or an outlier (Dukelow and Considine, 2014), although it is also categorised as a liberal regime for a number of reasons. Firstly, Ireland had a low level of social protection expenditure during the last 20 years as a percentage of GDP, compared to the EU average (Dukelow and Considine, 2017: 196). Secondly, means-testing has continued to occupy a central role in Ireland's welfare system, with over 30 per cent of social protection benefits means-tested in 2015, significantly higher than the EU27 average of 11 per cent (Eurostat, 2018a). As Ireland's social welfare system was formed before it gained independence from the UK, its early development has many characteristics of the British system. Many of these are based on UK legislation, such as the old-age pension and national insurance, and income support is provided through social insurance, social assistance or universal schemes. There are different layers of benefits, with public sector workers and those in some international companies receiving relatively generous provisions (such as occupational pension arrangements), whereas those in Ireland's services and manufacturing sector tend to rely on statutory benefits (Cousins, 2005). The provision of social protection in Ireland differs from some European countries in that it is not a corporatist system, where there is a stratification of insurance schemes for different categories of worker (Cousins, 2016).

Ireland and the UK have liberal features that, according to Ginsburg (2001: 183), 'have been enhanced by their state-sponsored exposure to economic globalisation since the 1980s'. Lacking an industrial base, Ireland positioned its economic strategy and industrial policies to encourage foreign direct investment and generate economic activity, particularly jobs in the services sector. The Irish State pursued pro-globalisation policies, which included a low competitive corporate tax rate and light touch regulation (Dukelow and Considine, 2017: 164). Following the success of this strategy, Ireland became the most foreign direct investment intensive economy in the EU by the mid-2000s (Barry and Welsum, 2005: 2). It is argued that globalisation has not only involved liberalisation of markets and changes in regulations which result in 'competitive individualism', but changes to social protection systems, all of which have led to a transfer of risks to workers and individuals (Standing, 2012: 588).

In the mid-2000s, the National Economic and Social Council (NESC), against the background of a strong economy, published a major report on the Developmental Welfare State (NESC, 2005). It recognised that Ireland's welfare state needed reform and improved social policies to tackle social disadvantage. The report concluded that cash transfers (as a percent of GNP) were low relative to other EU countries, due to the high use of means-testing, and that aspects of social protection were poorly designed. It referred to the hybrid nature of the welfare state, which it regarded as a 'potential strength' (2005: xvii) and recommended further universalism and extending social insurance.

Recent developments in social protection

Cantillon et al (2014: 181) argue that Ireland's level of poverty was reduced in the 2000s, as a result of improvements in social protection. This was supported by Watson and Maître (2013), who reported that social welfare has played a pivotal role in reducing poverty in Ireland, with the poverty reduction effectiveness of social transfers in 2010 above the EU15 average. Wang and Van Vliet (2016) found that from 1990 to 2009 underlying real benefit levels were enhanced in most countries, with Ireland recording the largest real increase across the Anglo-Saxon welfare regimes over nearly three decades (2016: 342). Although replacement levels reduced in most of the countries examined, they increased in Ireland by 2.5 per cent to 50.9 per cent over the period 1990–2009. The authors concluded from further qualitative research that the reason why replacement rates generally reduced was due to relatively higher wage increases, rather than benefit reductions. A widening difference between benefits and wage levels was aligned with a 'making work pay' agenda. Following the economic downturn from 2008, spending on social protection came under closer focus, with the dominant idea that public expenditure had become excessive (Dukelow and Considine, 2014: 421). Reflecting this narrative and the financial strictures, the response of the Irish Government was a series of austerity measures. The Budgets of 2009 to 2012 introduced a number of cuts to social security, including reducing social welfare, child benefit payments and housing benefits (Murphy, 2012: 349). Measures also included benefit reductions for lone parents living with young children and young job seekers. Although there were cuts in social welfare rates for all working-age beneficiaries, there was a particular focus on tightening eligibility requirements for some programmes. Changes to eligibility rules included restrictions on the duration and qualifying conditions for Jobseeker's Benefit. In 2013, the duration of Jobseeker's Benefit was reduced significantly, from 12 months to nine months for those with 260 or more Pay Related Social Insurance (PRSI) contributions (Citizens Information, 2021b).

Hick (2018) concluded that almost all the social security changes were decided on, if not implemented, before the Troika (European Commission, European Central Bank and International Monetary Fund) agreed in 2010 to provide Ireland with a three-year financial aid programme. However, as a result of the Troika intervention, there was a heightened level of pressure for further retrenchment of social protection programmes, as part of far-reaching austerity measures (Dukelow and Considine, 2014: 422). However, Hick (2018) noted that further cuts were resisted and it was pointed out that rates in Ireland may have appeared relatively generous compared to the UK, but this was not the case when reviewed against European standards (2018: 13). The Troika sought to spur on reform measures during their regular reviews, commenting that activation 'remains weak in relation … to European standards' (European Commission, 2012: 13). It was observed that welfare conditionality was not being implemented with the expected rigour and it was commented in a European Commission review (European Commission, 2011b: 32) that 'the use of financial sanctions for uncooperative unemployed is still very rare'. While Ireland operates activation policies, and recently introduced related sanctions for non-compliance, the rollout of the former has been relatively slow and there is evidence that the level of sanctioning for non-compliance has been low. The Minister for Social Protection (Dáil Éireann Debate, 2018) confirmed that 16,451 penalty deductions were applied to welfare payments in 2017, involving 13,503 individuals. In contrast, benefit sanctioning has been relatively frequent in the UK, with the National Audit Office (NAO) (2016: 6) reporting that 400,000 sanctions were imposed in 2015 (changes in the methodology for UK benefit sanctions statistics makes later comparison more difficult).

Studies have been carried out to monitor whether recipients of welfare support receive sufficient income to cover their essential living costs. MacMahon et al (2017) calculated the minimum average weekly cost of goods and services that will support a standard of living deemed sufficient to enable participation in the norms of Irish life (MESL). This research is based on a negotiated consensus view of what is necessary to have as the MESL, as determined by focus groups for each household type (MacMahon et al, 2006). MacMahon et al (2017) concluded that for all household types in the year to March 2017, apart from pensioners, social welfare support did not provide the MESL. Households with younger children were generally in a better position than those with secondary school children, reflecting the higher costs of older children. The largest shortfall was for households with teenage children, and single parents with teenagers fared worst. In these vulnerable households, social welfare income represented only 78 per cent of the minimum essential expenditure required by the household. The study also revealed that the minimum cost of food and utilities represented 42 per cent of a single person's social welfare payment. This is after an improvement during the last three years in the proportion of minimum costs that are met by welfare supports. The results for Ireland may be compared with research undertaken in 2020 by Safefood and the Food Standards Agency in Northern Ireland (FSA, 2021). This NI study was also 'consumer-led', being based on what consumers (rather than experts) regard as essential for a minimum standard of living. It was found that some low-income families have to spend between 24 per cent and 46 per cent of their income on a minimum food basket that meets basic nutritional requirements. Similar to Ireland, households with teenage children faced the largest expenditure, with a food basket costing approximately one third higher than for a comparable household with younger children.

Capacity for change

Following an assessment of welfare state development internationally over 40 years, Pierson (2011: 16) concluded that there was 'a striking story of stability at the level of core programs', as welfare states became change-resistant. However, Hemerijk (2013: 25) recognised that the recent economic recession resulted in a challenging combination of reduced government revenues, at the same time as higher expenditure on social protection. He argues that this squeeze on finances led governments to seek out policies that would ease the funding of the welfare state, by shifting some of the onus for welfare support to individual workers (2013: 33). While reforms in the UK have been driven by ideological and political considerations, Murphy (2012) argues that debate about reform in Ireland is muted and not as ambitious.

It was not until 1983 that the first fundamental review of social welfare in Ireland was undertaken. The Report of the Commission on Social Welfare was published in 1986 and recommended evolutionary reforms, rather than any change to the overall framework (Commission on Social Welfare, 1986). A critical review of income adequacy was an important part of the Commission's work and recommendations were made to increase social welfare payments, which was addressed by incremental progress in subsequent budgets (Curry, 2011: 37). McCashin (2015) concluded that there was considerable continuity in Irish social security during the 25 years leading up to the 2008 economic crisis. During this period of stability there was little evidence of either capacity or willingness to pursue structural reforms. Any changes were gradual, rather than 'root and branch', and this limited reform agenda suggests that the metaphor used by Palier and Martin (2007) about a 'frozen landscape' of reform in welfare systems could be applied to Ireland. Cousins has pointed out (2016: 39) that the social welfare system in Ireland is centralised, with all key areas, including planning and delivery, being the responsibility of the DSP. The DSP (2010) indicated that reforms were focused on incentivising people to take up employment. It acknowledged that changes have often been reactive and followed intervention from pressure groups, without adequate regard to the consequences for the overall direction of the social welfare system (2010: 72).

Stability over time in the welfare system has been explained as arising from an 'incremental policy culture' (Murphy, 2012: 359), with conservative social security policy that focuses on need, rather than redistribution. Although the Commission on Social Welfare (1986) argued that the social security system should have an explicit role related to redistribution, there is no evidence that this has translated into official policy. The lack of a progressive policy agenda also reflects limited ideological debate or public discussion about reforming social security. It is argued that this reflects the absence of significant ideologically based difference in policies between the two main political parties and that Irish political debate on the topic tends to be consensual in nature (Daly and Yeates, 2003: 88). Lynch suggests that, while Ireland is liberal leaning, there is 'a denial of ideology at the heart of party politics', with populist political parties that 'conceal their own ideological roots' (2010: 11). The literature thus indicates path dependency and little capacity for change or significant reform in social welfare programmes.

Carers

Census 2011 reported that 4.1 per cent (187,112) of the population in Ireland carried out regular unpaid caring work. Social welfare payments, which comprise a means-tested Carer's Allowance and a social insurance-based Carer's Benefit, provide limited support to family carers. The latter scheme allows two years of leave from employment to provide care, but there have been less than 2,000 annual claimants since the late 2000s (DSP, 2015). Caring responsibilities are a significant barrier to employment for carers who wish to join the labour force. The early welfare state in Ireland incorporated certain assumptions, including the male breadwinner model, with a gendered division of paid and unpaid work and where women would undertake any caring role necessary as part of family life. However, this model has been in decline over recent decades, as women have increasingly participated in the formal labour market. These changes exposed the extent of previously hidden care roles undertaken within families (Dukelow and Considine, 2017: 328).

Russell et al (2018) reported that childcare costs are a significant barrier to work for many households. Low-income families and lone parents were identified as having the greatest financial burden. The SVP (2014: 9) found that childcare was the second-largest expense for households after housing. This suggests that policies to address the costs of childcare are needed, with a particular focus on those most affected, who are already at a high risk of poverty. Ireland was positioned in joint last position in a UNICEF study carried out across 25 advanced countries on a range of indicators regarding early childhood education and care (Adamson, 2008). However, Ireland's Minister for Children and Youth Affairs has stated that it will take time to correct decades of under-investment in childcare (Zappone, 2018).

The private sector has dominated the provision of childcare services and state involvement remains relatively low, resulting in relatively high childcare costs for parents (Murray et al, 2016: 113). The lack of state funding for childcare and family policies still contributes to relatively low participation by women in the labour force. However, the increase in working mothers led to demand for state childcare provision, and the Report of the Partnership 2000 Expert Working Group on Childcare (Government of Ireland, 1999) recommended both tax breaks for employers and tax allowances for parents. The Government chose to increase places for childcare and subsequently raised child benefit payments (Curry, 2011: 261). It has recently expanded the Early Childhood Care and Education (ECCE) Scheme, which provides care and education for children of pre-school age. This is complemented by the Early Start Programme, which is targeted at schools in disadvantaged areas and provides one year to pre-school children, focused on helping their overall development (Department of Education and Skills [DOEAS], 2018).

Outside the childcare arena, the voluntary sector (including Church bodies and charities) plays a major role in providing a range of care services. However, this is declining, due to a range of factors arising from social change, including the lower levels of new entrants to religious orders. A nationwide carer consultation in 2007 focused on family carers supporting family members because of old age, disability or long-term illness. The report recommended more sharing of caring responsibilities by the state, improved income support for carers and support services that focus on carers' needs (Care Association et al, 2008: vi). According to Dukelow and Considine (2017: 321), the implementation of these actions would necessitate a significant overhaul of existing social services practices.

Illness and disability

A study by Watson et al (2016) reported on the relatively high levels of material deprivation and persistent poverty among households where an adult has an illness or disability. In part, this reflects the inequity of access to the Irish healthcare system (Dukelow and Considine, 2017: 237). Ireland has a dual system of private and public health provision, which includes private medical insurance, taken up by approximately half of the population, beds designated as public and private, and hospital consultants with different work practices and contracts (Curry, 2011: 158). There are long waiting lists in Ireland's health service for those who rely on the public system, which can prolong periods of unemployment for those waiting for some important medical procedures.

The primary care sector has historically been fragmented and poorly resourced (Dukelow and Considine, 2017: 230), and Ireland is the only EU country that does not have universal coverage (Wren and Connolly, 2016). There are different categories of entitlement to public health services, based on means-testing and residency (living in Ireland and intending to live in the country for at least one year). There was a 40 per cent increase in the number of medical cards to 1.7 million from 2007 to 2016 (CSO, 2016), although the share of medical card holders subsequently decreased to 32 per cent in 2018 (Statistica, 2019). Qualification for a medical card is linked to weekly income for family size, with holders entitled to a range of public health services without charge. These include GP visits, public out-patient and in-patient services, eye and ear tests and dental checks. The Euro Health Consumer Index (EHCI) monitors a range of indicators based on a combination of official statistics, patient surveys and independent research. In 2018, Ireland's healthcare system was ranked 22nd place in Europe overall and in the bottom position for accessibility (waiting times for treatment) (Björnberg and Phang, 2019). It also scored relatively poorly in other categories, including the range and reach of services provided.

An ESRI study found that, for people with disabilities, employment was an important factor in reducing the risk of poverty (Gannon and Nolan, 2006). It reported that over 80 per cent of disabled people who were also categorised as AROP lived in households where no one was in paid work. The employment rate in Ireland for working-age people with disabilities is low by international standards, with only 33 per cent of people in this category working (Government of Ireland, 2018a: 24).

Low pay and precarious employment

While low pay has undoubtedly contributed significantly to the problem of poverty, including food poverty, examination of the literature on the adequacy of the minimum or living wage reveals more complexity. Stabile (2008: 10; emphasis added) argues that 'low wage workers should earn a living wage as *defined by the standards of the community* in which they live and work', which illustrates that it is a relative concept which aligns with Townsend's understanding of poverty. The National Minimum Wage (NMW) in Ireland, which is set by the Low Pay Commission, has been increased on several occasions and, as of February 2020, was €10.10 for an experienced adult employee (Citizens Information, 2020). In Ireland, there is also a system of legally binding minimum wages across 11 sectors, which since the early 1900s have been set by Joint Labour Committees, and they are mostly above the NMW (O'Sullivan and Royle, 2014). The Living Wage for the Republic of Ireland, €12.30 an hour in 2020–21, is distinct from the minimum wage and based on the premise that income from employment should be sufficient to enable workers to afford a socially acceptable standard of living (Living Wage Ireland, 2020). In recent years, housing costs have been the main component driving increases in the Living Wage. However, it has limited influence as, unlike the NMW, it is an informal benchmark and not a legally enforceable pay rate.

In addition to the problem of low pay, recent trends in employment indicate an increased 'flexibilisation' of labour markets across Ireland, as well as other countries in the EU (Dukelow and Murphy, 2016: 19). The European Commission reports that, during the recent economic crisis, the loss of jobs in Ireland was accompanied by a growth in precarious work, particularly involuntary part-time work (European Commission, 2014). This was accompanied by an increasing trend towards a polarisation in the type of jobs available, particularly in the service sectors, with new jobs tending to be either relatively well-paid, high-skilled positions or low skilled and low-paid work (European Commission, 2014: 32). NESC reported (NESC, 2018a) that unemployed people supported by social welfare may have limited discretion over the work they choose and be obliged to take up jobs that may not provide a living wage, in order to avoid sanctions. The NESC study on moving from welfare to work reported that some of the unemployed felt they were offered no choice by social welfare service staff in relation to employment options and were obliged to take up precarious work, as a result of activation measures (NESC, 2018b).

Among OECD countries, Ireland had the third-highest proportion of low-paid workers in 2017 after Latvia and the US, on the basis of the share of workers earning lower than two thirds of median earnings (OECD, 2019b). The OECD (2017, 2019b) estimated that the proportion of low-paid workers in Ireland has been on an upward trajectory, from 17.8 per cent in 2000 to 23 per cent in 2017. Eurofound (2017b: 12) reported that the extent of low-paid work in Ireland is influenced by weak bargaining and a deregulated labour market. There are areas of the economy that employ a significant proportion on low pay, with many working in the wholesale, retail, food and hospitality sectors. According to Collins (2015), this is especially problematic for full-time working women, of whom approximately 30 per cent are low paid.

In-work poverty arises when an adult is working, but lives in a household that is below the AROP threshold, based on 60 per cent of the median household income (Watson et al, 2012: 59). In Ireland, the empirical evidence from EU-SILC data indicates that 6 per cent of the population were at risk of in-work poverty in 2014 (Eurofound, 2017b). This reflects a significant fall in median income during the global financial crisis (2017b: 16), rather than an improvement in living standards for the working poor. In-work poverty is a complex issue and, although low pay is an obvious cause, household composition is also key (2017b: 14). For example, the risk of in-work poverty is high for single-earner households with dependent children. Under-employment is also relevant, as 25 per cent of the low paid work less than 20 hours per week (Collins, 2015). Poverty rates are high in these 'low work intensity' households, which experience high unemployment, are often in the manual social class, have relatively low educational achievement and report higher levels of disability (NESC, 2018b). These households frequently include children, often with a lone parent, and accommodated in social housing.

Household type

The limited research carried out in Ireland on food costs for each main household type points to a higher risk of food poverty for certain households. The Vincentian Partnership for Social Justice's research on the MESL, discussed earlier in this chapter, reviewed food costs in 2018, which vary significantly for the six different household types examined (Safefood, 2019). The cost of a healthy food basket as a proportion of household take-home income (where receiving social welfare) is highest in households with a teenager. Two-parent/two-children households (with one child at secondary school) spend 30 per cent of their take-home income on food, if receiving social welfare. This reduces to 24 per cent if one parent is employed and receives the NMW. While single parents with young children (one pre-school and one primary school) spend 26 per cent, this proportion increases for older children. The lowest food basket cost relative to take-home income is for couples receiving the state pension, where the proportion is 16 per cent (the percentage varies, depending on pension entitlement).

Research in Northern Ireland on the drivers of food poverty has used focus groups to explore how those on low incomes manage food choices and diet, given difficult choices in terms of financial, social and other factors (Purdy et al, 2007). High-risk groups for food poverty were identified as lone-parent families, large families, older people and households with low incomes (often with the head of household unemployed). The aforementioned studies have conveyed the high risk of poverty in one-parent families, which aligns with other research in the EU (Chzhen and Bradshaw, 2012). Analysis of EU-SILC data for 2014 revealed that 40 per cent of these households in Ireland were AROP, which, after Bulgaria, was the highest level in the EU28 (European Institute of Gender Equality [EIGE], 2016).

The differences in relation to food consumption and attitudes of consumers across socio-economic groups in Ireland was investigated by Kearney et al (2008). The research identified young women living in disadvantaged urban environments as being at a higher risk of food poverty, in comparison to a reference group not living in such disadvantaged areas. Further research, using focus groups, identified the cost of food as an important factor in food choices. However, it played a 'subservient role' (2008: 15) when compared to other issues such as comfort-eating, due to social stresses. The stress triggers included insecure housing tenure, local crime, childcare demands and financial worries. A qualitative research study on the attitudes and behaviours of low-income households across the island of Ireland, in relation to food, studied four vulnerable household types: lone parents, two-parent families, single males and single older people (Safefood, 2011). The study found that food management was focused on the 'here and now' (2011: 63) and that food choices tended to be very conservative, due to limited budget flexibility. The majority of respondents did not link food with health and regarded 'eating badly' as often less costly than a healthy diet.

Housing

The prevailing housing crisis in Ireland is evidenced by long waiting lists for social housing, a shortage of affordable rental accommodation and persistent homelessness (Dukelow and Considine, 2017). Ireland's Celtic Tiger economy was accompanied by significant rises in house prices, which fell sharply during the recession that followed. The recent recovery and associated rising housing costs may be part of the explanation for food poverty. This is particularly the case for those who are not able to obtain social housing and those who rely on renting in the private sector. Those in social housing normally pay a differential rent calculated on the basis of household income, rather than on market conditions. However, renters are exposed to private rates, with a cumulative increase of nearly 50 per cent since 2012 (Residential Tenancies Board [RTB], 2018). For those in private rental accommodation, rent levels must be within designated limits in order to obtain rent support from their local authority, with some limited exceptions. The maximum limits for rents were raised in July 2016, but the benefit of these adjustments has eroded, as market rents have increased further. The result is limited availability of affordable accommodation, particularly in the Dublin area.

The evidence suggests that the cost of housing is having an increasing impact on family budgets. The Household Budget Survey 2015–16 ('HBS') reported that average weekly household expenditure in Ireland was €837, 3.3 per cent higher than in 2009–10 (CSO, 2012: 5). However, the proportion spent on food has declined steadily. In the HBS 2015–16, food accounted for only 14.7 per cent of total household expenditure, having fallen steadily since 1980, when it represented the largest proportion (27.7 per cent) of the total. In contrast, the proportion spent on housing costs has continued to rise, exceeding that of food for the first time in the 2009–10 HBS Survey and reaching 19.6 per cent in 2015–16 (CSO, 2018b). These results indicate that the average spent on food varied significantly by housing tenure. Those with a mortgage spent 13.1 per cent of their average weekly expenditure on food, compared to 13.9 per cent for those in privately rented accommodation and 20.1 per cent when in local authority housing (CSO, 2018b). A key aspect of the housing crisis in Ireland is homelessness, which remains a persistent problem, particularly in Dublin, where 70 per cent of the homeless are located (Department of Housing, Planning & Local Government, 2018). Hickey and Downey (2003) established a link between homelessness and food poverty.

Cost of food

The literature conveys that food represents a large expenditure category for low-income households. During the post-millennium period, both the Consumer Price Index (CPI) and the overall cost of food in Ireland peaked in 2008. It then commenced a downward trajectory, as the recession took hold in the Irish economy. Figure 3.2 illustrates these trends, indicating that the price of food has moved close to its level in 2001, while the CPI in 2020 is close to the 2008 peak. Despite this downward trend, in 2015 food prices in Ireland remained above the EU average (CSO, 2016).

In 2018, prices in Ireland for food and non-alcoholic beverages were 20 per cent above the EU28 average and approximately 13 per cent above the average for the eurozone (countries using the euro). Of the EU countries, Ireland and Finland were ranked as the fourth most expensive, while Ireland along with Finland were the third most expensive of the eurozone countries (CSO, 2020c). For eurozone countries in 2018, Ireland was ranked the fifth most expensive for bread and cereals, ninth most expensive for meat,

Figure 3.2: Ireland: trend in Consumer Price Index and Food Index, 2000–20

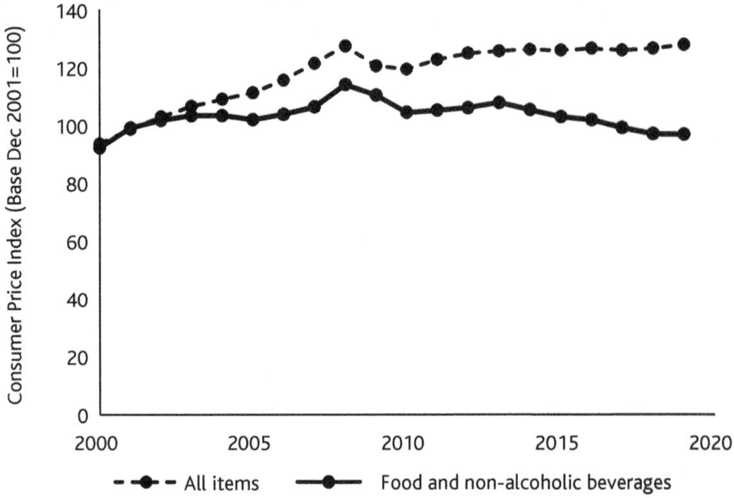

Source: Prepared by author based on data from CSO (2020b)

seventh most expensive for fish, fourth most expensive for milk, cheese and eggs and the joint third most expensive country for fruits, vegetables and potatoes (CSO, 2020c).

Food deserts

In Ireland, there have been few studies on 'food deserts', which occur when people live in locations from where they find it difficult to access affordable nutritious food, such as fresh fruit and vegetables. Apart from financial constraints, it has been argued that the main structural hindrance to healthy food choices in Ireland arises from physical constraints (Friel et al, 2006: 1013). In 2005, the issue of food deserts was raised by the SVP at an Oireachtas (Government) committee on food prices (Government of Ireland. Joint Committee on Enterprise and Small Business, 2005). It was pointed out that many households on low incomes are forced to rely on local shops, often with limited choices and higher prices, relative to large discount supermarkets. Layte et al (2011) analysed the Survey of Lifestyle, Attitudes and Nutrition 2007 (10,364 participants surveyed) and found that access to food outlets influenced the diet of individuals and may impact on socio-economic inequalities in health. Respondents who lived nearer to large food stores were found to have a superior diet, assessed on the basis of cardiovascular risk. Access to suitable transport is an important factor in location-based food poverty in Ireland, exacerbated by limitations in the public transport system and reliance on travel by car for shopping.

Policy and political profile of food poverty

In Ireland, political discourse on food poverty has been very limited, reflecting its surprisingly low profile compared to the UK, for example. A search of records on Irish Government debates over the last five years revealed only two references to the issue. In May 2018, Willie O'Dea TD, the spokesperson on Social Protection for the main opposition party, raised the issue of food poverty with the Minister for Employment Affairs and Social Protection (Dáil Éireann, 2018). The Minister accepted that preventing poverty, including food poverty, was an important role of her Department and specifically mentioned the role of social welfare income supports. The Minister agreed to review the funding mechanisms provided through the national anti-poverty strategy. The latest National Action Plan against Poverty and Social Inclusion (2015–17) made no reference to food poverty, although it contained specific goals to address energy poverty (DSP, 2016a: 10). However, the more recent Roadmap for Social Inclusion 2020–2025, published in January 2020, acknowledges that the level of food poverty in Ireland is of concern and indicates that measures will be taken to address the problem.

Another indication of the low profile of food poverty in Ireland is illustrated by the Government's approach in relation to the UN Sustainable Development Goals (SDGs). These global targets, which were set out by the United Nations General Assembly in 2015, include a goal to 'end hunger, achieve food security and improved nutrition' (UN, 2019). In the initial government approved Voluntary National Review report (Government of Ireland, 2018b), it was reported that 9.2 per cent of the population in Ireland experienced food poverty in 2016 (2018b: 28). However, in relation to SDGs, the report refers to two policy documents published by the Department of Foreign Affairs. These relate to Ireland's international development programme and make no reference to food poverty in Ireland. The report refers to the problem of obesity, specifically the national policy document 'A Healthy Weight for Ireland: Obesity Policy and Action Plan 2016–2025' (Department of Health, 2016). This document does not mention malnutrition or food poverty. In contrast, a similar assessment of performance against SDG targets in the UK specifically covers the problem of food poverty, in addition to obesity. The UK Stakeholders for Sustainable Development (UKSSD), which comprises organisations in the UK seeking to drive action on its SDG targets, has reviewed possible causes of food insecurity in the UK. It refers to food insecurity as a significant issue in the UK and has made specific recommendations, including the appointment of a government minister with responsibility and accountability for addressing the problem (UKSSD, 2018). However, at the time of writing, despite further calls from a cross-party group of MPs for a 'Minister for Food Security' in the context of the COVID-19 pandemic (UK Parliament, 2021), this has so far not been accepted by the UK Government.

It is difficult to explain why food poverty has such a low profile in Ireland. Possible reasons include the lack of media profile acting as an agent for change, as in some other countries. The UN Special Rapporteur on the Right to Food, De Schutter, has commented that many societies have kept food poverty largely out of view and public discourse (Riches and Silvasti, 2014). He argues that the emergence of food banks in advanced countries has provided a visible reminder of the problem. It can be argued that the relatively low number and discreet locations of food banks and other food aid outlets in Ireland compared with the UK, for example, has contributed to its low profile. The lack of a strong left-right political divide in Ireland could also be a contributory factor. However, in a further comparison with the UK, where there is arguably a broader political spectrum, it is of note that the members of the UK All-Party Parliamentary Group on Hunger and Food Poverty comprised a balance between the main Conservative and Labour parties.

Conclusions

The limited literature on food poverty in Ireland includes a quantitative assessment of its prevalence, indicating a reduction from a peak level of 13.2 per cent in 2013 to 7 per cent in 2018. A more detailed analysis of 2010 data by Carney and Maître (2012) revealed that the highest risk was for lone-parent families, although other families with two or more children were also at an elevated risk, together with the unemployed, those in low-paid work, ill/disabled, or undertaking home duties, such as caring roles. Although qualitative studies of low-income households in Ireland have not focused on food poverty, some have provided insights on the problem. The authors point to the need for a study dedicated to an investigation of food poverty.

The literature conveys that drivers of food poverty include a wide range of factors and policy issues, with many households facing multiple challenges. As evidenced by quantitative research, food poverty is a relatively high risk for those who are unemployed and rely on social protection. Ireland exhibits some key features of a liberal welfare regime, although is often regarded as a hybrid (McCashin, 2015). Social protection is characterised by extensive means-testing, with expenditure relatively low compared to the EU average and evidence pointing to low capacity for change or reform. Research indicates that social transfers do not provide an adequate level of income for most household types. In Ireland, families remain significant care providers and private provision is found to be too costly for many households. Improved state support for carers' needs would require significant reform of existing social services, which remain a barrier to employment. Adults with an illness or disability experience relatively high levels of poverty. This is exacerbated by Ireland's health system, which is challenged by inequities, particularly in relation to access. Medical costs increase financial difficulties for the unemployed and those on low incomes, while barriers to employment include long waiting lists for treatment. For those with disabilities, paid work helps to reduce the risk of poverty, but the employment rate in Ireland for working-age people with disabilities is relatively low. For the employed, food poverty is of concern more than low pay, with factors such as household composition and the number of dependents critical in determining the risk of poverty. Although the prevalence of low-paid precarious work is increasing, working poverty often arises from under-employment, where low income is due to limited hours worked.

Other explanations for food poverty include the relatively high cost of food, with Ireland the third most expensive country in the eurozone. Despite this increased cost, the proportion of household expenditure on food has continued to reduce. This reflects other pressures on household budgets, with housing costs and utilities regarded as essential to pay, in order to avoid homelessness and maintain a functioning household. In particular, housing has become a significant risk factor for food poverty in Ireland and household expenditure on accommodation has become the largest cost category. Research on food deserts has also identified an enhanced risk of food poverty for those having difficulty accessing food stores, due to their physical location.

4

Interpreting the data

Introduction

This chapter examines the extent of food poverty in Ireland, including trends over time, and provides a comparative quantitative analysis of Ireland with EU15. A review of food poverty indicators in Ireland is undertaken, based on an analysis of the latest secondary data available, including recent evidence regarding the impact of the COVID-19 pandemic. The analysis explores the characteristics of those experiencing food poverty in Ireland and considers factors that may predict food poverty. These data align with the timing of the interviews of food bank users. The chapter then focuses on comparing Ireland with other EU15 countries. Following a discussion of the results in the context of previous research, the conclusion summarises the key messages.

Prevalence of food poverty in Ireland, 2006–18

Two sources providing comparable data on food poverty are the EU-SILC and an OECD survey carried out by Gallup World Poll. Data on food insecurity in European countries were obtained from the UN FAO. Background on the secondary analysis of survey data in this study is set out in Appendix 1.

Figure 4.1 provides an overview of the four food-related deprivation items from EU-SILC in 2006, 2013 and 2018, which allows an assessment of food poverty in Ireland between 2006 and 2018. This timespan straddled a period of economic growth, followed by the onset of recession in 2008 and subsequent emerging recovery. Overall, it confirms that food poverty increased in the period to 2013, at least partly reflecting the impact of Ireland's recession on living standards. This is evidenced by the significant increases in all 11 deprivation indicators measured in the same period (Central Statistics Office [CSO], 2015: 17). In 2018, the four food deprivation indicators recorded an improvement, which was consistent with the developing economic recovery.

The four items each increased significantly during the seven-year period to 2013, before commencing a downward trajectory. The social aspect of food poverty is at a significantly higher level than the other items. The

Figure 4.1: Food poverty, Ireland, 2006, 2013 and 2018

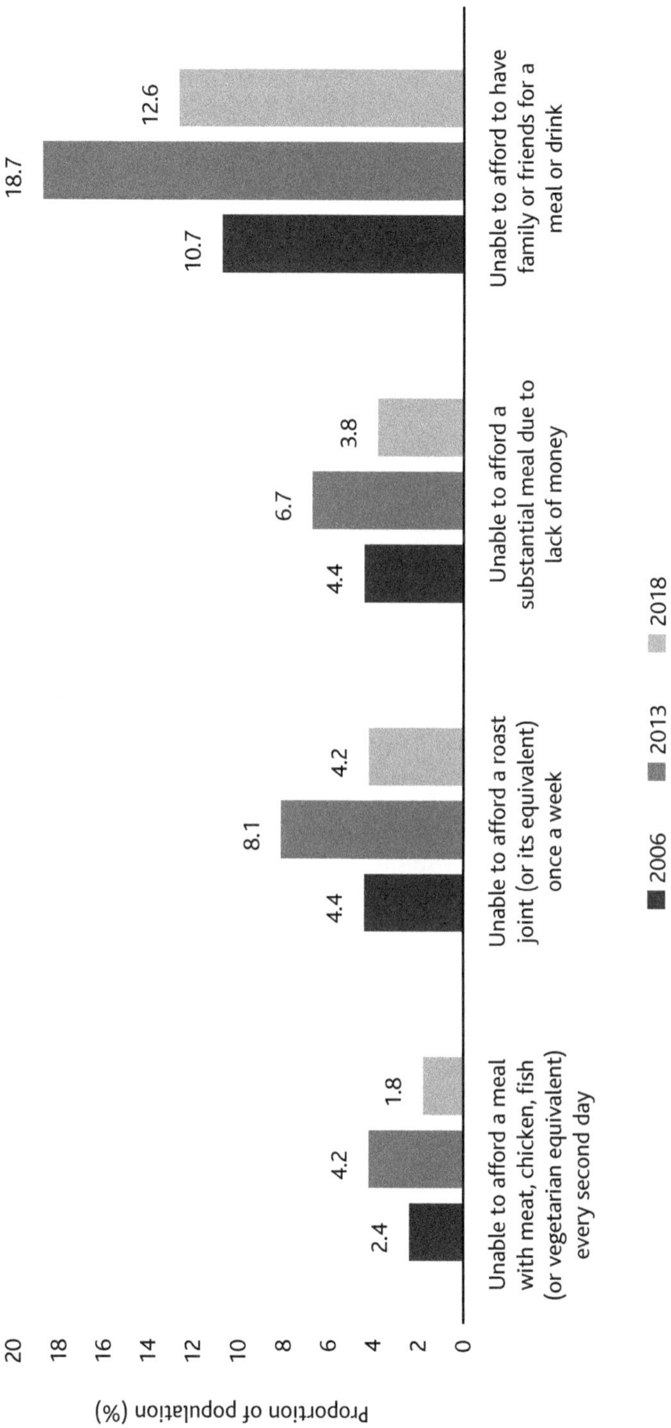

Source: CSO SILC (2006, 2013 and 2018), analysis by author

proportion reporting inability to afford to have family or friends for a meal or drink was up from 10.7 per cent in 2006 to 18.7 per cent in 2013, falling back to 12.6 per cent for 2018.

In order to avoid over reliance on one measure, the following analysis is based on a composite measure of food poverty for Ireland, which was put forward by Carney and Maître (2012) and is now regarded as the official food poverty indicator. It combines three of the food deprivation items. The measure 'unable to afford to have family or friends for a meal or drink' is excluded, in line with the approach of Carney and Maître (2012: 24), as it differs from the other questions by addressing social aspects relating to food and drink. Eating out with family and/or friends is important and has been described as an 'essential form of social and cultural participation' (Pfeiffer et al, 2011: 417), although the reference to 'drink' arguably extends the measurement to wider issues than those involving food. Healy (2019) has taken issue with the exclusion of this item from official estimates, arguing that it restricts measurement to items covering nutritional adequacy, food deprivation and cultural deprivation. While these are important aspects, this approach effectively ignores an important aspect of social inclusion, where the level of deprivation is comparatively high. It may be concluded that, given the relatively elevated proportion of respondents reporting this type of social deprivation, the official approach may underestimate food poverty in Ireland. Healy (2019: 114) has carried out an analysis of 2015 SILC data, demonstrating that the inclusion of the measure regarding meeting family or friends for a meal or drink would result in a nearly doubling of the reported prevalence of food poverty in Ireland. However, while the social dimension of food poverty is important, it was decided to use the official measure in this work.

Food poverty, using the official composite measure, is assessed by determining the level of deprivation in one or more of the other three items. On this basis, the level of food poverty is set out in Figure 4.2. It indicates that food poverty declined from 2006 to 2007, then remained relatively flat over the following two-year period, before a sharp increase to 10.1 per cent in 2010. The upward trend continued, with food poverty levels peaking at 13.2 per cent in 2013, before commencing a downward trajectory to 7.3 per cent in 2018. This level suggests that food poverty affects over a third of a million people in Ireland.

The composite food poverty indicator conveys the impact of the recession on household circumstances. It is useful to compare this trend with the AROP rate (60 per cent of median income after pensions and social transfers), which is illustrated in Figure 4.3. This income poverty measure declined between 2006 and 2009 but, unlike food poverty, did not increase significantly over the subsequent period and peaked at 17.3 per cent in 2012. It remained stable around this level, before commencing a downward trajectory. This

Figure 4.2: Trend in food poverty in Ireland, 2006–18

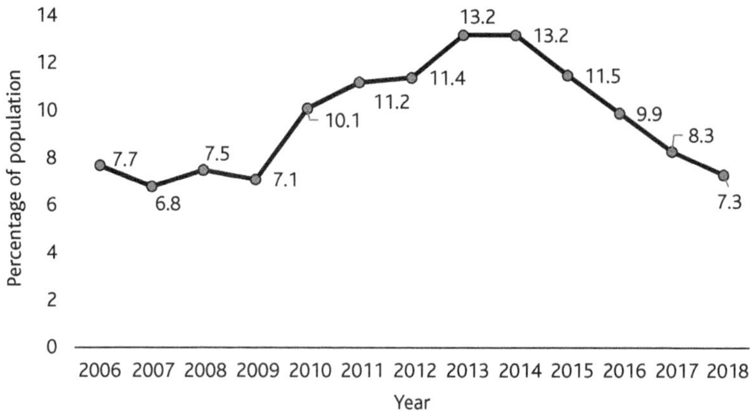

Note: The composite indicator was created from three of the food-related deprivation indicators used in the SILC. The measure is based on a threshold of reporting any one from the three items.
Source: EU SILC (2006 to 2018), analysis by author

Figure 4.3: Poverty in Ireland (AROP) v food poverty (composite indicator), 2006–18

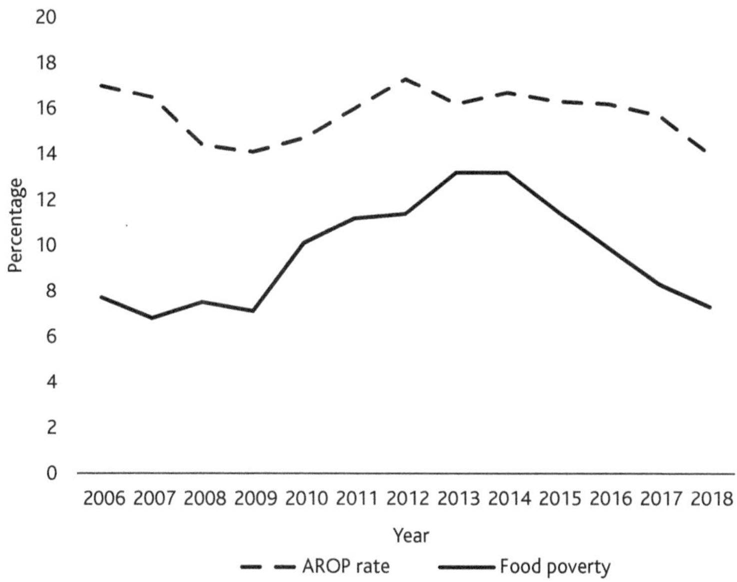

Source: CSO and EU-SILC (2006 to 2018), analysis by author

Figure 4.4: Trend in food poverty (composite indicator) in Ireland, by region, 2012–18

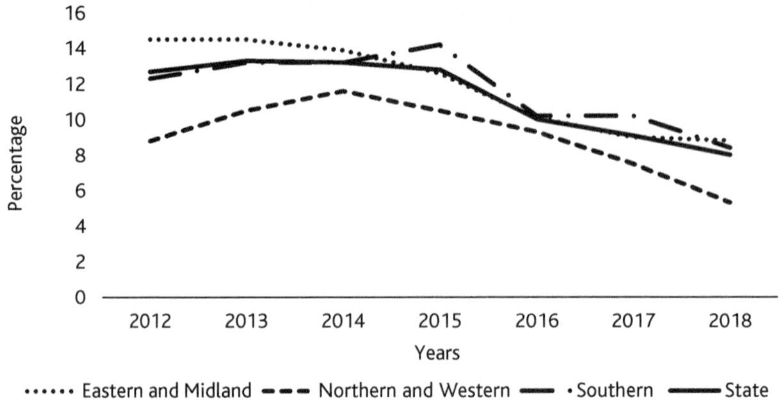

Source: CSO (2021: Table 1.2), analysis by author

can be explained because AROP is determined based on median incomes, which fell during the recession (Watson et al, 2018). However, it illustrates the value of non-monetary deprivation indicators in measuring food poverty, compared with solely income-based measures.

A regional analysis of food poverty in Ireland from 2012 to 2018 is set out in Figure 4.4, based on data provided by the CSO (2021). It shows that the prevalence of food poverty was highest in the Eastern and Midland region (8.8 per cent), while the lowest was in the Northern and Western region (5.3 per cent). While no further analysis is provided, the explanation for the higher level in the Eastern and Midland region may be associated with the increased risk of food poverty in the conurbation of Dublin. This reflects the higher risk of food poverty in urban locations, compared to rural areas (see Table 4.1).

Characteristics of those experiencing food poverty in Ireland

This section complements the preceding review of the extent and trends in food poverty, by examining the demographic and socio-economic profile of those experiencing food poverty, using 2016 EU-SILC. The characteristics explored were gender, marital status, composition of household, education, income, social class, principal economic status, housing tenure, health profile and location. The characteristics of those experiencing the highest risk of food poverty are summarised in Figure 4.5. The most important factors included where the HRP was a lone parent with children (25 per cent), renting below the market rate (24 per cent), unemployed (23 per cent), ill/disabled (21 per cent), separated/divorced (19 per cent), renting

Table 4.1: Risk of food poverty by demographic and socio-economic factors, 2016

HRP Gender	Male	9%
	Female	11%
HRP Marital status	Single	13%
	Married	6%
	Widowed	10%
	Separated/divorced	19%
Household composition	1 adult, no children under 18 years	12%
	2 adults, no children under 18 years	7%
	3 or more adults, no children under 18 years	7%
	1 adult, 1 or more children under 18 years	25%
	2 adults, 1 to 3 children under 18 years	9%
	Other households with children under 18 years	11%
Number of children under 18 in the household	0	8%
	1	12%
	2	9%
	3+	14%
HRP Education	None or primary	13%
	Junior Cert (Intermediate) Level	12%
	Leaving Cert Level	11%
	Low Tertiary Level	8%
	High Tertiary Level	5%
HRP Income	Lowest and second quintile	12%
	Fourth and highest quintile	6%
Social class	Higher and lower professional	4%
	Clerical and secretarial	5%
	Self employed	5%
	Lower service/technical and routine	12%
HRP Principal economic status	At work	6%
	Unemployed	23%
	Student	10%
	On home duties	12%
	Retired	5%
	Ill/disabled	21%
	Other	12%

(continued)

Table 4.1: Risk of food poverty by demographic and socio-economic factors, 2016 (continued)

HRP Tenure status	Owner occupied	7%
	Rented at market rate	15%
	Rented below market rate or rent free	24%
Health status (self-reported)	Very good and good	9%
	Fair, bad and very bad	12%
Chronic illness or condition	Chronic illness	14%
	No chronic illness	7%
Limited activities due to a health problem	Very limited and limited	17%
	Not limited	9%
Location	Urban	11%
	Rural	8%
Total		10%

Source: CSO SILC (2016), analysis by author

Figure 4.5: Risk of food poverty: summary chart of most important demographic and socio-economic factors, 2016

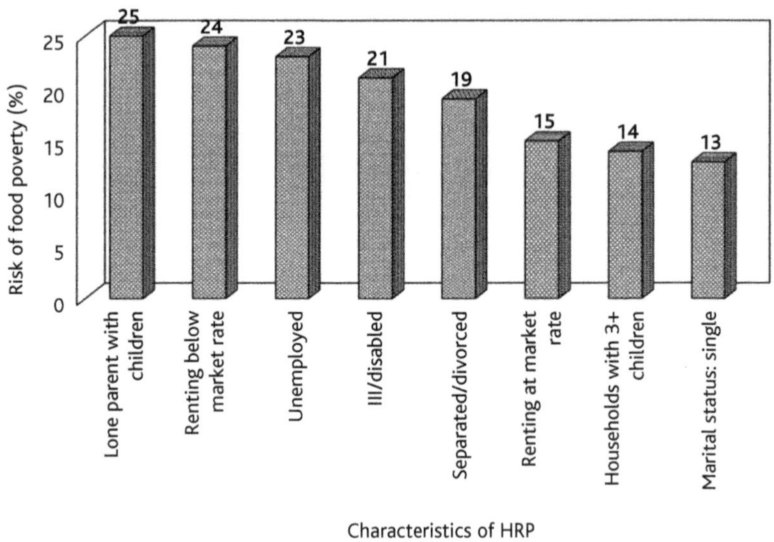

Source: CSO SILC (2016), analysis by author

at market rate (15 per cent), large families (3+ children) or single people (13 per cent).

The more detailed results are set out in Table 4.1, which reveals other interesting findings. While there was a slightly higher than average risk of food poverty for females, there was a higher level for single adults and those who are separated/divorced, which included those who may be caring for children alone. The risk of food poverty was higher in households with children and single-adult households without children. It was particularly prevalent (25 per cent) for lone parents with one or more children aged under 18 years. Food poverty was less prominent among those with higher levels of educational attainment. The highest rates occurred where the HRP was educated to intermediate level or lower. Those living in urban locations reported a higher rate of food poverty (11 per cent) than the rural population (8 per cent).

The food poverty rates for the top and bottom two income quintiles are set out in Table 4.1. This illustrates the contrast, with the risk of food poverty in the bottom 40 per cent of income distribution, twice as high as in the top 40 per cent. In relation to the HRP's principal economic status, the risk is highest for those who are unemployed or are ill/disabled and lowest for those who report being at work or retired. Food poverty was relatively low among professional, clerical workers and self-employed, in contrast to the significantly higher rate for those in lower social groups. The risk of food poverty was three times higher among those employed in lower service, technical and routine work than for the professional category. In relation to housing tenure, the risk of food poverty was significantly higher for those in rented accommodation, particularly those renting below the market rate (for example social housing).

Three health-related questions are asked in SILC: self-reported health status, whether the HRP reports having a chronic illness or condition and whether the respondent is limited in activities due to a health problem. There was a higher risk of food poverty for those who reported fair, bad and very bad health, with food poverty rates increasing as health declined. In households where the HRP reported a chronic illness or condition, the level of food poverty (14 per cent) was reported as twice that in other households (7 per cent). In households where the HRP reported either being very limited or limited in daily activities, food poverty (17 per cent) was found to be nearly twice that in other households (9 per cent).

Logistic regression was carried out in order to assess the relative impact of a range of characteristics on the likelihood that respondents would report experiencing food poverty. The model used the composite food poverty indicator as the dependent variable and a range of predictor (independent) variables were chosen, as the literature review and previous analysis indicated a relationship between them and with food poverty:

- HRP Gender
- HRP Age
- HRP Marital status
- Household composition
- HRP Principal economic status
- HRP Socio-economic group
- HRP Education
- HRP Health
- HRP AROP
- Housing tenure

In interpreting the analysis, the focus was mostly on individual statistically significant results. The model indicates that age was a predictor of food poverty. Those aged 24 years or under were over two and a half times more likely to experience food poverty than those 65 years and over (the reference category). In cases where the HRP was aged between 25 and 64 years the odds were also significantly higher, particularly in the age range 25 to 49 years, where they were over twice as high as for those aged 65 years and over. Marital status was also a significant predictor, with all 'not currently married' groups (single, divorced, separated or widowed) reporting higher odds than those who were married. Those who were divorced, separated or widowed had over twice the odds of those who were married, while those reporting as single nearly twice the odds.

The principal economic status (PES) of the HRP was also a significant predictor of food poverty. For the unemployed, the odds of being in food poverty were over twice as high as for those in work. Odds of food poverty were also higher where the HRP was either ill/disabled or occupied with home duties. Socio-economic status was also a significant predictor, with the odds of food poverty over one and a half times higher for those in non-professional households. In relation to education, the odds of food poverty were higher for those educated to intermediate level or lower, compared with those who completed second level or a higher level of attainment.

The health of the HRP was another significant predictor of being in food poverty. For respondents self-reporting health problems, the odds of food poverty were over twice as high as households where the HRP was in good health. Housing tenure was a significant predictor of food poverty. The odds were nearly two times higher for those in renting below the market rate, compared to owner occupiers, and one and a half times higher in cases where the property was rented at the market rate. The poverty measure, AROP, was found to be a good predictor, although not as strong as other characteristics, such as age, marital status, health or housing tenure.

The impact of the COVID-19 pandemic

At the time of writing, the latest data available from EU-SILC and other official sources pre-dates the onset of COVID-19 in early 2020. However, there is little doubt from other evidence that the pandemic has given rise to an upturn of food poverty in Ireland and many other countries. As discussed earlier in this chapter, unemployment has been shown to be a predictor of food poverty, and data from the European Commission indicate that the impact of the pandemic on employment in Ireland has been relatively severe. Workers in precarious jobs have been particularly exposed to loss of employment, with those on temporary contracts in the hospitality, food services, travel and retail sectors most affected (Eurofound, 2021). In Ireland, these workers experienced a fall in income (compared to 2019) that was twice that of employees on higher salaries (European Commission, 2020) and the fifth highest rate among low wage earners across the EU27. However, the economic impact on families was cushioned by government compensation measures. This policy response to the crisis, including the Pandemic Unemployment Payment and Employee Wage Subsidy Scheme, mitigated significant income losses (Beirne et al, 2020).

A 2020 Eurofound survey (see Figure 4.6) reported a relatively low proportion of households in Ireland (compared to EU14) experiencing either difficulty or great difficulty (14 per cent) making ends meet during

Figure 4.6: Percentage of households experiencing difficulty/great difficulty (%) making ends meet during COVID-19, 2020

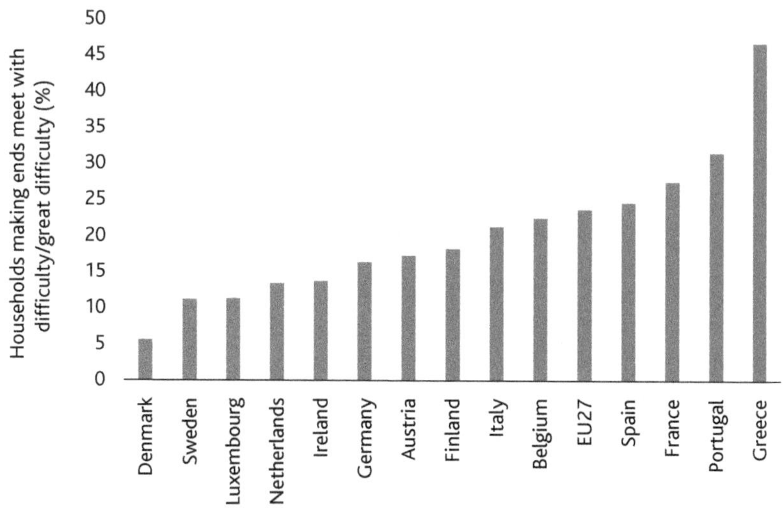

Source: Eurofound (2020), analysis by author

the pandemic. However, the results of two studies during COVID-19 illustrate that groups more vulnerable to poverty before the pandemic experienced a disproportionate impact during the outbreak. A food-related study by Gibney et al (2020) on the early impact of COVID-19 in Ireland and Northern Ireland was undertaken during spring 2020. It reported, based on a survey of 4,000 participants, that 20 per cent of respondents worried about not having sufficient food for their families during COVID-19. This was particularly the case during school closures, when children were not able to access school meals schemes. The study included interviews with community and advocacy groups, which revealed an increase in families needing food aid during the pandemic, often due to unemployment. This particularly affected vulnerable groups, who experienced food poverty, in addition to serious financial strain and social isolation.

A further study was undertaken by the Society of St Vincent de Paul (SVP) (2021a) on the financial impact of COVID-19 in Ireland, including online interviews carried out with over a thousand respondents in January 2021 by RED C (market research company). While it found that 15 per cent of all respondents reported restricting food costs due to financial strain, the pandemic exacerbated the existing situation of vulnerable groups. The unemployed were most affected, with 29 per cent cutting back on food due to costs, while 21 per cent of those unable to work due to illness or disability also reported having to reduce expenditure on food. In addition, a quarter of single people with children had to cut their food expenditure, as they found it difficult to cope financially with additional household costs, due to the lockdown and related school closures.

Some studies have monitored responses to food poverty arising from the additional problems in accessing food during the COVID-19 pandemic. In the UK, for example, Lambie-Mumford et al (2020) assessed interventions to help those unable to leave home to shop for food, or who have experienced income loss as a result of the crisis. Responses to food poverty, including during the COVID-19 outbreak, are discussed in Chapter 8.

Food poverty: Ireland in comparative context

Food poverty

Ireland's SILC questionnaire includes four questions that relate to food poverty. However, there is only one food poverty question that is asked consistently in surveys across all EU28 countries over time: the inability to afford a meal with meat, chicken, fish (or vegetarian equivalent) every second day. This allows a comparative analysis of this question for Ireland and other member states between 2006 and 2018 to investigate the extent, changes over time and role of welfare regimes in food poverty outcomes.

Figure 4.7: Trends in food poverty for Ireland, EU15 and EU28, 2006–18

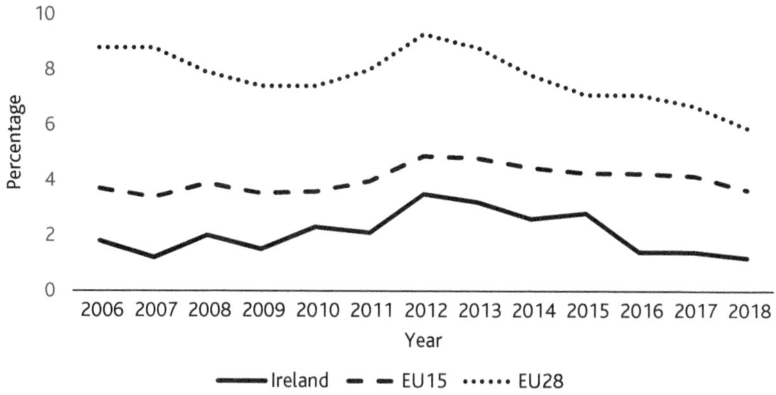

Note: In relation to EU28 trend line, EU27 data is used for 2006–09 (before the accession of Croatia)
Source: Eurostat (2018b), analysis by author

The analysis is restricted to EU15 countries, as Eastern European countries have very significantly higher levels of both food poverty and AROP levels, reflecting a lower standard of living (Böhnke, 2008). The rationale for focusing on EU15 is illustrated by Figure 4.7, which includes plots of food poverty for Ireland, EU15 and EU27/EU28 over the period 2006 to 2018. It illustrates that the high prevalence of food poverty in Eastern European countries had a significant influence on overall EU28 levels, compared to EU15. In addition, it shows that the level of food poverty in Ireland, based on one indicator, has been consistently below EU15. The trends in Ireland, EU15 and EU28 have been similar, with a marked rise during the recession to a peak in 2012 and subsequent improvements each year. There appears to be a delay between the onset of the economic crisis in 2008 and the peak levels of food poverty in 2012.

Figure 4.8 illustrates that Ireland had a relatively low rate of food poverty in 2018, as measured by this one item. At 1.2 per cent in 2018, Ireland recorded the fourth lowest rate across the EU15, with six countries at a level below 2 per cent (including Denmark, Netherlands, Sweden, Luxembourg and Portugal). This level was below the 1.8 per cent recorded in 2006, before an increase to 3.2 per cent in 2013, as a result of the deteriorating economic situation. A similar pattern was recorded by many countries, with the average across the EU15 increasing from 3.7 per cent to 4.8 per cent between 2006 and 2013, before reducing to 3.6 per cent in the latest available year. In 2018, the highest levels across the EU15 were reported by Greece (10.9 per cent) and Italy (9.8 per cent).

Analysis of OECD data highlights the problem of food poverty in many advanced countries. Similar to the EU-SILC data, this analysis is also

Figure 4.8: 'Unable to afford a meal with meat, chicken, fish (or vegetarian equivalent) every second day' by EU15 countries, in 2006, 2013 and 2018

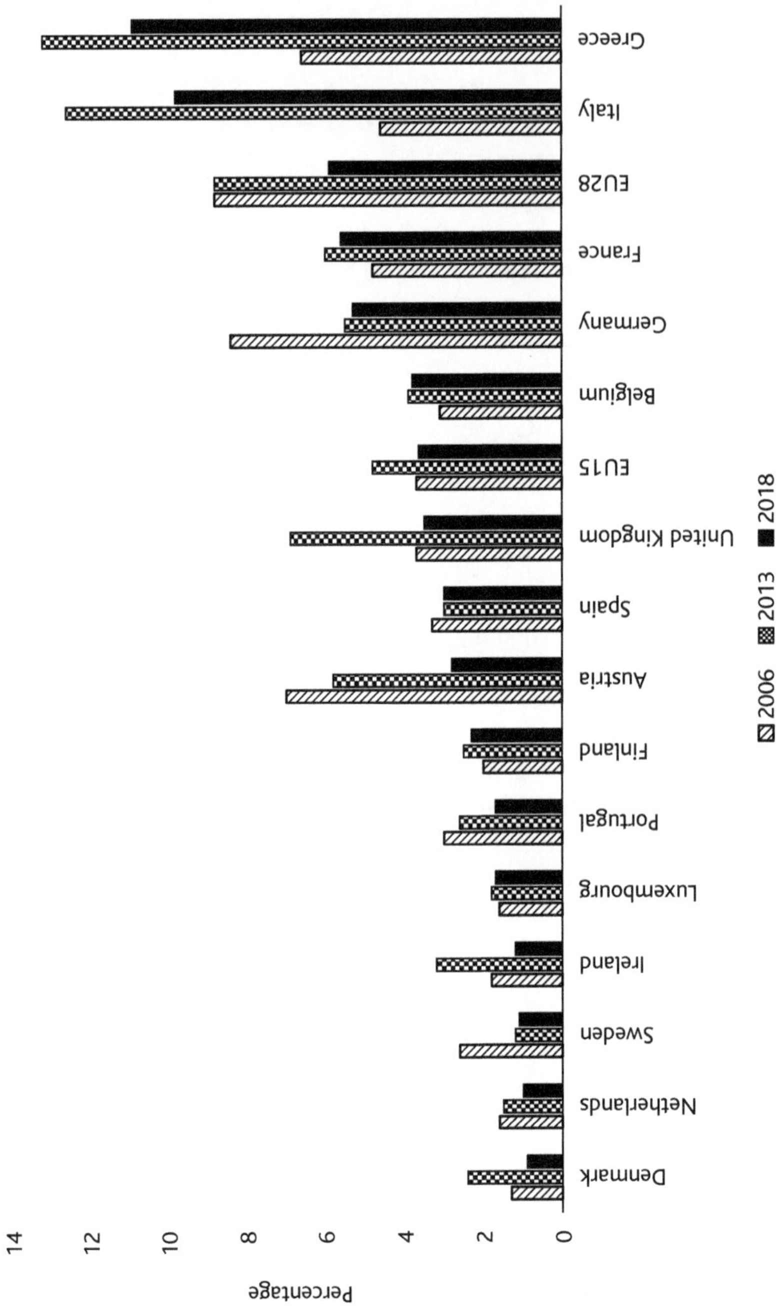

Source: Eurostat (2006, 2013 and 2018), analysis by author

based on one measure of food poverty, which is part of the Gallup World Poll that is tracked consistently across the OECD. This poll is a private dataset, designed to be nationally representative. It has a relatively small sample size (approximately 1,000) and sampling was via telephone (OECD, 2014b). The question asks respondents: 'Have there been times in the last 12 months when you did not have enough money to buy food that you or your family needed?'

Results for the EU15 countries are set out in Figure 4.9. In Ireland, the percentage of respondents who reported that they did not have enough money to buy food increased from 4 per cent to 9 per cent between 2006 and 2007 and 2011 and 2012. This was one of the lowest rates in 2006 and the sixth highest in 2011/12, after the Mediterranean countries. Improvements were made in Germany, Denmark, the UK and France during that period.

Food insecurity

Food insecurity is a phenomenon that is closely aligned to food poverty. The UN FAO carries out regular assessments of global food insecurity. Measurement of the severity of food insecurity is undertaken, according to a scale developed by the UN FAO, by asking respondents eight food-related questions. Results for the EU15 countries are set out in Figure 4.10, which ranks EU15 countries in terms of the level of moderate and severe food insecurity for 2017–19. A three-year average is presented to reduce the margin of error (UN FAO, 2020: 176). The data indicate that 7 per cent of people aged 15 and over in Ireland were food insecure (moderate or severe) over this period. This means that they experienced difficulty getting enough to eat, because they did not have enough money or other resources to obtain adequate food. The total of respondents classified as food insecure includes 3.5 per cent who reported severe food insecurity, which typically involves going without eating for a whole day due to lack of money for food. Results for this separate category of severe food insecurity are included in Figure 4.10.

In comparative terms, the level of food insecurity in Ireland at 7 per cent was just above the EU15 average (6.9 per cent) in 2017–19 and in ninth position out of 15 countries. In relation to those who experienced severe food insecurity, Ireland reported the second highest level of 3.5 per cent, just behind Belgium (3.6 per cent). A comparison between the latest three-year average periods (Figure 4.11) illustrates the overall fall in food insecurity in Ireland, from 8.9 per cent (2014–16) to 7 per cent (2017–19). Most EU countries also showed an improving trend, although food insecurity increased in Sweden, Spain and Belgium. Ireland's relative position improved from 11th position to ninth over the period.

Figure 4.9: 'In the past 12 months were there times when you did not have enough money to buy food that you or your family needed?' (%=yes), EU15, 2006–07 and 2011–12

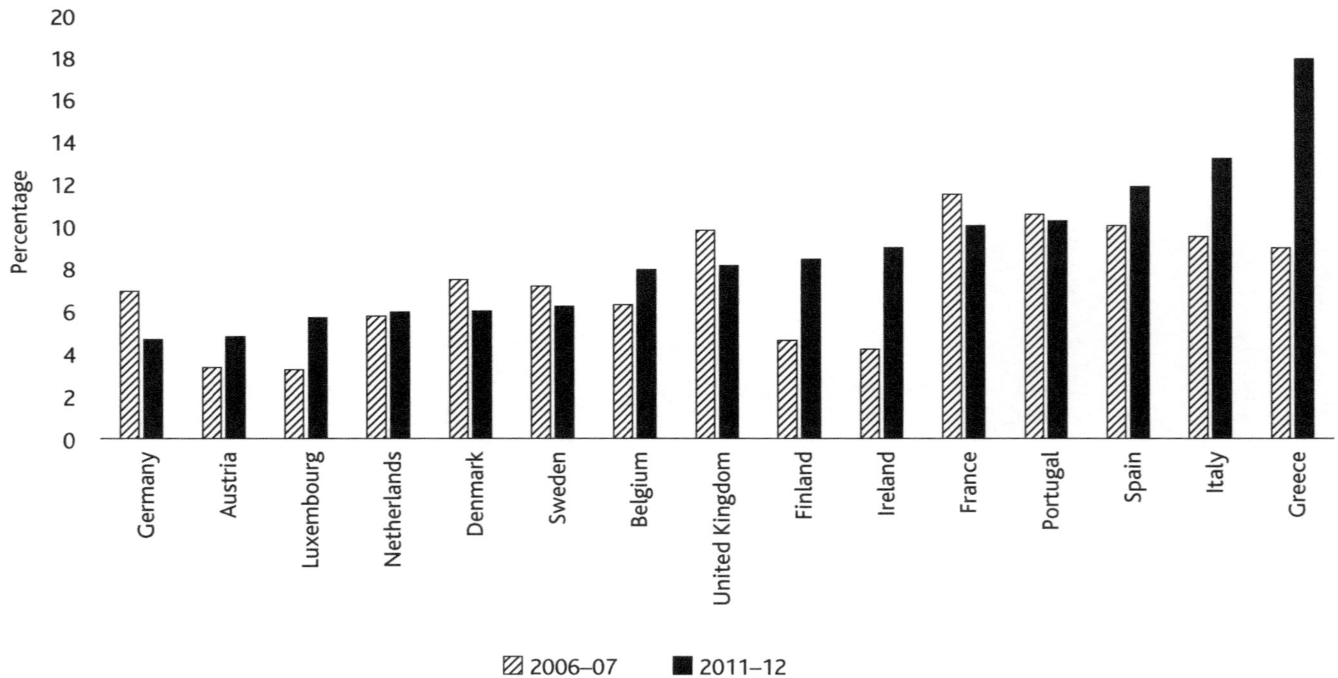

Note: The share of 'yes' responses to this question have been averaged over two-year periods (2006–07 and 2011–12) to adjust for fluctuations (with the exception of Luxembourg, where 2008 data are used, instead of 2006–07).
Source: Based on OECD (2014b)

Figure 4.10: Food insecurity in Ireland, EU15, 2017–19 (three-year average)

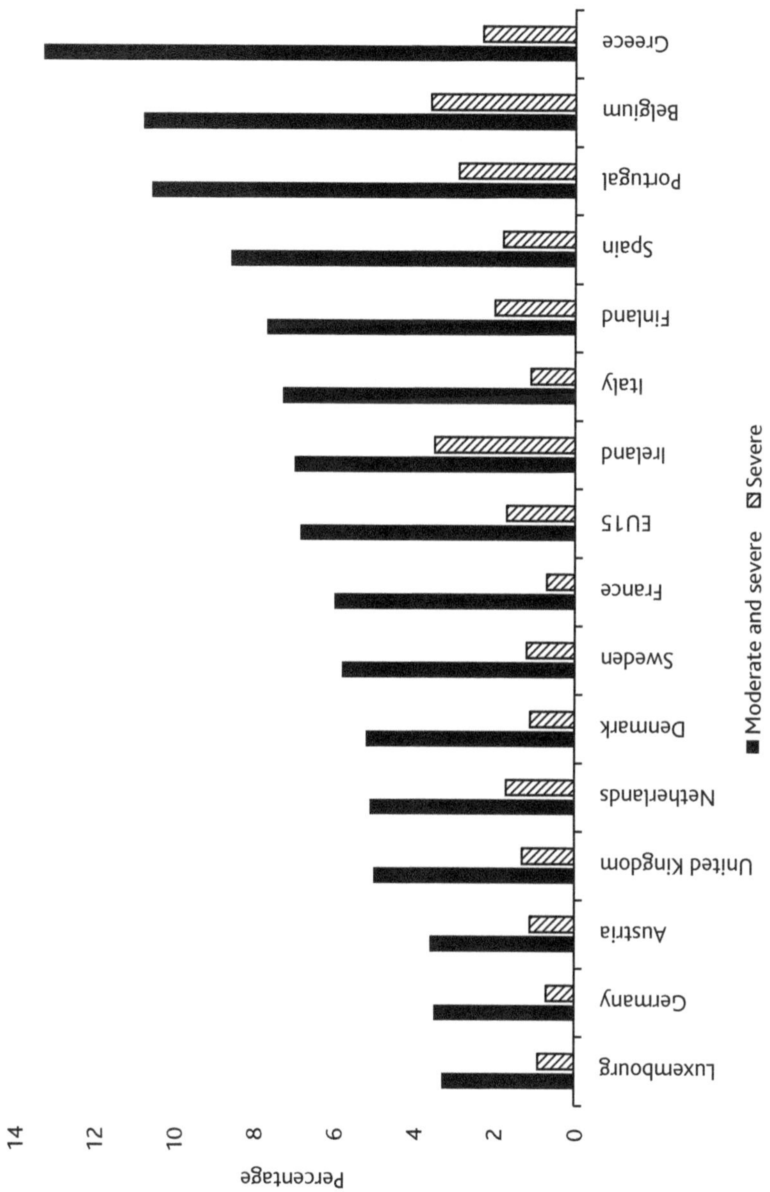

Source: UN FAO (2020), analysis by author

Figure 4.11: Food insecurity in Ireland, EU15, 2014–16 and 2017–19

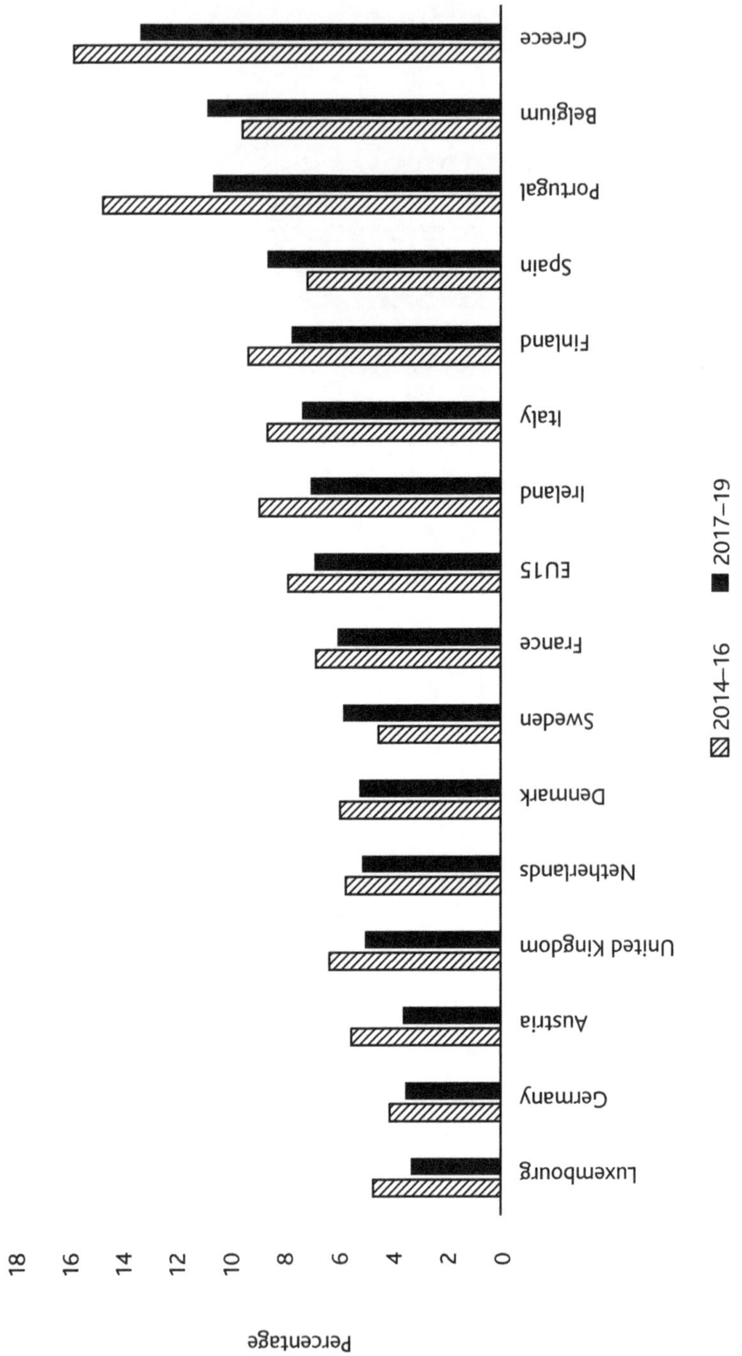

Source: UN FAO (2020), analysis by author

Conclusions

This chapter examined the available data regarding the prevalence of food poverty in Ireland and how it compares with EU15. The lack of an official definition of food poverty and the use of different terminology present challenges in measuring its extent. In Ireland, the only food-related question used by EU-SILC consistently across the EU indicated a low rate of food poverty (1.2 per cent) in 2018. However, the most recent OECD survey (2011/12) recorded a rate of 9 per cent, while UN FAO reported food insecurity at 7 per cent in 2017–19. Different results would be expected from different questions at different times, particularly during a period of economic crisis. There is an argument for not relying on one measure to assess food poverty, as no one indicator can capture all the information to make an assessment (Maître et al, 2006: 1). A composite indicator using three deprivation indicators from the EU-SILC survey conveys that approximately 7 per cent of the Irish population experienced food poverty in 2018. The recent trend in food poverty followed a crisis pattern, which peaked in 2013–14 and subsequently reduced in line with the emerging economic recovery. The sharp increase in food poverty between 2009 and 2010 may be linked to the onset of recession, as real GDP in Ireland fell significantly during 2008 and unemployment rose sharply, from 5 per cent in 2007 to 16 per cent in 2010. Household incomes in Ireland experienced one of the biggest falls in the EU15 during the recession (OECD, 2014b). While there is evidence that food poverty levels are declining as the economy improves, it remains a significant problem. At a level of 7 per cent, food poverty affects the lives of over a third of a million people in Ireland.

Analysis of surveys that report the prevalence of food poverty across EU15 indicates different relative positions for Ireland. In relation to the EU-SILC survey, having only one food-related deprivation indicator in use across all countries in EU28 limits scope for comparative analysis. EU-SILC data indicate that Ireland recorded the fourth lowest rate (1.2 per cent) of food poverty across the EU15 in 2018. This measure reveals a significantly lower level of food poverty than the other surveys, which suggests that it may understate the problem, at least for Ireland. If we turn to UN data from 2017–19, which provide an indication of food insecurity based on broader measures, Ireland was positioned ninth in EU15 on moderate and severe food insecurity. The results indicate that the level in Ireland was slightly above the EU15 average at 7 per cent.

It is instructive to locate the level of food poverty and food insecurity in Ireland relative to other EU15 countries, in the context of income poverty levels (AROP) and welfare typologies. If we consider these results in terms of welfare regimes, we can conclude that Ireland generally had higher food poverty levels and AROP compared to the Nordic welfare states. Finland and Denmark had the lowest poverty levels in 2018 based on the AROP measure, while Sweden was close to the EU15 average (Figure 4.12). However, although food poverty and food insecurity in Scandinavia were generally low, the level in Finland was arguably higher than might be expected from its low level of poverty (see Silvasti and Tikka (2020) for discussion of this issue). Ireland recorded different relative positions compared with the UK, with EU-SILC indicating a much lower level of food poverty in Ireland, but UN data suggesting a higher level of food insecurity. A closer alignment might be expected, given that Ireland is often categorised together with the UK as a liberal welfare regime (Castles and Mitchell, 1993; Saint-Arnaud and Bernard, 2003; Powell and Barrientos, 2004; Nolan and Whelan, 2011), although others (Bambra (2006) and Scruggs and Allan (2006)) view Ireland as being in a conservative type grouping. While most Continental European countries reported poverty levels in a middle grouping, no consistent pattern is apparent when comparing levels of food poverty and food insecurity in these countries. Mediterranean-type countries recorded (with some exceptions) the highest levels of poverty and food poverty (particularly Italy, Portugal and Greece). Overall, countries have tended to cluster geographically and these datasets convey that Ireland is positioned with higher food poverty and food insecurity than Scandinavian welfare states, but below those in most Mediterranean countries.

An analysis of the socio-demographic profile of those experiencing food poverty in 2016 points to a higher risk for certain household types. The highest risk of food poverty arises for a lone parent with children, those who are renting below the market rate, the unemployed, ill/disabled, separated/divorced and those renting at market rate. There are no official data on the prevalence of food poverty in minority ethnic communities in Ireland. However, other research data indicates a serious problem of food poverty for Roma and this situation is likely to be mirrored in some other ethnic groups, including Travellers. This points to the importance of enhancing official surveys to include disaggregated data that will provide this information. This enhancement would contribute towards informed decisions on targeted measures to help address food poverty in these communities. Due to the lag in dissemination of official national statistics, official sources of national data, such as EU-SILC, are not yet available for the period covering the COVID-19 pandemic. This has resulted in reliance on surveys by charities and other sources, which suggests that the outbreak resulted in a significant increase in food poverty. Vulnerable groups who were most at risk before the outbreak, such as the unemployed and single parents, were disproportionately affected.

Predictive factors of food poverty identified by statistical analysis include the HRP being of working age; single or divorced/separated/widowed; unemployed; in lower social classes; having a relatively low level of

Figure 4.12: Poverty in Ireland (AROP), EU15, 2018

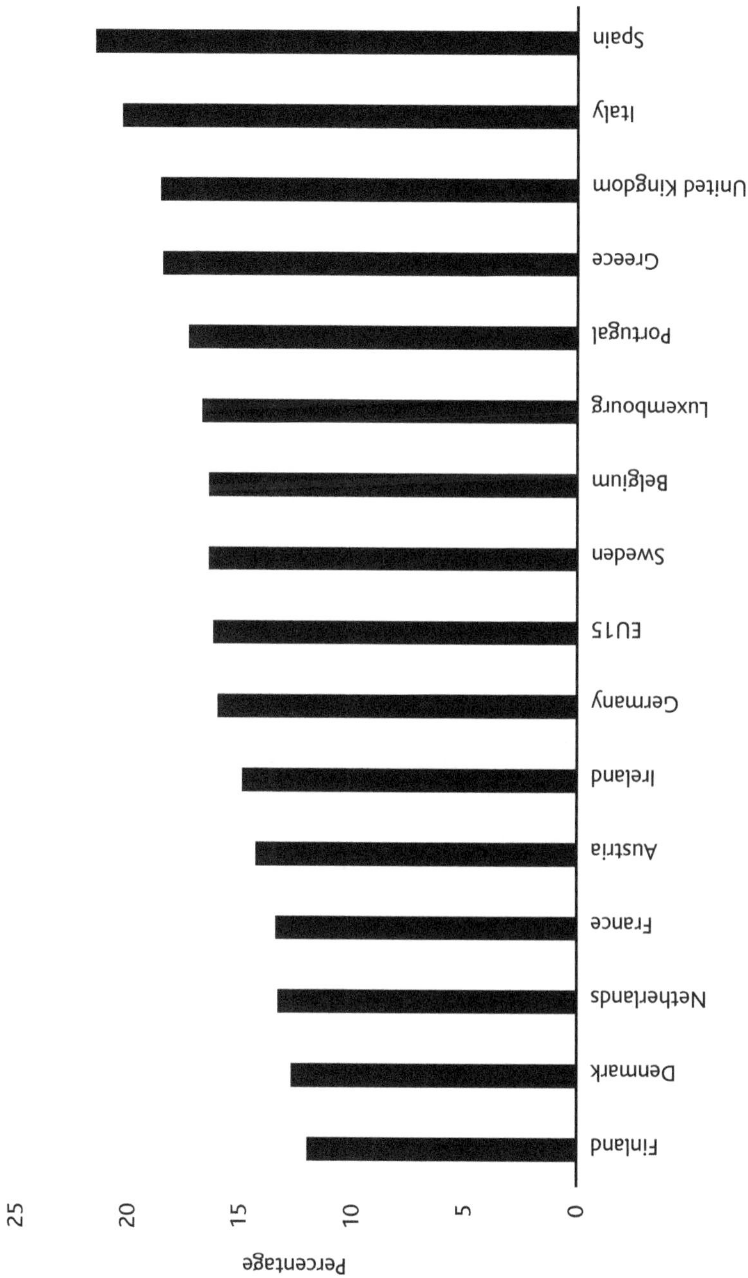

Source: Eurostat (2021), analysis by author

educational attainment; in rented accommodation or in bad health. The relatively high risk of food poverty for lone parents aligns with recent research in Ireland which reported that they are a vulnerable group with high poverty risk, who experience a much higher rate of material deprivation than other working-age adults (Watson et al, 2018). By way of international comparison, research in the United States (Coleman-Jensen et al, 2017: 13) found that the prevalence of food insecurity was particularly high for households with children headed by a single parent (32 per cent when headed by a single woman and 22 per cent for a single man). In Ireland, all households with children were found to be at a higher than average risk of food poverty.

Higher rates of food poverty were reported where the HRP was unemployed. Social welfare payments provide essential support for households, but recent research found that over 70 per cent of households reviewed had insufficient income to meet the MESL (MacMahon et al, 2017). The highest risk of income inadequacy was for one-parent families. Although unemployment rates have declined significantly following the economic crisis, many people are in involuntary part-time jobs. This may involve relatively low hours, which negatively impacts on their income. Research indicates that work available for those with low educational attainment is more likely to be precarious in nature, with nearly a third of workers in Ireland in low-paid, part-time work or reduced working hours and employed on temporary contracts (Collins and Murphy, 2016: 89). Food poverty is higher for lower socio-economic groups compared with professional, clerical workers and self-employed. There were higher rates of food poverty where the HRP was not educated above Junior Certificate level. Lower levels of achievement may be class-related, as those from lower socio-economic groups are more at risk of educational disadvantage (Dukelow and Considine, 2017: 260). For example, the disproportionately high participation levels in higher level education by children of higher and lower professional levels was illustrated starkly by O'Connell et al (2006) in relation to college entrants in Ireland during 2004. In turn, lower educational achievement has been shown to significantly reduce employment prospects and affect earnings potential (Dukelow and Considine, 2017: 246). Fahey et al (2012) argue that the most important public policy measure to combat family problems involves addressing educational disadvantage. They find a strong influence of parental education on family well-being.

In relation to health, food poverty was higher for those reporting a relatively poorer health status, those with a chronic illness and those whose activities are restricted by their health condition. This is consistent with studies by Solar and Irwin (2010), who investigated the social determinants of health and reported that it is influenced by food poverty, among a range of other problems. Those who have a poorer health status may require medication and incur a range of additional medical-related costs, such as prescription charges or medical equipment. In addition, this may affect their ability to shop, particularly if they are poorly serviced by suitable food outlets locally, or do not have access to a car. Research by the ESRI reveals that, together with lone parents, working-age adults with disabilities tend to have a much higher level of material deprivation than other working-age adults (Watson et al, 2018). According to the authors of this report, these social risk groups have a similar pattern in relation to persistent deprivation. Their difficulties in achieving an adequate standard of living arise from barriers to participation in the workforce. There is a range of health policy issues in Ireland, such as waiting times for access to hospital care in the public system, that may exacerbate the problem of food poverty.

The survey data indicated that the risk of food poverty was significantly higher for those in rented accommodation, particularly those renting below the market rate (for example, in social housing). Housing tenure has been linked to the food security of low-income households in Canada (Kirkpatrick and Tarasuk, 2011). Similarly, research in the UK found that even significant subsidies, inherent in below market rent levels, and housing benefit for private renters do not prevent high rates of chronic poverty in these groups (Stephens and Leishman, 2017). The risk of food poverty is reported as higher in urban locations, which is consistent with findings in the international literature. For example, Kirkpatrick and Tarusuk (2011: 284) found higher rates of food poverty in urban areas compared with rural areas across the US and Canada. Distance from suitable food outlets has been identified as a risk factor in the literature, suggesting physical access to food outlets may exacerbate food poverty. Layte et al (2011) carried out a study in Ireland which analysed food availability in terms of the distance to and density of a variety of food outlets. They found a marked gradient in distances to the nearest food stores and diet quality across socio-economic groups. There is related research in Ireland (Poole and Parker, 1990) which indicates that urban development, particularly out-of-town shopping centres, has made food access more difficult for some social groups. This is likely to have some influence on food poverty, particularly for those without access to a car, or adequate public transport.

Measuring food poverty is challenging and highlights the value of carrying out qualitative research on the topic to complement quantitative findings. Empirical evidence provides an opportunity to explore the complex nature of food poverty and gain further insights in relation to the characteristics of those experiencing food poverty and the factors that contribute to the problem. The following qualitative chapters will aim to understand how these risk factors are interrelated.

5

Pathways into food poverty

Introduction

This chapter explores the main pathways into food poverty, based on interviewing a sample of food aid users. The literature indicates that there are often multiple drivers that result in poverty and this is also the case for food poverty. Chapter 4 has shown that there is a relatively high risk of food poverty for those who are unemployed and rely on social protection. There is an increased prevalence for those in low-paid and precarious employment, although working poverty often arises from low work intensity, due to limited paid hours at work. Yet, given the quantitative and cross-sectional nature of research, little is known about the biographical pathways into food poverty and the underlying causal mechanisms that lead to the use of food aid. Given the lack of qualitative research on food poverty in Ireland, this chapter aims to address this gap in knowledge.

The qualitative research investigated users of food aid through a total of 42 semi-structured interviews. These were held at food banks in locations spread around Dublin, which were convenient for confidential interviews with respondents. Throughout this research, pseudonyms were used in order to preserve the anonymity of participants. The food bank users received referrals from charities such as the SVP, which provides vouchers for this purpose. The intention is that the food aid provides relief to help the recipient cope with a short-term emergency, although many users seek ongoing assistance. It should be noted that food bank users are a sub-sample of those experiencing food poverty. There is a range of other types of food assistance available, depending on location, and some of those affected by food poverty are not able or willing to avail of food aid.

The interviews sought to explore why each respondent needed food aid and probed their pathways into, through and out of food poverty. A summary of the methodology for the study is set out in Appendix 2. The results of this qualitative output were then analysed to review the characteristics of food bank users, what drives the need for food aid and the experience of food poverty. The data from these research strands informed a review of how to improve the conceptualisation and operationalisation of food poverty and key policies that drive food poverty. These issues are discussed in later chapters.

Pathways into food poverty

Inadequate social security

Income protection

Most respondents in this study were unemployed and relied entirely on social welfare support. This reflected multiple issues, including difficulties in finding suitable employment and barriers to work, such as illness/disability and care responsibilities. As many respondents found that their social welfare payment was inadequate to cover their necessary weekly expenditure, help with food was needed:

> 'So you don't have bills building up, because you are living beyond your means … you're getting €188 per week, you've got your rent to pay, you've got kids to support, you've got bills to pay … out of €188. It's not enough. This (food bank) would put your head above water … barely enough, but it puts you above water … it makes a difference.' (John)

> 'I had lost my job. I didn't know about the food bank, but I'd gone to Vincent de Paul and they suggested the food bank as a helping hand for me, because I was struggling to pay bills and put food on the table.' (Barbara)

Another respondent explained how, after essential costs were met, she had little money left for food expenditure:

> 'By the time I pay €44 on rent, €20 on heating and then maybe €40 to €50 on electricity for the week, because of the children, doing their washing, watching the television … all round, it's very, very hard … and then I have to pay for the bins, so I have hardly anything left for cleaning stuff or food.' (Sheila)

In addition to providing inadequate income, respondents also found that the welfare system lacked flexibility and responsiveness. This was reflected in difficulties receiving welfare payments when circumstances changed, particularly after becoming unemployed between periods of paid work. Issues arose for respondents who worked intermittently or on a part-time basis, reflecting the increasing casualisation of work, which tends to blur the boundaries between working and being unemployed. During periods of unemployment, the social welfare safety net did not always keep up with these irregular work patterns and resultant delays in payments meant families struggled financially and needed help to feed their families. This is illustrated by a single mother with four children, who had recently completed a vocational course and obtained employment on a temporary basis. She subsequently lost her job and was waiting for her social welfare payment to be increased to reflect her new status: "I haven't got the rest of the social welfare back yet. … so I'm still living on €185 and trying to do it all and get through" (Grainne). Another respondent needed food aid, as a result of a similar delay in receiving her social welfare entitlement after a period in employment: "If I was on my full social welfare payment, then it would be ok, as I would have that extra €100. That's my only issue at the moment. I'm trying to get that sorted with them. I have an appeal in" (Eimer). In another illustration of the lack of responsiveness of the welfare system, a respondent explained that, following a period of employment, she recently had to give up work to look after her son. She had subsequently waited three months to get a reduction of her payment reinstated and had an appeal pending:

> 'Ideally, I would be able to get a job, I'd be financially secure. At the moment, I am having problems with my son, so I feel that I can't go to work full time … but if I get the social welfare thing sorted, I'll have extra money for the food.' (Eimer)

Respondents provided a variety of examples of situations when they found their payments inadequate. John, who shared care of his three boys, explained that he was unemployed and recently sent on a training course to improve his job prospects. However, his bus fares to attend the course were higher than the related travel allowance he obtained from social welfare:

> 'I get €188 from the social welfare payment and I get a travel allowance. They give me €17 towards my travel … my bus fare is €30 per week. So, out of the €188 that I get from the social welfare, before anything I've got to take €13 out of that to put towards my bus fares. So that's gone from €188 to €175 … that's what I have left to pay the rent, the kids' maintenance, food and bills.' (John)

John also found that his social welfare payment had recently been cut, as he had missed a day of training. Ireland has increased its use of sanctions as part of welfare conditionality, where benefits are made dependent on the recipient first agreeing to meet certain obligations, such as attending training or interviews: "If I'm late in or miss a day, I get docked. I got docked last week as I took a personal day over depression, because of my mother's death, and they docked me €40" (John). Providing for teenage children was a challenge for many respondents. Child Benefit is paid to parents or guardians of children who are under 18 years, provided they are in full-time education. Parents were struggling to feed children who had left school, but were not yet in employment. Christine, a mother of three teenage sons, explained that her eldest son recently reached the age of 18, when a child is no longer categorised as dependent and some benefits are stopped (Citizens Information, 2018a): "I have a lad at home who is in between school and college and he is looking for … work. I don't get paid for him, so it's a struggle to provide for another adult" (Christine). John was separated from his partner and needed help from the food bank, as he was providing for his children, who came to stay at weekends. He explained that, although reluctant to do so, he had regularly asked his ex-partner to contribute towards the cost of food for his children. However, as this had become problematic due to ongoing challenges by social welfare officers, he needed help from the food bank:

> 'I've had to ask their mum … when you're coming up, bring some bits and pieces with them. There are regularly times when I've had to ask … will you put a tenner in my account … it's for food. Every so often, the social welfare call you down for a meeting and want the last 6 months' bank statements. And they say "Why is she giving you money?" Can you get a letter off her to say this … she's given me a fiver or a tenner … towards a bit of food for the kids … and I've got to go and explain … this is exactly what happens.' (John)

Respondents explained that the cost of heating was a major burden during the winter months. A Fuel Allowance at a rate of €28 per week (from January 2021) is paid under the National Fuel Scheme to recipients of long-term social welfare, in order to assist with home heating costs for six months of the year. However, Carol found that it was difficult to keep her house adequately heated, particularly for her children. She experienced particular difficulties, as the allowance was not paid until after the end of March, when it was often still cold:

> 'We get the fuel allowance, but that's going to stop in March. It's very tough trying to heat the house. I have a bale of briquettes to do me, but I have no coal or anything for the next 6 weeks. It's going to be really cold, like winter, the next 6 weeks, so it's trying to keep the house heated and warm as well.' (Carol)

Unexpected expenditure frequently posed difficulties for respondents. Living on social welfare left little or no spare money to provide a buffer for unanticipated costs. As an illustrative case, Lisa was struggling to cope with extra expenses, which included a family bereavement. In addition, she had recently moved to new social housing. Her child had to change school and she was facing additional unplanned expenses for the child's new school uniform and books. As a result, she needed help from the food bank:

> 'My nanny passed away on Saturday … flowers are expensive … that's why I came today, because I knew I'd have to pay for flowers.' (Lisa)

> 'Now I'm getting a different house, I have to pay for it all again. Whatever I paid the school already, they can't transfer it to the new school. I have to pay it again.' (Lisa)

Respondents also reported difficulty affording to repair or replace defective household items, such as a fridge or freezer. It was necessary to apply to the DSP, including certification from a registered gas or electricity agent. This service involved paying the agent in advance, without any certainty of obtaining approval to go ahead with the repair work or replacement. The DSP makes Exceptional Needs Payments under the Supplementary Welfare Allowance Scheme, which are intended to meet such one-off exceptional expenditure. According to the DSP, each case is subject to a means test and decided 'on its own merits' by the DSP's representative (formerly known as the Community Welfare Officer).

> 'The fridge … I am going to have to go up to the relieving officer [DSP representative] … there is something wrong with the fridge and I will have to get a new one.' (Janet)

> 'You have to pay for the man to come and have a look … to make sure it's not working … you have to get a registered gas man or a shop that does reconditioned fridges or cookers, you have to pay them 20 euro … to come out. Then they give you a receipt, then you bring it up to them [Social Welfare] and then they look at it and they say "yes" or say "no". If they say "no", you might not get your money back … you've lost.' (Michael)

The need to find money to repair or replace an essential household item was one reason why respondents resorted to moneylenders. This reflected their predicament when income from social welfare payments left no capacity for unexpected expenditure. Sometimes support from family and friends had been exhausted, following repeated requests for help, while in other cases respondents wanted to keep others from knowing that they were going through tough times. For those on a low income, there was a variety of reasons why moneylenders were used. A financial crisis could arise from various pressure points, such as children's return to school, Christmas, family religious ceremonies or other unforeseen costs. Despite the high cost of borrowing, in such circumstances resorting to a moneylender was sometimes felt to provide a quick solution, as explained by one respondent: "If you are desperately panicked about something, it gets rid of that panic for that instant. It just stretches out the panic and makes it a little bit easier" (Patricia). While no respondent recommended moneylenders, there was a general understanding as to why people got involved: "If you are in a dilemma where you need to feed your kids … or need to provide" (Christine). "Usually something comes up that you have to [use a moneylender]. It gets you out of a hole, but then you are thinking how long it is stretching out paying this money" (Patricia).

Most respondents who had used moneylenders were acutely conscious that starting to use them could give rise to difficulties. In some cases, respondents were encouraged to continue borrowing until the interest payment amounted to a significant proportion of their weekly income, which impacted on paying for essentials such as food:

> 'At one stage, I had owed, I think it was over €2,000 and that was over probably a two or three year period … that €20 interest could have got me three days food … it could have fed them [children] for three days … it was frustrating that I got myself into that position.' (Christine)

Weekly loan repayments became a priority item, similar to rent, with difficulty affording money for food. Pressure to repay debt was illustrated by one respondent, who expressed concern that there could be serious consequences if repayments were not made: "I don't know what would happen if I didn't pay it. He would be sleeping in my apartment" (Uta). As an illustration of gaps in the safety net of social welfare protection, some non-EU migrants were receiving food aid. As most had no local connections, they were not in a position to seek support from family or friends living in Ireland. Their predicament arose for several reasons, including the requirement to meet the habitual residence condition to be eligible for most social welfare payments. This condition requires that you are residing in Ireland and can demonstrate a close link to the state (DSP, 2020a). However, the term 'habitually resident' is not defined in Irish law, which leaves the onus on applicants to prove to the social welfare deciding officer that they have the right to live in the state and have a 'close link' to Ireland. As an illustrative example, one Nigerian mother, whose residency permission required her to be fully financially self-sufficient, needed food aid for her children: "I couldn't provide food for the children. It was really bad" (Ibekwe).

As a non-EU migrant, Ibekwe was not entitled to welfare payments and was totally dependent on remittances from her husband, who remained working in Nigeria. It was a condition of her visa that she would not be eligible for social welfare (Irish Naturalisation and Immigration Services [INIS], 2017). Due to recent problems in the Nigerian economy, the currency weakened sharply and remittances from her husband had become worth much less in euro, giving rise to the need for food aid to help feed her family: "In my letter from the Department of Justice … it states 'do not be a burden on the State', so I'm not on social [welfare]" (Ibekwe).

Housing

Respondents lived in a range of housing tenures, with most in social rented accommodation or renting from a private landlord. Almost without exception, keeping up with rent was top priority in terms of expenditure, as respondents were acutely aware of the importance of maintaining a 'roof over the head': "If you don't pay your rent, you're out" (John). In some cases, the importance of keeping up with rent was born out of a concern to avoid homelessness:

> 'I would say rent first … I would have said food first, but only because we were renting … high rent … before, and we ended up homeless. So it's immensely important that we have a roof over our head. Food would be first, only we've had this perspective from the homeless side of it.' (Darren)

Those in housing provided by the local authority or an approved housing body, such as a not-for-profit housing association, paid rent based on household income. This meant that they were protected from the private market and could obtain rental housing at a relatively affordable cost. Clúid is the largest approved housing body in Ireland, providing over 8,000 units for people who cannot afford to buy their own home or pay for private rented housing (Clúid, 2021): "We are lucky at the moment. We're with Clúid Housing, so they can reduce the rent a lot for us. Otherwise, we'd find it very high to pay private rental" (Darren).

Many respondents were living in the private rented sector while on a long waiting list for social housing, which totals approximately 69,000 households across Ireland (Clúid, 2021). The problem is particularly serious in Dublin and other large urban centres. For example, in the South Dublin area, where a significant number of respondents lived, there were 7,156 households on the waiting list for housing as at October 2020 (O'Flaherty, 2020). For those on the waiting list, DSP provides a range of housing allowances, principally through the Housing Assistance Payment (HAP), Rental Accommodation Scheme or the Rent Supplement (RS). Those with the RS pay the total rent to their landlord and receive a supplement, which is capped for each local authority area. The prevailing high level of market rent caused serious difficulty for those struggling to bridge the gap between their monthly rent and the RS: "You just can't make ends meet any more. I'm in rented accommodation, which would be €1,400 per month. I would get €900 a month, so I have to make up €500 per month, which is a lot of money …

you would be struggling" (Joy). This situation puts considerable pressure on family finances and can increase the risk of food poverty:

> 'I got a notice of eviction from my landlord, because I couldn't pay the rent. So I needed to pay the rent and, in order to pay the rent, I had to come up here and get food. Rather than spend an extra €20 or €30 on shopping, I'd have to put it towards the rent.' (Joy)

Some respondents were able to avail of the Rental Accommodation Scheme, which is more secure for tenants deemed to have a long-term housing need. In this scheme, the local authority puts a contract in place and pays the rent directly to the landlord. The tenant makes a specified contribution to this rental cost, according to household income, but pays it to the local authority (Dublin City Council, 2021). Although Janet said she had "cut back on everything", she quickly added, "I always pay my rent, that's the first thing I pay" and revealed that: "My rent is nearly half of it (social welfare payment) … and that's a hugely reduced rent, as it is a Rental Accommodation Scheme. I don't know what I'd do if I had a mortgage or something like that" (Janet). A significant difficulty with renting in the private sector arises because the tenure is insecure and, in some cases, can lead to homelessness. This is a devastating experience for families, who may face multiple problems, including food poverty. Respondents described a range of their experiences of homelessness, where help from the food bank proved vital to provide for themselves and their families. In one case, a respondent, Margaret, explained that her family, which included six children, was recently forced to leave rented accommodation, as the landlord decided it was too small for their needs. Her family was provided with emergency accommodation in two hotel rooms. They had no kitchen in which to prepare meals and lacked even basic facilities, such as a microwave or toaster. Since moving there, three months prior to the interview, Margaret was occupied every day trying to cater for her family's food needs, spending €70 to €80 daily on food and seeking to get a balance of hot and cold foods to provide for her husband and children. Her husband's wages from full-time employment, augmented by the Working Family Payment (WFP), left them financially stretched, but she was stoical about it: "There was enough but now, we are having difficulty … but when I get a house, it's ok" (Margaret). Another case of homelessness arose from a family break-up, arising when one member left the family home without access to accommodation. Following the breakdown of his marriage, John lived for a protracted period in a variety of supported temporary accommodation provided by homeless services, until he was able to obtain a home from Túath (a voluntary housing association). The food bank was a great help when his children came to visit: "I got divorced from the boys' mum and, when I moved out, I had nowhere to go. I was homeless for two years" (John). In another case, a respondent's husband died while in homeless accommodation. Her loss was framed in terms of worry about costs, as she had to deal with an unexpected financial crisis and needed help from the food bank:

> 'He died in a homeless unit, my husband, and then they put us into a hostel in the city and we just broke down because we had no money, no way of burying my partner and then I had to turn him over to his family, which was very hard … it broke my heart … and then they paid for the headstone. … I was lost in the world.' (Sheila)

A young Traveller faced homelessness when she was forced to leave her family home after becoming pregnant. The respondent, who could not read or write, was reliant on the food bank due to multiple factors, which included educational disadvantage and childcare problems: "Well, I don't have my parents because I had a baby as a sole person and I'm a Traveller, so it didn't work out. I've just been homeless since I had my daughter" (Lisa). Housing was highlighted by respondents as of vital importance. For those reliant on state support to meet their housing needs, lack of available social housing resulted in most respondents having to live in the private rented sector. Ongoing concerns with privatised solutions included inadequate supply, insecure tenure and the threat of homelessness. Each type of housing allowance presented different challenges, with some respondents forced to pay top-ups to landlords or lose their home.

Illness/disability

Many respondents were from families experiencing either mental or physical health problems. They were often not fit to work or were full-time carers and thus unable to work. This overall picture is consistent with the findings of Daly and Kelly's study of families and poverty in Ireland, where nearly two thirds of poor families were affected by serious illness or disability (2015: 42). Family situations often involved complex issues, with a significant proportion of respondents having children with health issues. Daly and Kelly reported a 'very striking' finding that, during interviews with families, there were many references to the poor health of children (2015: 37). Many respondents found that their Disability Allowance was insufficient and they needed food aid:

> 'For me, on my social welfare, I'm not dissing social welfare, I'm very lucky to have had it all these years. I've made several attempts to go back working, but it just hasn't worked out for me because of my health. I feel the rising cost of living in this country has made surviving on social welfare, well, not totally impossible, but nearly … it's a very

> difficult thing to do. I would say that's why a lot of people are going for food aid … because they need to survive.' (Kathleen)

> 'I had a massive heart attack and then a mild stroke after it. And then I've had another one recently, in the year just gone, and a lot of heavy medical problems. I needed some help and … I'd be lost without it (food aid), because at the end of the day with €188 on your Disability and then you have to pay your rent and then gas/electric, it doesn't give you an awful lot to play around with.' (Mark)

A mother with three teenagers, who was caring for her husband, had difficulty getting through the week on his Disability Allowance, resulting in the need for food aid:

> 'I have a husband and three sons and my husband is on Disability [Allowance]. It's just, come Sunday, the food is really starting to run out and on Monday I don't have very much. I would be really struggling on the Tuesday … to try and have dinners. So I find it fantastic, the help which you get [from the food bank].' (Carol)

Darren felt that the level of welfare payments was not sufficient to provide for his family. In particular, he voiced a concern in relation to the way entitlements were calculated between himself, his wife and child:

> 'You are pushed below the line of survival really, because what you earned when you were fit enough to earn, is sliced to nearly a third of what you expect three people to live on. That's hard to describe to you, but because of my disabilities I get €341 … that's for the three of us. I get €188 for myself, €124, however they calculate it, is for Penny [wife] … it's two thirds they say … and then Eva [daughter] is considered a third of a person, €29 … not even a single person can live on €300 when you take into consideration your rent.' (Darren)

His wife, Penny, explained that their daughter's health problems meant that the family had to allocate a significant proportion of their total weekly income to support her. The cost of special foods and medical needs had contributed to their financial difficulties and resulted in the need for food aid: "Unfortunately, she has been very sick herself for the last year and she's on a lot of medication as well" (Penny). In another example, an Armenian migrant couple were in need of food aid, as they struggled with health problems and a new baby. Alexander was in receipt of a Disability Allowance and a dependent adult allowance. His partner was not eligible for Maternity Benefit paid by DSP, as she had not worked in Ireland:

> 'I have some food, but not much. Because she (my partner) was that time pregnant and needed to eat good food and I buy some medication … and that time she had a … very hard operation … I needed to buy good food and lots of medication, that time, a heavy time. She is not taking maternity benefit. She is not getting nothing.' (Alexander)

Another respondent was struggling on a Disability Allowance, supporting her two grandchildren as well as her own children, one of whom had an addiction problem and provided only occasional financial assistance. In another illustrative case, an adult son with a disability was living at home. Although he was entitled to social welfare, this was not shared with the care provider and resulted in the respondent needing help from the food bank:

> 'I was on sick benefit when I came out of work. … My daughter is going into rehab for five months … now there are weeks that she might throw me a few bob and there are weeks that she wouldn't … so I'm left to do all the household bills, everything out of €180. The eldest lad is 14 and my other granddaughter is six … they need to be clothed, there is schooling and I need a bit of help.' (Alice)

> 'I'm on Disability [Allowance], so it's even harder, because I've no dependent child now, because he is 18 and has a boxed foot. He doesn't give me zilch.' (Janet)

In one serious case of food poverty, the perceived lack of responsiveness of the social welfare system aggravated an already difficult situation for a disabled lone parent. Deirdre, who was supporting her twenty-year-old son on her Disability Allowance, was required to pay extra rent for him, as he was an adult living in the same house. However, her son was not able to leave the house to make his own claim, due to a serious medically diagnosed anxiety problem. Deirdre was in need of help from the food bank, while her case was under appeal:

> 'We are in the midst of having major problems trying to get the social welfare to pay my son, because he can't apply for Jobseeker's because he is not available for work and he can't get the Disability Allowance because he can't go and get assessed. … Even though our doctor … he has had a psychological report … they are all saying that he can't go and do this. We have had the doctor come to the house and the psychologist come to the house to do the reports.' (Deirdre)

Some respondents faced difficulty affording a special diet needed for medical reasons:

> 'I have to stay on a healthy diet. So, my biggest problem would be because they cost dearer and I can't afford the dearer food. So there are special foods that I can eat and there are foods that I can't. … I have to be on a special diet.' (Mary)

> 'I'm a coeliac and it's so expensive to buy food, so that sometimes I actually just eat ordinary food and I would be really ill. I know I shouldn't, I keep on saying that I know I shouldn't, but I just can't afford it.' (Cathy)

One respondent was anxious to get back to work after experiencing health problems in the last couple of years. However, waiting for treatment in the health system was delaying his return to work and prolonging reliance on the food bank. According to a report by the Health Consumer Powerhouse (Björnberg and Phang, 2019: 15), the Health Service Executive (HSE) has indicated that improving waiting lists is a key objective for the health services. The HSE seeks to attain a target of no more than 18 months' wait for a specialist appointment, although the report indicates that this still represents the worst waiting time situation in Europe: "There are delays … there is the waiting period in the public health system. It's slow … waiting for appointments, waiting for procedures to get done. I think it keeps you out (of work) longer" (Darren). Respondents found that illness or disability often gave rise to additional costs, such as prescription charges, medical supplies or the cost of transport to and from hospital appointments: "You run out of it [social welfare] sometimes, because you have to pay extra bills … and extra when you need to get your medication and … when you need to go to hospital and bus fares and stuff like that … that all costs" (Mary). The cost of medicines was a serious financial burden on some respondents, who had to find the money from their social welfare payment to pay for medical expenses that were not covered by their medical card. Many respondents qualified for the medical card issued by the HSE, as their income was below the designated threshold for their family size. This card provided access to many health services free of charge, including GP visits, public out-patient and in-patient services and dental checks. However, there is a prescription charge of €1.50 for each item that is dispensed (reduced from €2.50 at the time of the interviews). This cost, which is capped at €15 per month (€25 during interviews), presented a financial challenge for Deirdre:

> 'My prescriptions are €25, so the week that I have to pay for that … that's a bad week, because I have to pay for my prescription, which is taking a quarter of my income for that week. If you work it that way, it's bad. I get €144, so €25 out of that is an awful lot. But you

have to buy the prescriptions, there is no let up from it, it just doesn't stop.' (Deirdre)

Prescription charges were also a problem for Linda, but other medical costs were an additional burden that gave rise to the need for food aid:

> 'Just to pick up my medication from the chemist costs €25 per month and that must be paid for. That's only for the covered medication … covered under the medical card … and then I have medication that is not covered under the medical card that I have to buy independently. So that's why I have found the food a huge help, in order to leave me with some income to pay for my most necessary medication.' (Linda)

In addition, Linda was prescribed items that were not included on the list of medicines provided under the medical card. She was required to purchase these as a private customer from the pharmacy, which for one item would cost her €100 per month. Linda was trying to get this medication included on the approved list, otherwise she has to do without it and face the resulting consequences:

> 'I can't afford to buy what I need to buy. I am doing without certain medications … medications that can make me a lot better are too costly for me to buy. So I have to do without them. I could be taking a lot healthier medication for my condition that would give me a better quality of life.' (Linda)

A Hardship Scheme is available for people to access medical supplies that are not available directly through the medical card, subject to a supporting General Practitioner prescription (HSE, 2016). However, some respondents reported that medical supplies often gave rise to additional costs not covered under this scheme, which left little money for food. For example, Kathleen needed support stockings, but only two pairs per year were covered. This resulted in additional expenses: "I have to wear support stockings 24/7, 365 days a year … they are very expensive. I get two pairs from the HSE, but the two pairs would not last me a year … they only last a certain length of time, as they lose their stretchiness" (Kathleen).

Low pay and precarious employment

Employment

While most of the respondents were unemployed, a small number were in families with one member in full-time employment and others were engaged in part-time work. The interviews revealed the diverse work patterns of respondents and their families. In Ireland, a significant proportion of the working-age population (approximately 23 per cent) are defined as low-wage workers, earning less than two thirds of median wages in 2017 (OECD, 2019b). In-work poverty arises from inadequate working hours, as well as low wages. Research indicates that very low work intensity (VLWI), where households have a work intensity of less than 20 per cent, is a particular problem in Ireland. The ESRI reported (Watson et al, 2012) that VLWI households in Ireland were twice the average across Europe (EU15). In particular, the study pointed to the higher risk of low work intensity for lone-parent households and those with an adult reporting a disability, with these two groups accounting for over 50 per cent of these households. In a representative case, a respondent with two children, whose husband worked full-time in the public sector, found it difficult to cope on his earnings: "On a typical week we are surviving hand to mouth. We are left with basically nothing ... probably €20 to cover us for milk and bread during the week. When anything else happens ... there is nothing there" (Cathy). A combination of tax increases and wage cuts during the recession made it necessary for some to seek food aid:

> 'The budgets came in and he got cut left, right and centre in his wages. They seemed to be cut every time the budget came in. I feel that we are like the new poor now and, whereas it wasn't like that for us seven years ago, it's like that for me now and my family ... and my husband works full-time.' (Cathy)

The WFP is a weekly tax-free payment for families at work on low pay. This is the primary in-work social welfare payment for households with children, where the rate of payment is based on the level of earned income, coupled with the number of children in the household. In a European comparison, Lohmann and Marx (2008: 27) argued that Ireland, in addition to the UK, has 'gone the furthest' in putting in place 'in work' benefits such as WFP. Despite this, another example illustrates that some families receiving WFP still need help with food. Margaret's family included six children. Her husband worked full-time, with his income supplemented by the WFP: "I need this help for the children and not for me and my husband. My husband works and I have the Family Supplement as well" (Margaret). In a case illustrating the casualisation of segments of the workforce, a respondent needed food aid, as he was experiencing difficulty obtaining a social welfare payment following a period of paid employment. Paddy, a construction worker who supported nine children, had found it difficult to obtain a permanent work contract, as employers offered short-term temporary work only. While Paddy found it difficult to earn more than he could obtain on social welfare, WFP provided an incentive to obtain employment and boost his income beyond the level of unemployment payments:

> 'I can't work for any less than €600 per week. … I get €570 on the dole. I haven't had dole in two weeks because of problems beyond my control. When I'm working, I'm lucky to get €600 a week. I've been urged to find a job, because they are going to put me on a FIS [Family Income Supplement; now WFP] payment, which means that if I can find a full time job I will get help from the State … top-up money to bring my money up to what I should be getting … with nine children.' (Paddy)

Paddy's previous employer required him to register as self-employed, so that it avoided paying PRSI and pension contributions. This practice has been described as 'bogus self-employment' (Irish Congress of Trade Unions, 2015), whereby workers are labelled as self-employed contractors and deprived of a range of social protection. Unfortunately, Paddy had not understood the implications for his family, which included loss of social welfare entitlement, no holiday pay and no paid sick leave. As a result, Paddy needed help from the food bank to provide for his family, while he tried to sort out the problem with Social Welfare:

> 'With the [employment] agencies … you are not working for the builder … *they* are working for the builder. So the builder rings them and fills the site with ten or 20 fellas to get a load of work done in a hurry. And then the next week … we are ahead of the posse … we'll send most of those home. There is no such thing as a Bank Holiday payment. You don't get holiday pay … you are not entitled to nothing. If you get sick and are supposed to be in work and you ring in sick, they say, "Sure, no problem, we'll give you a ring." They ring somebody else to take over from you and you have no more work there.' (Paddy)

As pointed out by Andress and Lohnmann (2008: 4), a single mother's wage may be sufficient for herself, but may be inadequate for herself and her children. Elaine, a lone parent with one teenage son, had recently set up her own business, so that she was not reliant on social welfare. In the start-up period, she was supported by the Back to Work Family Dividend scheme, which provides social welfare support for two years, with the benefits tapering off in the second year. Because her income from employment was low, she needed help with food, mainly to feed her teenage son:

> 'My income has been reduced, because I'm on the Back to Work [Allowance] so, if I don't get any work, I have €160 a week to pay my bills and feed us. It's impossible … I just couldn't cope anymore … and I knew that they had help available … he was eating so much, that I just wanted help.' (Elaine)

Employment and caring

Many respondents were not available for paid employment as they were carrying out unpaid caring for family members. Respondents in this situation were mainly single parents with school-age children or parents of unemployed adult children and, in some cases, grandchildren. The cost and availability of childcare meant that many single parents were not available to work full-time or participate in either training or further education. Some reported challenges in finding part-time work that fitted in with school hours and the availability of affordable after-school care. Other barriers to taking full-time paid education arose for single mothers, who felt it was a priority for them to care for young children or those with serious health issues. In some cases, single parents could seek increased part-time work, as their children's school day became longer. As an example, Christine, a single mother with three sons, explained that her youngest child recently moved to secondary school, which allowed her to work additional hours: "I'm available for work from 9am until 2.30pm … it used to be 9am until 1.30pm … it's just finding something that will suit those hours. The plan is to stay in employment and to get more work" (Christine).

In some cases, respondents were not able to seek paid employment as they were caring for adult children, as illustrated by two cases. One respondent, Brian, needed food aid to feed his grown-up son, who was homeless. In the second case, Becky was struggling to care for both her adult children and grandchildren. One of her children was drug dependent and, as a result, Becky received no financial support and needed help with food:

> 'I needed help as I have a young lad with me that shouldn't be with me anyway. He would eat me out of house and home. He was on the streets and I took him in, but he eats most of that food. That's why I need the service, as he is a big lad.' (Brian)

> 'Because I have two daughters at home. Each has two children … one is partially blind … a girl called Ciara. The other girl is on drugs. There is more of my family now than when I was rearing my own … in my house. I say to myself, "I'll go to work and earn a few bob" so that I'm not looking for help. I'd love to be a day worker, but I can't with the two grandchildren, they are in my care.' (Becky)

Conclusions

The interviews revealed a complex picture, reflecting the multidimensionality of food poverty. While some respondents needed help to overcome temporary difficulties obtaining food, many interviews revealed longer-term food poverty, arising from a combination of factors, similar to those described as a 'toxic cocktail' by Daly and Kelly (2015: 41). This typically included low-paid work or no employment, because of ill health, disability or full-time caring responsibilities. It often involved accumulating high-cost credit from moneylenders. Respondents relied on the safety net of social welfare as their main source of income. They found that their welfare payment was inadequate to cover their necessary weekly expenditure, and issues with these payments were frequently the trigger that resulted in the need for food aid. Examples provided by respondents included delays in payments being adjusted, following changes in employment status. These difficulties suggested a lack of responsiveness and flexibility in the support system that tended to exacerbate their underlying problems. For respondents in paid employment, low-pay or low work intensity, together with issues arising from the casualisation of the workforce, this posed difficulties in being able to earn enough money to meet essential needs. Responses indicated that these structural issues have combined, together with lack of affordable childcare, high healthcare costs and the housing crisis, to present very serious challenges to respondents. As a result, little money was left for food after paying rent, utilities and sometimes loan repayments. Even for those coping within their limited income, the absence of a buffer meant that a relatively small additional cost for the family could give rise to a financial crisis and the resultant need for food aid.

6

Pathways through food poverty

Introduction

This chapter investigates the main pathways through food poverty, by exploring the experience of food aid recipients. Respondents described the impact of living through food poverty and it clearly affected their lives in many different ways. Food bank users in Dublin were asked about the difficulty of having no food and the experience of hunger, maintaining an appropriate diet, emotional experiences and social exclusion. The chapter presents important coping strategies, as respondents struggled to make ends meet and prioritise their spending. Respondents were asked about food shopping, providing for children and coping with special occasions when money was scarce. Finally, the use of moneylenders and support networks at pressure points in their lives was explored.

Impacts of food poverty

Hunger and running out of food

Many respondents reported they had experienced hunger after running out of food. Respondents described the different ways that hunger affected them, including food cravings, insomnia and a feeling that eating any food was better than going without:

> 'I go to bed hungry and then I find it hard to go to sleep. I'd move around a lot and find it hard to sleep.' (Barry)

> 'When you're very hungry, you don't really care what you are getting, to be honest with you.' (Kathleen)

> 'That would be terrible, as you have a craving for different things, like people might have a bar of chocolate in front of you and you feel like grabbing that. You have to do without it, because they have it, you haven't got it.' (Mary)

Respondents also experienced hunger when they had little remaining food, but not sufficient for their needs: "We would have probably gone to bed hungry because we would not have eaten as well as we would have liked. We do our best with what we have. If we go hungry, we go hungry"

(Kathleen). Respondents described how occasionally there would be little or no food left in the home:

> 'Nothing … sitting in the cold, with no gas, no electricity and no food. No money. I can't go into a shop … I can't go in and get milk and bread every day … I can't do that. I have actually got nothing in my fridge at the moment. Nothing. Some people might say "nothing" and there would be an onion or a potato in the bottom, but there is nothing in my fridge at the moment.' (Deirdre)

These responses show occasional and repeated experiences of hunger, followed by periods of sufficient supplies. The result is long-term negative effects on the family, as the following sections will show. Hunger often affected all members of the family, as children could not be protected if there was no food left in the home. However, the predominant view was that children should be shielded from hunger if at all possible, and parents often missed meals in order to have enough to feed them:

> 'There are times when I've nearly collapsed with the hunger … they [children] are more important.' (Grainne)

> 'The majority of times the kids are here for the weekends they will eat. I won't … I will pick. I will put their plates first and, if there is anything left in the soup bowl, I'll have it or I'll pick … or I'll have a couple of bowls of cereal during the day just to fill me up.' (John)

Running out of food causes the whole family distress. In one case, a woman described how her children worried about her: "They turn around and say, 'I'm hungry, I'm hungry' and when they see me they say, 'Mam, you're going to start losing weight again'. They are not just worrying about themselves, they are worrying about me as well. 'Mam, you have to eat, you have to eat'" (Carol). As was noted in Chapter 5, many of the respondents were living on social welfare. However, some respondents described how they experienced hunger while in employment: "When I had the kids that time, we often went hungry … I was working at [X company] at the time.… I couldn't … with the money … with the mortgage and everything" (Brian). A shortage of food may cause serious medical problems. A respondent explained that she needed to have adequate food in order to take her medication safely:

> 'You see, if I don't eat, I can't take a lot of my medication, because I have to take it on a full stomach, or at certain times of the day … and if I can't take my medicines, I get sicker and some weeks I get caught in that, which is dreadful.' (Deirdre)

These sections show that hunger is interrelated with employment conditions, family situations and health. Additional family members coupled with poor health amplify the experience of hunger and can lead to a vicious cycle of prolonged food poverty and deteriorating well-being.

Healthy eating and special diets

Some respondents reported that they were not able to afford a healthy or special diet required for medical reasons. They felt this had a detrimental effect on their health: "It wrecked my health. I ended up with all sorts of conditions and problems due to a bad diet" (Christine). This situation was not due to a lack of knowledge about the importance of a good diet, as respondents said they were felt well-informed about healthy eating, but found it financially beyond their reach. Some respondents were particularly concerned about eating processed food, which they felt was not nourishing:

> 'I just had to cut back … I went to a course on healthy eating and eating properly. It's really, really expensive to have fruit every day in your diet. It's so expensive for five people. Because you cannot afford the good stuff, the healthy stuff, you go back to processed rubbish.' (Cathy)

> 'You just don't put yourself as a priority. It probably sounds funny, you know you would be looking at programmes … healthy eating and 'go on a diet' … I couldn't afford to go on a diet.' (Patricia)

> 'If you want to eat anything of quality that is not processed or whatever, it still costs money and the money just isn't there.' (Elaine)

Respondents felt that their children were well-informed about healthy eating. As an illustration, Carol explained that this sometimes resulted in pressure at home. This arose when her son requested organic food, which she could not afford:

> 'The eldest son … he is into healthy eating, but a lot of the healthy eating stuff is very expensive and I wouldn't be able to afford it … he'd say, "I'd like the organic pasta" and I'd say, "You can't have that … you'll just have to get whatever you get".' (Carol)

A respondent reported that she found it would be less expensive to provide fast food for her family, than what she felt would be a healthy lunch: "You wouldn't be able to eat healthily in this country, because it's more expensive. It would be easier for me to get a €3 meal in McDonalds for the lunch, rather than an apple, a sandwich, a yoghurt and a drink for the kids" (Joy). Reflecting the significant number of respondents with an illness or disability in their household, many family members required a special diet for medical reasons, in order to avoid adverse consequences for their health. The difficulty of maintaining a diet recommended by their doctor was illustrated by two respondents:

> 'I am diabetic and I am supposed to only eat certain foods. The doctor said to me, "Don't eat this, don't eat that", but I don't have a choice … what I am supposed to eat, I can't afford.' (Kevin)

> 'Darren [husband] is meant to be on a specific diet, because he has diverticulitis. Sometimes we can't afford to buy specific food for him … we just don't have the money.' (Penny)

While respondents displayed knowledge and desire to eat healthily, this was constrained by lack of affordability, given that healthy eating and special diets were found to be relatively costly.

Emotions

Many respondents experienced high levels of stress as they tried to survive on a low income. There was a constant worry to provide enough food of sufficient quality, including special diets required for themselves and their family. The days prior to being paid were found to be particularly stressful, as illustrated by the following examples:

> 'My presses would be empty and the fridge is empty on the Sunday or the Monday. It's the worry and seeing how little you have … three sons that you have to feed and then a husband as well.' (Carol)

> 'Bread … fresh milk. If I have no money, I have no money. We would be looking around the house to make up €2. That is the truth. I would be looking in pockets, bags, everywhere for money.' (Linda)

Anxiety about getting enough food for their children was a recurring theme in the interviews with parents:

> 'It's very stressing, isn't it? You just want for the kids to have what they want … they are my priority, so they come first, before me.' (Jackie)

> 'I used to spend days thinking what will I put in their lunchboxes or what I don't have, or where I'm going to get it … or what's for breakfast, lunch, dinner and tea … or whether they would even get two meals.' (Christine, single mother of three)

Respondents also worried about the quality of the food they were able to give their family. In some cases, this meant not being able to provide their children with the special diets they required:

> 'I worry about them not being healthy and eating takeaways, because it's cheaper. Not having enough healthy food … in their diet … the two oldest ones would be overweight.' (Joy)

> 'I don't really worry about me at all. It's especially the little one, as she is coeliac as well.' (Cathy)

Some noted that their anxiety levels were accentuated when children referred to food shortages in the home. Parents sought to protect their children from worrying about the family's situation by covering up when there was not enough food for everyone. One respondent described how she would pretend to her children that she was not hungry. However, parents were aware that children were often able to sense that there was a problem:

> 'They say, "Mummy, there is not enough food in the presses … did you not do your shopping this week?"' (Terry)

> 'I don't share with them that I might have had a sleepless night the night before, because I am worried about having to pay for something. … It does affect them, as they can see it in my eyes at times … they can see it in my demeanour.' (Bridie)

Some parents decided to be open with their children about their financial difficulties:

> 'I think with me and with my two kids, we would talk openly and be honest with each other … I sat them down and said … this is how bad it is … this is what we have to do … now it broke my heart … because I am a single mother and I always want to provide for my kids.' (Barbara)

In another example, a parent revealed that the combination of stress and hunger had affected her behaviour towards her children: "I'm sure it did [affect sons] when they saw me. When you get hungry, you get really aggressive or worn down and tired … so it would affect them if I was in a bad humour. It was hard going" (Christine). Some respondents reported feeling depressed about their situation, which could arise on all kinds of occasions. One woman revealed that she had contemplated suicide, as financial stress was a constant in her life and she could see no clear path out of her difficulties:

> 'When I get into negative mode and I think that … I'm not going to be able to pay the bills, that's when it's dangerous times for me, because I was suicidal there ten days ago. I was in touch with the psychiatric services and I rang the Samaritans that night as well. It comes down to finances, because I find it difficult to survive.' (Kathleen)

These interviews illustrate the cumulative negative impact on the respondents' mental and physical health of living on a low income. Examples include the constant stress of having to pay bills and purchase food:

> 'I was struggling to pay everything else, because when you're not paying something else, then you have them on your back … and it just gets very frustrating.' (Barbara)

> 'When you are going around the shops, sometimes you do feel really down, because you are picking up the same "cheapest of the cheap" stuff every week. Sometimes it gets in on you. It might be a really cheap packet of burgers that you know no one really likes, but it will go with potatoes.' (Patricia)

Stress levels were particularly high when unexpected costs arose or were anticipated. Examples given were when a household appliance broke down, or when facing a potentially large car repair bill following a National Car Test (MOT): "When the car goes for the NCT … it's a week of sleepless nights, in case it doesn't pass, because where are you going to get the money to get it fixed, because you need it" (Bridie). In some cases, this tension had a detrimental effect on relationships with partners: "It causes tension between us, but we have been together a long time and we get through, but it does … it does cause a bit of tension" (Darren). Some respondents conveyed that they were embarrassed to let others know their financial difficulties. As an illustration, two food bank users explained that, even when they were so desperate that they were tempted to borrow from neighbours, they could not bring themselves to ask for help: "We try not to let people know we are in that predicament. We try not to say, 'Can we have €20 to buy the children food?'" (Declan). "I was tempted to ask my neighbours, but I was too embarrassed to do so. You couldn't … you'd die of embarrassment" (Kevin). The individual stress of respondents also had cumulative negative effects on the family members, in particular children. While parents tried to shield their children from these worries and negative emotions, the feeling of hunger makes it more difficult to control their emotions and respondents reported how children were also worrying.

The embarrassment of a food bank visit was inescapable. Seeking food aid was something that respondents felt they had to do, because they had exhausted other options available, such as support from family and friends. Most respondents found that their initial visit to the food bank was extremely difficult, with many having negative feelings about themselves. Respondents expressed a range of emotions, including shame, especially the first time they used the food bank:

> 'It's very daunting coming down at first because, in actual fact, you're begging … that's what it feels like.' (Barbara)

> 'Traumatised. Because I worked all my life … I just got sick … I was diagnosed with an illness and I couldn't work. I was devastated the first time and I still find it very hard.' (Deirdre)

Most users found that subsequent visits were less difficult, but never a comfortable experience: "I cried. But I feel fine now. I think you are under so much stress for so long and then it's a release, even though it's not all your problems" (Patricia). Many respondents blamed themselves for getting into a situation where they needed to resort to food aid. They described their sense of personal failure and felt they had let down their family:

> 'When I came here first I was just broken. … I felt so bad about myself. … I felt that I was a failure as a mother, because I wasn't able to provide for my daughter.' (Kathleen)

> 'The first time I came here, I was very apprehensive and I didn't know what to expect. And I think it was more my own … it was disappointment in myself.' (Barbara)

> 'I was not impressed with my own self having to come here. I'm not a drunk, I'm just struggling with nine kids at home.' (Paddy)

Shame and embarrassment about receiving food aid was felt by many respondents, worried that they would meet a neighbour or friend: "I was embarrassed, in case I'd bump into someone else that I knew" (Cathy). "Sometimes you would be embarrassed, if you met one of the neighbours … we are all here for the same reason. And that's why I would be saying she'll only see me, if she's here herself" (Joy). For some food bank users, the sense of embarrassment was a serious deterrent to seeking help. This issue is illustrated by a respondent who said he was sent by his wife, as she was too embarrassed to be seen at the food bank. He knew of other families in a similar situation:

> 'Just everyone seeing you coming down. We try not to let people know we are in that predicament. Coming down, people hear you

are here and you feel discriminated. At first, that's why she wouldn't come down, she felt embarrassed. And I know loads of people who do not turn up to this place.' (Declan)

While many were anxious to avoid meeting neighbours or family, one respondent said she was comforted during her visit to the food bank by knowing that her family's situation was no different from others: "I feel grand, because everybody that I know is here. So, you are not on your own … there are other people out there that are in the same situation" (Mary). Respondents were also keen to point out that their visit was made less difficult by the staff and volunteers at the food bank, who were felt to be empathetic, friendly and non-judgemental:

> 'I felt very, very good … that they were there to help. When you're in need, you're in need.' (Sheila)

> 'When you come here first, you don't want to be asking for stuff, you don't feel that it's right, you feel that you're not worthy of taking the stuff … all these feelings of embarrassment and what people think of you coming down. That's laid to rest as soon as you come through the door here. You are welcomed, you are offered, you are told where things are.' (Darren)

> 'You are not judged, which is very important. That was my … maybe it's pride.' (Penny)

> 'I have always been treated really nicely and very respectfully.' (Deirdre)

> 'I'm humbled.' (Christine)

Staff and volunteers clearly made a difference to the experience of food bank users, who were keen to express their appreciation.

Social exclusion

Many respondents found that they had become isolated from their communities, because they did not have the resources to participate in social activities. This included the difficulty of engaging in activities that most people would consider normal, such as meeting a friend at a shopping centre:

> 'The days that other people expect you to be able to just do stuff, with nothing … and you get a lot of "Why can't you go?" or "Why can't you meet me in Dundrum [shopping centre]?" It's very hard to say

I can't go, because I literally haven't got one penny … to pick up a bottle of water while I'm walking around looking at the shop windows … never mind going in to buy stuff. It's tough.' (Deirdre)

For some respondents, living on a low income severely curtailed family activities:

> 'Well, we don't go anywhere, we don't do anything … we don't go out socialising … you don't bring [children] to activities or anything like that. It's all that kind of stuff that they don't have. It's just food and bits, food and bits, and food and bits.' (Patricia)

> 'Like taking the kids out … I can't remember the last time I took them out.' (Ibekwe)

Respondents explained that this withdrawal was at least in part driven by the desire to avoid letting others know their financial situation was so bad. While they conveyed the stigma of using a food bank, respondents were also ashamed to let neighbours know of their difficulties. One respondent explained that it was not even straightforward to ask a friend to visit her at home. If she wanted to offer the simple hospitality of a hot drink, this could present her with practical difficulties: "You can't even invite people in for a cup of tea. I'd have tea bags, but I wouldn't have milk" (Deirdre). During the year, special events arise and food plays an important part in how families celebrate these occasions. However, respondents found that such family occasions, particularly Christmas, were very difficult for them. As a result, some respondents preferred to withdraw from participating in social events, rather than face embarrassment when relations became aware of their situation: "Christmas is really, really, hard. I'd imagine birthdays. If there is anything going on in the families … weddings or christenings … we tend to back away from all those and make up an excuse that we can't go … rather than let people know that things are really that bad" (Cathy). Another respondent explained that the cost of inviting friends to participate in special occasions meant that her family were in financial difficulty for weeks after the event. As a result, they decided to withdraw from such events:

> 'A few years ago, if it was something big to celebrate, I was inviting friends but, in the past few years, it's no point to invite, say, eight or ten adults just to eat food today and for next few weeks to be in arrears, so we are trying to survive on our own.' (Uta)

One respondent described how his situation had resulted in being cut off from the community: "I have no other connection with family. I don't talk to neighbours … only to say hello. I don't get mixed with them at all. I'm in isolation" (Barry). Some were reluctant to seek help from family members because they were also in a similar situation, or they felt they had called on them for help too often: "I have family, but they are all finding it hard enough as well" (Carol). "Not any more … you'd exhaust it. I would have had help from my oldest sister, but you can't keep on going back to the same person" (Joy). In a situation where they felt isolated from family and friends, some respondents explained that they had no option but to try to manage on their own and be self-reliant:

> 'I'll try to manage … I'll try to do something [with] what I have at home, before asking for help. I am trying to rely on me, if you understand.' (Uta)

> 'You learn to deal with stuff yourself … you wouldn't ask anybody else … you were brought up not to ask anyone else. You would just do without it.' (Mary)

Some respondents pointed out that their visit to the food bank had a social aspect and felt a sense of community there:

> 'Coming here for me is not just a case of coming to get food and having food to put on the table. It's also the social aspect of interacting, as I might not always see someone from one end of the week to the other or through the day.' (Kathleen)

> 'When I come around here on a Wednesday morning, I meet people and it's nice to meet them. They always have something to say to me, they smile and they are just nice guys. That gets me out of the house for half an hour, or whatever, and that for me is brilliant.' (Kevin)

Coping strategies

Making ends meet

Respondents regularly found themselves faced with the dilemma of prioritising between very important items of expenditure. Sometimes hard choices would affect critical aspects of their lives, such as the risk of homelessness, health and having adequate food. The top priority was invariably paying rent, and some stated that this was a higher priority than money for food: "Well, we would have no roof … nowhere to eat it under … if I didn't pay [the rent] first" (Christine). "I always pay my rent, that's the first thing I pay. I've really cut back on everything" (Eimer). "It would be the rent, that's the most important thing" (Carol). One couple explained that their priority to pay the rent first was influenced by their previous experience of being homeless: "It's immensely important that we have a roof over our head. Food would be first, only we've had this perspective from the homeless side of it" (Penny). After paying rent, most respondents regarded heating and other utility costs as their next priority. However, many respondents had to cut back on heating or could not keep their home sufficiently warm for their family:

> 'Sometimes you have to go without heating … my house is like an ice box.' (Grainne)

> 'It's very tough trying to heat the house. I have a bale of briquettes to do me, but I have no coal or anything for the next six weeks … it's trying to keep the house heated.' (Carol)

Sometimes being without heating could involve serious health consequences, as illustrated by one respondent: "If I had the operation that I am supposed to have … I wouldn't survive if I was in the cold, no way. I have high blood pressure … so I need heat. I have arthritis. I need electricity" (Janet).

Respondents found that using meters for electricity was of help in avoiding large bills. However, a prepayment meter is more expensive than a standard billing arrangement (Electric Ireland, 2021), and there is a lack of flexibility that can present challenges: "I have my electricity and my heating on a meter, which means I can't say I'll buy extra food this week and I won't buy electricity, so I have to put the money in, or we will be sitting in the dark" (Deirdre). In the days immediately before her welfare transfer, Deirdre found that visiting the food bank helped her to stay warm: "I don't have any electricity or heating at the moment at home, because I don't get paid until tomorrow. And it was cold, so I came here … that happens regularly. It's really bad" (Deirdre). Other respondents reported that running out of power was a regular occurrence, with some regularly having to spend periods living in the dark:

> 'I do spend one or two days a week sitting in the dark.' (Deirdre)

> 'I often run out of ESB (electricity). … I don't mind staying in the dark. I'm on a meter now … it's down to 48 cents, but I get paid today, so I will be able to top up today.' (Brian)

Another respondent explained that maintaining the electricity supply was a priority, in order to keep his children entertained: "Obviously tele for the kids, so they have something to do" (John). In contrast with rent and utility costs, food was regarded as a relatively low priority. It was accepted that spending on food was a more flexible part of the budget and available from what was left over after other more important items of expenditure. However, respondents were acutely aware that, if their family used more heat or had additional bills to pay, this impacted on what was left for food: "If you are using more ESB, more gas and other bills that come in … for the schools or whatever, we would obviously have less money to spend on food" (Marie). As food expenditure had such a relatively low priority, this frequently resulted in little money left for shopping:

> 'The bills are paid first and then, if we eat, it's a bonus.' (Deirdre)

> 'Sometimes I am left with €50 for shopping, sometimes I am not left with a penny.' (Tom)

> 'Food … if you have to do without it, you have to do without it.' (Mary)

> 'It's last. You tend to go hungry yourself.' (Joy)

Although the focus of the interviews was the topic of food poverty, respondents explained that prioritising expenditure usually resulted in some other basic necessities ranking lower than food purchases. Basic household items needed for daily living were sometimes out of financial reach for respondents. Items such as toiletries and new clothes were often regarded as luxury items of expenditure:

> 'It's super tight … sometimes you have to choose between the toilet paper and the light bulb.' (Elaine)

> 'I've no light bulbs upstairs in my house for the last 11 days. I can't afford to buy light bulbs … it's really bad. It's very hard.' (Deirdre)

> 'Say, like shower gels … washing powder, toiletries and stuff like that.' (John)

> 'Even this morning … I used the smallest amount of toothpaste, because there was barely enough left to make sure the others had some.' (Christine)

> 'Me and my wife always do without important things … it doesn't bother me doing without, once the kids have it … as I said, roof, gas, electric and them clean.' (Paddy)

Funeral costs were also a significant issue for some respondents, with one expressing concern about the cost of her own funeral: "God forbid, if I die tomorrow morning, I've got no way of burying myself. That's really hard. It's a sad thing to say. Very, very sad" (Sheila). Respondents reported that significant expenses arose from time to time. By way of illustration, Patricia explained that she could not afford the cost of having her washing machine repaired. The consequence of this was that her family's clothes would have to be washed in cold water:

> 'Big stuff like the washing machine breaking down … you couldn't afford to just go out and buy a washing machine. … If I had to get this done this week, the rent wouldn't get paid, we definitely wouldn't pay the bins, you wouldn't be paying UPC [former Irish telephone, broadband and TV provider] … there would be three or four things that you would have to leave out to cover that … if something like that comes up and you don't pay two or three things, it's the catching up. … It's going to be wash with a cold wash.' (Patricia)

Respondents were asked whether, in a typical week, they were able to make ends meet. All respondents found that this was difficult and, for some, it was not possible to afford basic meals and essential necessities each week: "I would never go a full week with two meals a day and constant heat, electric. No, never, not in a long time" (Deirdre). Respondents who were able to get through the week on their income were usually left with little at the end. Most respondents received weekly income and, in the days immediately before their next payment, there was often a risk that money would run out:

> 'Thursday is ok as I get my social welfare … but Monday, Tuesday, over there is hard. Sometimes when you can't afford to pay the bills … and you have to leave things back … that's hard.' (Terry)

> 'Every weekend … you always feel on the Sunday or Monday that you are really going down … it's tough every week.' (Carol)

Unexpected events could easily throw respondents off course and result in food poverty. In illustrative cases which demonstrate the variety of problems faced, respondents explained the type of difficulties they encountered:

> 'Two weeks ago, the girl [daughter] who is on drugs stole my bill money. Since she took the money … it was €275 for my bills … gas and ESB … and my messages [other expenditure] … I don't seem to be able to get back on top, because I am paying extra off my bills as I missed out on that week. I have a television … it's a meter television … she robbed the money out of that … the man came to collect it and, when he opened the back, there was no money in it.' (Becky)

A visit to a doctor, dentist or optician often involved significant costs, which could not be afforded:

> 'I can't afford to get sick. The alternative is that, if I get sick, I go to a doctor and it's going to cost me €50 and it's going to cost me money for medication. I can't see what's written on the wall over there … that sign there … I can't see what's on it. I need glasses. I can't afford them.' (John)

> 'Even the medical care … I have to look for home remedies and the children … I can't take them to the dentist.' (Ibekwe)

Respondents found that budgeting was essential to help make ends meet and ensure that their money lasted until the next pay day. It helped to map out meals for the week and prepare a shopping list with planned food expenditure:

> 'I budget my bills all the time, so I know how much per week I have to pay off. Then whatever is left is for shopping and then for the bread and milk during the week. When I'm writing out my shopping list, I write down what I'm having on Monday for dinner, Tuesday and all the week through.' (Carol)

Respondents were asked about food choices when money was tight, in order to focus on the type of meals they were able to have on a low income. One respondent explained the limitations in her family: "We only get one or two meals a day. A good dinner would be enough where you push your plate away without it being cleaned … it would be nice. I couldn't tell you the last time I had a roast dinner … or meat and vegetables and potatoes" (Deirdre). Respondents were asked about a typical main meal on a day when money was tight. The option cited most often was a fried meal: "It would be frozen pizza, chicken dippers, frozen skinny fries. Ridiculous disgusting food I abhor, but I have to put something on the table … they are very cheap" (Cathy). Popular options were also pasta meals or other options that did not involve the expense of meat: "They'd get a bowl of pasta with tomato sauce on it … I wouldn't let them know that money was tight. They'd still have a meal. I'd make a meal out of whatever I have" (Alice). "If it was a really hard day, probably beans and toast, or something like that" (Terry). Most respondents indicated that they had adequate kitchen facilities. However, some lacked basic kitchen appliances, utensils or sufficient storage space for groceries:

> 'I don't have space for storing food. I just have a kitchen, so we store the food underneath the cabinets.' (Ibekwe)

> 'I need a freezer. … I keep saying to myself I am going to have a look and see … on eBay … is that what you call it … or on Facebook or whatever.' (Janet)

As Janet had no freezer, budgeting was more of a challenge, as it was more difficult to take advantages of bargain food offers when shopping.

Food shopping

Reflecting the relatively low prioritisation of food, as discussed earlier, respondents were left with little money for food shopping. This had implications for the type of food they could buy: "I have to go for the cheapest food in the store" (Jackie). "We've cut back completely on the type of food we eat and look for cheaper … more processed, I would imagine … which is not good for me or my daughter … because we are both coeliac" (Cathy). The following three illustrative cases convey that respondents normally had a routine for food shopping. Paddy had recently taken on the food shopping for his family of nine children. He explained why it was necessary to carry out the main shopping immediately after picking up his social welfare payment:

> 'I get paid on a Monday, normally and, before I leave the Post Office, the gas and electricity and rent are paid. Then I get the bus down to the Square and do about €50 worth of shopping in Dunnes … the likes of stuff you can't buy in Aldi. Then you go and do about €150 of shopping in Aldi … then you run out during the week for the likes of bread and milk and stuff like that. If we don't do the shopping on Monday, Tuesday comes and most of the money is gone, because the kids are rushing across to (local convenience store) all day … their charges are enormous.' (Paddy)

Patricia's family included three teenage boys:

> 'You'd be sticking to the same thing every week. I would go in and pick up potatoes, a packet of mince, packet of mash, packet of sausages and cereal for the breakfast and there would be nothing else outside of that. You would try and pick up seven things to go with seven dinners.' (Patricia)

Respondents used various coping mechanisms to provide for themselves and their families. This meant careful shopping and hunting out special offers: "I am looking for sales or something like that in the shops, so I can buy it. I am waiting until the evening time, or the special offers time, to buy"

(Uta). "Unless something is on special offer, it doesn't go into the fridge" (Linda). Planning a visit to the shops was important, and respondents had ways to avoid impulse purchases that they could not afford:

> 'What you do is you bring over just enough money, because if you bring over extra, you'll do the impulse buying … once you get the impulse, I'll want to buy a bottle of Coca Cola, I'll want to buy a packet of crisps. The knock-on effect a couple of days later is huge … for a bottle of Coke.' (John)

> 'I just put as much money in my pocket as I can afford. … I don't bring any more money. So, I won't be tempted to spend any more.' (Kathleen)

Respondents found that local convenience stores were often too expensive, apart from using them occasionally for small purchases. Discount food stores, such as Lidl and Aldi, were popular with respondents, who took advantage of their special offers and items on the reduced shelves:

> 'We will watch for the ads … you know, the way you get papers through the door … it's just watching for the cheap sales.' (Jackie)

> 'Sometimes, if there is stuff that is reduced … that's where you go first … to the reduced section. Some things are all right to use … on the sell-by date and others aren't.' (Joy)

However, despite planning their shopping carefully, some respondents expressed a fear of being embarrassed at the supermarket till:

> 'I have a huge headache in the shop, because there are lots of things you want to buy but, as you are taking them off the shelf, you are calculating in your head. Sometimes I have to bring out my phone to make sure that I don't get to the till and become embarrassed. So, I use my calculator and enter the amounts.' (Ibekwe)

> 'When I go shopping for food, I might not have the full amount to pay for it. I might have to put back something out of the food that I would need for the kids.' (Jackie)

Providing for children

Providing for children's meals was a priority for all families. Parents reported that they often had to go without, in order to feed their children: "I'd rather do without it myself and let the children eat it" (Sheila). "You'd find yourselves not being a priority. If you opened a packet of burgers and there was only four in it, you'd give one to everyone else and just wouldn't have one yourself" (Patricia). Some respondents found that it was difficult to cope with the appetite of teenagers and explained that it was sometimes necessary to ration the weekly food, so that it lasted until the next shopping trip:

> 'The biggest problem buying food is trying to keep the food. The two boys eat more than I would ever eat.' (Janet)

> 'He [son] eats twice as much as me ... and it's absolutely impossible.' (Elaine)

> 'The lads are getting older and eating more. They were saying, "I'm hungry" and "there's nothing here, there's nothing to eat". I just kept saying, "I'm doing my best," which they do know I'm doing my best. I was saying, "You can't have that, that's for tomorrow and this is for the next day".' (Carol)

Some respondents resorted to desperate measures:

> 'At one stage, when the two older boys were getting bigger and harder to feed, I would put the week's shopping in the fridge on a Friday and then maybe I would be out ... and when I came back, the whole lot would be gone. They would have eaten everything, or most of it. I used to fight with them over this ... really badly ... because it was a worry ... and at one stage, I found myself putting a twisty bicycle lock on the fridge ... which was totally wrong ... because they would have eaten the whole week's lunches or put a good dint in them ... and then I thought to myself, that's really wrong ... really mean ... so I didn't do that again.' (Christine)

After deciding not to lock the fridge, Christine considered other measures to ensure that her food shopping lasted until the next payment: "I felt really bad about it. I thought I would either hide the shopping in the boot of the car or just do it on a Sunday ... or do it day by day" (Christine). In another example, a father of nine children explained that when he ran out of food for his family, he took extreme measures to provide for them. He felt that this was necessary for his family's survival:

> 'I went and I robbed. Seriously. I'm sorry for those things. I never robbed a person or never did anyone's house in my life. It was a couple of occasions. I robbed pubs when they were closed, cigarettes and drink, you can always sell them. I always find that's the very, very, last

> resort … so I try my best not to do it. You have to do what you have to do to make ends meet … to survive. If you haven't got it, you do without and make sure the kids have it.' (Paddy)

Both examples show how parents felt that they had to take extreme measures to feed their children and were also ashamed of their actions. The well-being of their children was a priority that made them resort to such extreme measures.

Special occasions

Respondents found that at certain times or occasions during the year it was particularly difficult to afford food. Christmas was most regularly cited, with many respondents worried about the expense but, at the same time, conscious of its particular importance for their children: "Christmas is difficult. We spend more money … Christmas for the children" (Margaret). "Christmas is an expensive time of the year … you don't want to let down children" (Linda). Some respondents found that providing for the family on a low income made it a time of stress and worry, which could spoil the festive enjoyment. As a result, one respondent, Kathleen, declared that she "hated" Christmas, as it nearly caused her to have a nervous breakdown in the previous year. However, despite difficulties, most respondents found ways to cope with the additional expenditure. Some were able to put aside small amounts of money in advance, while others resorted to borrowing: "Christmas this year was rough enough … it has to be done. I put an extra … the boys don't know … three euro into a box, just to have it there for an emergency only" (Terry). "At Christmas I'd have to get a loan … from the loan shark" (Larry). Some respondents managed the additional expenditure for Christmas by cutting back in the run-up to the occasion:

> 'At Christmas … we do without … all the way up to Christmas. It's called a feast or a famine. You have the famine for a couple of weeks and then a feast for Christmas.' (Paddy)

> 'Last year I found … coming up to Christmas … you are cutting out on your foods. Buying a present is a problem, two children are in my care, I cut down on food to get presents.' (Becky)

> 'It's … Christmas, getting everything and whatnot … having money left over for food.' (Jackie)

Given the demands on limited resources at Christmas, many found that there was little money left for food. For some families, the pressure of their budget at Christmas was alleviated by assistance from charities: "The SVP have been extremely good in providing us with help for the last two years. They have provided us with a very nice Christmas dinner" (Linda). Apart from Christmas, there were other special occasions during the year that were particularly challenging for families with children. For example, the back to school period was found to be difficult: "Yes, August and September. Because of going back to school … it's draining" (Ibekwe). "There are certain times of the year when you are knocked with expenses, like books" (Linda). A range of coping mechanisms were used to manage this situation. Two cases illustrate different approaches. In one case, a respondent explained how it was necessary to cut back in other areas, which sometimes included reducing expenditure on food. In another example, a respondent explained that, in addition to economising, she tried to save small amounts regularly, in order to help offset the school expenditure: "We cut back, because the uniforms cost a lot, the books cost a lot, the fares cost a lot, and then they've got [to have] shoes" (Michael). "I kinda put whatever I can, even if it is 2 or 3 or 5 euro aside and try and forget that it's there" (Christine).

Moneylenders

Personal and household debt emerged as a theme for respondents coping with food poverty. For those struggling on a low income, there was a thin line between making ends meet and slipping behind with bills. When an emergency situation arose, resorting to borrowing was sometimes felt to provide a quick solution. However, respondents were acutely conscious that solving a short-term need could give rise to further problems, which could create a spiral of difficulties. In an illustrative case, a respondent explained that she purchased a freezer with her credit card and was struggling to repay the debt:

> 'I had to get a new freezer there before Christmas … it was rusty and the dial on it wasn't working … I used my credit card to buy one … so I'm just trying to bring it down each month when they ask for the minimum payment … I put in whatever I can. But that's how easy things can just slide and I'm careful with my money.' (Kathleen)

Most respondents who borrowed had to use moneylenders, as they were not able to access cheaper loans. However, they were aware of the drawbacks:

> 'It's a high paying interest rate. You borrow €300 and you pay back €390. I wouldn't recommend that to anyone.' (Ibekwe)

> 'I did get moneylenders … the more that you would borrow, the more you would be in trouble.' (Mary)

'I was sky high trying to pay them back. They are too expensive.' (Grainne)

Moneylenders would often grant new loans to existing borrowers, trapping them in a cycle of debt, from which it was difficult to escape:

'Once you get them in, you'd never get them off your back.' (Michael)

'I hope it never comes to it again … with the moneylender … it's just what you are paying back, you know, and the hassle of them at your door … they are nearly in the door on top of you … if you don't have the money.' (Declan)

Social networks

Respondents found that occasionally they were able to call on help from their support network, which included family, friends or neighbours: "Now and again you don't mind asking a neighbour or a friend or family member … look, I'm stuck … could you give me a tenner or whatever … give us a bit of bread or milk" (Christine). Most respondents reported that their closest support was from family members, particularly parents and, to a lesser extent, siblings. Respondents described the importance of emotional support, as well as practical help:

'My mum and my dad … they would help out now as well. I'd have to say they're very good and I'd be lost without them … lost. We're very close now … when I actually lost my job, I was very down and they were there for me at that time as well.' (Barbara)

'I wouldn't ask anyone else. She just knows what it's like. She understands. I'd never let anyone [else] know my business.' (Cathy)

Another respondent, who minded his children at the weekend, following his divorce, also reported that his close relations were his main source of support: "If I get stuck for food, I can go down to my mother or my sister for dinner" (John). Some respondents were able to call on other family members when needed: "At Christmas, I got a bit of money off her [sister]. I used to go to the Provident [high cost credit provider] and I cleared them" (Patricia). "Only my brother sometimes, he would lend us some money, when he has got it" (Michael). Some respondents found that their best source of help was from their adult children. In one example, a respondent with five children still at home explained that her adult daughters were her only source of help and provided financial assistance when needed. Another respondent reported that her son regularly contributed towards the cost of utilities, which she found to be a big help: "I just go to my daughters. They give me a lend and I give it back" (Jackie). "One of my sons would come in and say to me, 'Mam, there is €20' and that €20 would go on the electric or the gas" (Janet). Many respondents were reluctant to ask for help from family members, as they felt they were in similar difficulties. One man explained that he was unwilling to ask for help from family as, if he received a loan, he felt he would be obliged to repay it quickly. Another respondent, who lived on a Traveller site with three married sisters, summed up how many felt about asking for help: "Most on the site … in the Travelling community … they all have big families … some of them out there have 12 children. I can't go out there and take, because I know they don't have it either" (Terry). Friends were also an important source of support. The type of help that was most frequently mentioned by respondents was a loan: "I have very good friends. They have helped me on many, many occasions. One in particular, she gives me the shirt of her back … literally" (Bridie). "You would have to get a lend of money off someone until it's payday … and give it back to that person on payday" (Jackie). Some respondents felt in a position to ask neighbours, particularly those who lived in a close community:

> 'I'm very lucky where I am. If I'm short of milk, I run across to my neighbour … and she'll give me milk. If she was rooting for eggs, I'd give her an egg, you know that way. I live in a wonderful community, which is great.' (Elaine)

> 'We have great neighbours. If they have it, or we have it, we share.' (Tom)

For some, respondents explained that if the arrangement was reciprocal, this made it easier to ask for help when needed: "Sometimes you'd have the neighbours dropping in and we just share … that's no problem" (Elaine). "I've often had to ask a neighbour … they were ok, as they've often had to ask me when I've had money" (Larry). A small number of respondents explained that they had no one to turn to for help or did not want to let friends or family know their plight. In these cases, respondents often sought help from a charity, such as SVP:

> 'I come [to the food bank] as I am too proud to ask my family or friends.' (Kathleen)

> 'I picked up the phone … I was a little bit embarrassed the first time I thought about it … the second time I thought about it I said I have

to just ask. They [SVP] surprised me … they were really great about it.' (Christine)

Conclusions

This study reveals that the consequences of living through food poverty manifest themselves in multiple ways. The impacts include experiencing hunger and not being able to afford the right type of food to sustain good health. The experience of food poverty often involves significant stress, mostly driven by the struggle to survive on a low income and provide for families. While the food aid was given free, there was evidence of the hidden cost to users in terms of its emotional impact, including shame and embarrassment. In the literature, definitions of food poverty overlook these important aspects of the experience of food poverty. The findings of this study also demonstrate how food poverty is interwoven with other aspects of poverty, including energy poverty and social exclusion. This aligns with previous research on poverty, which indicates that material deprivation on one dimension often brings about a higher risk of deprivation on others (Hick, 2016).

Respondents in this study used a range of coping mechanisms to try to make ends meet. They struggled with difficult decisions regarding how best to prioritise their limited resources. Examples of hard choices were between maintaining the family home, ensuring adequate heating or light, meeting essential medical costs or providing food for themselves and their family. A key finding is that respondents ranked rent and utility costs ahead of expenditure on food. As a result, many families had insufficient money to spend on food, which severely restricted their food choices and raises concern about the quality of food being consumed. Providing for children was always regarded as a priority, although this was put under particular strain on special occasions, such as Christmas. The study revealed that some respondents resorted to desperate measures, including theft, as they tried to overcome their difficulties. Social networks provided a key resource for many respondents, although in some cases was limited, as friends and family members were in similar difficulties. Some respondents had to resort to moneylenders to provide temporary financial relief, although they found that this usually exacerbated their difficulties over the longer term.

7

Investigating the policy drivers

Introduction

Many findings from the quantitative and qualitative data on food poverty set out in this book are linked to or have implications for the policies and practices of government, employers and other relevant stakeholders. Drawing on the relevant literature and key findings from primary and secondary data analysis, this chapter discusses the most prominent of these issues. These include problems regarding social protection, housing, illness/disability, caring, low-pay and precarious employment. In particular, it highlights issues which, if addressed, may elucidate pathways out of food poverty. The conclusion summarises the key policy implications.

Inadequate social protection

Income protection

Most food bank users in this study were reliant on social protection. A key theme that emerged from respondents was the inadequacy of welfare support. In Ireland, social transfers play an important role in reducing poverty (Watson and Maître, 2013), but levels of deprivation during the last recession were likely to have been exacerbated by cuts to social welfare benefits, including Child Benefit and Jobseeker's payments (Murphy, 2012). In relative terms, social transfers may have helped significantly to reduce poverty, but a closer review indicates that social welfare support has been inadequate, particularly for some household types. Research on welfare support levels in Ireland across a range of households demonstrated that, apart from pensioners, it does not provide an adequate income for the MESL (MacMahon et al, 2017). This ties in with OECD data for 2012 which indicated that, except for one-earner married households, with or without children, Ireland had replacement rates below the EU and OECD median values (Nevin Economic Research Institute [NERI], 2014: 94). Watson et al (2016) revealed that during the recession Ireland was the least effective EU member state, together with the UK, at safeguarding the living standards of vulnerable groups. For example, the gap in persistent deprivation levels, measured over two years between lone parents and other adults aged 30 to 65 years, increased by 12 per cent from 2005 to 2014.

Two groups which stood out as having a high prevalence of food poverty were lone parents and those with an illness or disability. Over one third of food bank users were lone parents and 2016 EU-SILC data corresponding to the period of interviews (Chapter 4) showed they had a higher risk of food poverty. MacMahon et al (2017) found that lone parents fared least well in terms of social welfare, particularly families with older children. In single-parent households with teenagers, social welfare income represented only 78 per cent of the minimum essential expenditure required. This impacted on poverty levels, with Watson et al (2016: 40) reporting that material deprivation levels in Ireland were the highest for lone parents, increasing from 39 per cent in 2004 to 58 per cent in 2013. A child of a lone parent was found to have an even higher deprivation level of 61 per cent in 2013. Apart from lone parents, approximately one third of food bank users in this study reported having a disability. This group was identified, from analysis of 2016 EU-SILC data, as having a higher risk of food poverty. Watson et al (2016: 40) found that material deprivation levels for working-age disabled adults were 49 per cent in 2013, having increased significantly from 24 per cent in 2004. Deprivation levels for children of disabled adults was slightly higher in 2013, at 51 per cent.

Some food bank users found that income protection was inflexible and unresponsive to their needs. While respondents showed great resourcefulness, interruptions in welfare payments presented them with extremely serious challenges, as they tried to make ends meet. Having no buffer (for example, savings) to help them cope with this situation, they found that assistance from a food bank was essential. Respondents expressed concern about cuts or interruptions to their social welfare payments when taking up part-time work, moving from one job to another, or periods out of work between jobs. Problems with payments were often experienced, due to a lack of responsiveness by the social welfare system in dealing with such transitions. The system did not cope adequately with the fundamental changes in work patterns that have arisen from the trend towards increasing casualisation of work. Worry about an interruption in transfers was a deterrent to seeking paid work, given that respondents often had little or no spare resources to fall back on and their support networks lacked capacity to assist financially. The provision of medical cards also illustrates the inflexibility of social protection. This was an area of significant concern to respondents, especially those who were ill or disabled, as applicants were in a very uncertain position when the issuance of these valuable cards was at the discretion of social welfare officers. An expert panel review (HSE, 2014) commented on the complexity and inefficiency of the medical card system and the risk of inconsistent assessment of eligibility.

Reform of the Irish social protection system has been limited in tackling issues such as social welfare traps and adjusting to changes in the nature of work, such as the increase in non-standard employment. Indeed, McCashin (2015: 212) contends that Irish social protection management and administrative structures have changed very little over 50 years. Viebrock and Clasen (2009) argue that traditional social protection programmes are increasingly incapable of keeping pace with the needs of employees with different work patterns. Social support systems have been built over time and assume a stable, long-term contract with one employer (Kiss, 2017: 5). During the global financial crisis and Ireland's Economic Adjustment Programme (2010–13), the Troika identified issues impeding employment in Ireland, including social welfare traps (Dukelow and Considine, 2014: 425). Subsequently, the Irish Government's National Action Plan for Social Inclusion 2015–17 (NAPinclusion) sought to 'avoid poverty traps and disincentives to work' (DSP, 2016b: 4). However, a respondent in this study raised the issue of the 'three-day rule', which made it difficult for her to accept available work without losing welfare benefits. At the time of writing, a person must be unemployed for at least four days out of the seven-day week to be eligible for Jobseeker's Allowance/Jobseeker's Benefit (Citizens Information, 2021a). This rule means that someone who works a total of 15 hours over three days of the week will receive two fifths of their normal welfare payment, but another earning the same income from the same number of hours over five days would receive no payment. The respondent reported that she would much prefer to get a full-time job, even though she would lose her benefits. However, as she was only able to obtain part-time work, the additional welfare support was vital, in order to top up her income and meet basic needs. The system lacked flexibility, as any part-time work would need to be for no more than three days per week, in order to avoid loss of welfare payment. The rule does not recognise the reality of the situation for many part-time workers, who do not have control over the number of hours or days of work they will be allocated each week.

Murphy (2012: 351) argues that the DSP has a limited capacity to develop policy and tends to focus on administration and service delivery. However, recent reforms in relation to labour market activation, including incentivisation of employment take-up, were problematic for some food bank users. DSP activation policies, which were set out in the 'Pathways to Work 2016–2020' programme, include welfare conditionality and many transitioning from unemployment find themselves having to accept a low-paid job to avoid sanctioning (Boland and Griffin, 2015). The type of employment offered may include low-paid, part-time or temporary work which sometimes represents little more than subsistence living. Moreover, it may present difficulties advancing to better-paid employment, as a result of fewer training opportunities and other factors. Ó Riain (2017) describes this predicament as a 'low learning trap', where precarious work, without skills and education, can keep people and families in poverty. Morel et al (2012: 29) argue that the state should be engaged in 'preparing' instead of 'repairing' workers for our economy, where skills and competences need to be constantly developed and renewed. This requires public investment, not just in early childhood care and education, but lifelong learning and training for adults. Although the provision of a precarious job may be regarded as a success in terms of transitioning someone into work, over the longer term it is unlikely to be successful in reducing poverty.

Social welfare conditionality has recently been applied in Ireland via DSP sanctions to payments for lack of engagement, or compliance with job seeking and training requirements. Food bank users in this study felt that these were sometimes implemented unfairly. One respondent reported that he had received a permanent sanction of €40 for failure to attend one day of a training course, while he was mourning his mother's recent death. This unexpected cut in his social welfare payment left him short of money for food. Data on payment sanctioning in Ireland are difficult to obtain, relying on responses to parliamentary questions. The Minister of Social Protection (Dáil Éireann Debate, 2018) confirmed that sanction levels have risen and 16,451 penalty deductions were applied to welfare payments in 2017, involving 13,503 individuals. An increasing use of sanctioning via cuts in welfare payments is likely to have an impact on social welfare recipients, including the need for food aid.

Many food bank users were unable to heat their homes adequately, while providing sufficient food for themselves and their families. The winter fuel allowance was considered both inadequate and paid for too short a period. Research in the UK indicates that householders give priority to paying for goods or services where the consequence of default is severe (Hossain et al, 2011). For example, electricity meters have to be topped up to avoid loss of supply. In addition, demands for payment of bills may arise from suppliers or other agencies, who can threaten or impose fines (Wanless, 2002). Despite the importance of keeping their home adequately heated and maintaining household energy supplies, food bank users found that prioritisation strategies were often not enough to make ends meet. The issue has been referred to in the UK context as the 'heat or eat' dilemma (Snell et al, 2018). This oversimplifies the situation, as in practice there is nuance in such household decisions, with respondents having to restrict their heating to fewer hours and also cut back expenditure on food. Snell's study found that there was often an impact on the quality of food consumed.

Housing

The importance of a 'roof over the head' was conveyed by respondents, who highlighted that their top financial priority was to pay their rent and keep their home. The affordability and availability of adequate housing was a particular concern for respondents, many of whom were experiencing problems with the cost and insecurity of living in private rented housing. This reflects limited public provision of social housing, with waiting lists of 61,880 households across Ireland in November 2020 (Housing Agency, 2021). About 27 per cent of these applicants were on waiting lists for more than seven years. This has resulted in many low-income households relying on housing allowances in the private rented sector. Analysis of EU-SILC (Chapter 4) revealed a higher risk of food poverty among those who were renting. Housing affordability has been confirmed as a problem, particularly in Dublin, by both international and domestic analyses (Housing Agency, 2017).

Respondents in private rented accommodation were in receipt of a range of housing allowances, but difficulties arose from serious drawbacks in each scheme. Many were in receipt of RS, a housing allowance for those who are not in full-time employment and which is paid by the tenant directly to the private landlord. Affordability issues arose for food bank users on this form of housing support. This is not surprising, given the findings of one study that RS tenants faced the highest rent burden compared with tenants on other types of housing allowances (MacMahon et al, 2017: 37). DSP publish rent limits as part of their eligibility criteria for RS. These limits vary by area to reflect market conditions and, in principle, no housing allowance is payable if the rent exceeds the limit. Private rent levels increased by an average of 9.2 per cent nationally in the 12 months ending March 2016, with a cumulative increase over the three years to 2016 averaging over 30 per cent (MacMahon et al, 2016: 9). Reflecting this upward trend, particularly in Dublin, renters can experience problems where there is little or no rental accommodation within the prescribed DSP limit. As a result, many households receiving RS must make 'top-up' payments to their landlord, to bridge the gap between the DSP rent limit and the actual rent (Threshold, 2014). Finnerty et al (2016) report that covert payments of this type by RS recipients have been a feature of the sector for several years. Respondents in this study who were obliged to make such additional payments to landlords found that this significantly increased their financial strain and contributed to their need for food aid. One particular area of concern was the loss of RS, with respondents very concerned about the potential consequences of putting this housing allowance at risk, if they took up employment. RS is not payable to those working 30 hours or more per week. For those working fewer hours, a reduced amount is calculated according to a formula determined by the DSP.

This particular deterrent to taking up employment was addressed in the HAP scheme, which was introduced in 2013 and is intended to eventually replace long-term RS. Applicants for HAP can take up full-time employment and retain their housing support, subject to meeting income criteria and other eligibility requirements. Unlike RS, the local authority pays the rent directly to the landlord, but it is the responsibility of the tenant to find suitable accommodation within specified rent limits. As with RS and all private renters, HAP recipients do not have adequate security of tenure, as they may be forced to relocate if the landlord decides to sell or refurbish the property. In such circumstances, tenants must find alternative private rented accommodation as they are removed from the social housing waiting list as soon as they move to HAP. Consequently, in areas with high rent levels, families are forced to move to more affordable areas, often quite distant from their community, schools and networks.

Social housing represents a small proportion (about 9 per cent) of the Irish housing stock, and new output collapsed after the onset of the economic crisis in 2008 (Norris and Byrne, 2018). However, the limited provision of social housing for low-income households is largely a continuation of policies originating well before the recent economic downturn (Norris and Byrne, 2017). Although the Government's policy is to increase the level of social housing, progress has been slow. Norris and Byrne (2017) argue that the heavy reliance on subsidising private rented accommodation is therefore likely to continue over at least the short and medium term. Capital grants have recently been sanctioned for additional social housing, but public spending and borrowing constraints restrict significant further investment in this area. Following the recent global financial crisis, Ireland's national debt (which includes borrowings by local authorities) increased to a significantly high level and a major constraint arises from IMF/EU restrictions on borrowing, including that for social housing. This has resulted in increased use of housing allowances to accommodate low-income households in the private rented sector, which has led to inflated private rents (DSP, 2015). The Simon Community (2018) reported that 92 per cent of properties available to rent were above government-imposed rent allowance limits. In addition, the shortage of private rental accommodation is likely to result in tenants facing rent increases they cannot afford (Drudy, 2016). Given that respondents in this study prioritised paying rent, financial hardship and an increased risk of food poverty is inevitable for many families.

Difficulties in accessing private rented accommodation by housing allowance claimants has contributed to a recent rise in homelessness in Dublin (DSP, 2015; Threshold, 2018). In December 2020, there were 8,200 homeless people in Ireland, including approximately 2,300 children in emergency homeless accommodation with their families (Focus Ireland, 2021). Experiences of homelessness were recounted in this study. One food bank user with six children was forced to leave their private rented accommodation at the request of the landlord and became homeless. At the time of interview, the family were living in a Dublin hotel, where they were experiencing severe deprivation and required food aid. In another case, family breakdown had resulted in one partner leaving the home and having to stay in a homeless hostel, as private rented accommodation was unaffordable.

Illness/disability

The impact of illness or disability on food poverty was a major theme that emerged from this study. Analysis of secondary data (Chapter 4) revealed a higher risk of food poverty for those who reported bad health, chronic illness or were limited in their daily activities. In general, food poverty rates increased as health declined. A significant proportion (over 30 per cent) of food bank users reported a chronic illness or disability. There is an established link between income and health, which is affected by a range of problems associated with trying to make ends meet on a low income (Kempson, 1996: 57). Doyal and Gough (1991: 53) argue that health is a basic need that must be met, in order to take part in society. The investigation of pathways through food poverty (Chapter 6) illustrated that food poverty resulted in respondents experiencing hunger, difficulties affording special diets for medical conditions and associated worry and anxiety about being able to provide for themselves and their families. These impacts of food poverty, including coping strategies used, are likely to affect respondents' physical and mental well-being.

Those with an illness or disability often live on a low income, because they are not able to take up paid employment. A Disability Allowance is payable to applicants with an injury, disease or disability that is expected to continue for over a year and results in the applicant being 'substantially restricted' in undertaking work (McManus, 2003). Many respondents found this support inadequate, with the situation exacerbated by additional medical-related out-of-pocket expenses (for example prescription charges, certain prescribed medicines, special diets, medical socks, heating). This was a general issue raised by respondents who were experiencing health-related issues, either themselves or in their family. These essential health-related expenses reduced respondents' ability to meet other necessary costs, such as food. Research studies show relatively high levels of material deprivation and persistent household poverty for adults with an illness or disability (for example, Kemp, 2005; Watson et al, 2018). Watson et al (2018) reported that, on average across 11 EU countries, 28 per cent of disabled working-age adults experienced material deprivation, compared to 13 per cent for other adults. Watson et al (2016: 40) found that, in 2013, working-age disabled adults in Ireland experienced the second highest material deprivation level, after lone parents.

A significant factor contributing to these deprivation levels is that working-age adults with a disability encounter particular difficulties in accessing the labour market. The Comprehensive Employment Strategy for People with Disabilities 2015–2024 (Government of Ireland, 2018a) identified structural barriers to labour market participation. These included concerns regarding loss of benefits and lack of knowledge by employers. According to the National Disability Survey 2006 (Central Statistics Office [CSO], 2010), the main perceived barrier articulated by people with disabilities was their need for flexible work arrangements. In order to facilitate this, the Government needs to work with employers to address the creation of more disability-friendly workplaces. Over one third of those with disabilities expressed an interest in working, and this rose to over 60 per cent for those in the 18–34 year age range. Those with disabilities may be restricted in terms of the type of work that they can undertake although, according to survey data, about 15 per cent of those who experience difficulties working are actually in employment (Government of Ireland, 2018a: 26). However, despite this willingness to consider and undertake work, people with disabilities experience challenges, both in finding work and being able to remain in employment.

As many of those with disabilities wish to work, adequately paid employment should help to alleviate poverty experienced by this group. Research indicates that those with disabilities generally have lower qualifications and skills, compared with the overall population (Watson et al, 2015). As employment levels and earning capacity are linked to educational achievements (Watson et al, 2015), initiatives to encourage those with disabilities to improve their qualifications and skills should enhance their chance of finding suitable work. Active recruitment strategies for the public and private sector, including activation policies to encourage job seekers with disabilities, also need to be accompanied by a range of supports, to ensure a successful transition to employment. This would be helped if the Government actively promotes the provision by employers of more disability-friendly workplaces, as people with disabilities may have special requirements, or be restricted in terms of the work that they can undertake.

Access to healthcare was also reported as a problem by some food bank users. This presented a significant barrier to work for respondents, who experienced delays in obtaining health treatments, which prolonged their experience of food poverty. Long waiting lists in Ireland's health service are a burden for those who rely on the public system. This arises from the lack of reform in the two-tier public/private health system (Dukelow and Considine, 2017: 235). In the primary care sector, many respondents in this study held a medical card, which they regarded as an important and valuable asset, as it gives entitlement to a range of public health services, without charge. Entitlement to the medical card is primarily assessed by income, but there is an element of discretion by social welfare officers (Citizens Information, 2018b). The Government has disclosed (Dáil Éireann Debate, 2016a) a significant increase in the issuance of cards on a discretionary basis and has indicated that it will continue to adopt a 'humane approach' to issuing them. However, the policy of leaving significant discretion to a social welfare officer gives rise to considerable uncertainty for those seeking this valuable benefit.

Caring

Many respondents were caring full- or part-time for children, their partners and other adults. Apart from the impact of illness/disability on those who were not able to work, this study revealed significant adverse implications for family members who were in a full-time caring role and thus also not available for work. Food bank users reported limited state support for their caring responsibilities. Those who received the Carer's Allowance, a non-contributory social assistance payment, found it difficult to manage on this payment. The pathways analysis illustrated the range of challenges encountered in relation to childcare. These included the difficulty of finding suitable work that could be arranged around school timetables, availability of affordable childcare and parents caring for adult children. Structural issues, such as the high cost and limited supply of childcare, have contributed significantly to this problem, reflecting relatively low state investment in childcare (OECD, 2019a). As a result, the cost of formal care for pre-school children in Ireland is one of the highest, relative to household income, in the OECD (2014d). The high cost of private childcare is a particular barrier to employment for low-income households. Respondents found that childcare became more manageable as children grew up, permitting them to work longer hours, if suitable work could be found. However, issues raised included reductions in welfare benefits if respondents worked significant hours, the cost of transport to and from work and out-of-pocket expenses. These concerns motivated some respondents to risk taking up casual work in the informal economy, where they were paid in cash and felt they could avoid paying tax, while retaining their full social assistance payment.

Some progress has been made in addressing the affordability of childcare, including the free pre-school Early Childhood Care and Education Scheme. However, the OECD has recommended further measures to address obstacles to work, particularly for lone parents. In November 2019, the National Childcare Scheme (2021) was launched to replace existing childcare support programmes and the universal childcare subsidy with a single scheme. This provides subsidies to families with children (up to 15 years) who are attending officially recognised childcare services. It provides financial support for parents, including a blend of universal and targeted payments towards the cost of childcare, which are particularly beneficial to lower-income households with children (MacMahon et al, 2017).

Low pay and precarious employment

Most food bank users who were in paid employment reported that they were undertaking part-time, temporary work, which was usually in low-paid sectors (for example, homecare). The term 'precarious employment' is often used to describe this type of low-wage, insecure work (Nugent, 2018). An increasing trend to 'de-standardisation' of employment (Bonoli, 2007: 500) has resulted in what Standing (2016) has described as a new socio-economic group, 'the precariat'. The recent recession resulted in higher levels of involuntary temporary and part-time employment, with only 59 per cent of employees in the EU having a permanent contract in 2016 (Broughton et al, 2016). In Ireland, research suggests that precarious work is particularly prevalent in certain areas of employment, such as childcare, postal and telecommunications, and third level education (Pembroke et al, 2017). Outsourcing has become the preferred model, and roles that were traditionally occupied by workers with full-time permanent contracts and represented by trades' unions have been replaced by precarious employment relationships. Respondents in this study included workers undertaking roles such as cleaning and homecare assistants. In Ireland, Nugent (2018) reported that workers in these occupations experienced a high rate of involuntary temporary and part-time work, together with labourers, food preparation assistants and refuse operators. Furthermore, the study found that the deprivation rate for workers in these occupations rose significantly between 2004 and 2015 (from 13 per cent to 23 per cent) and almost 80 per cent found it difficult to manage within their means in 2015.

Non-standard employment is driven by the development of employment legislation across different sectors (Nugent, 2018). In Ireland, low employment protection has facilitated the significant increase in these types of contracts and provides insufficient safeguards for workers. This is evidenced by Ireland's position in the 2015 Employment Protection Law index, where it was ranked in 27th position of 28 European countries for permanent workers, and in 23rd position out of 26 countries for temporary employment (OECD, 2018). Shin and Ylä-Anttila (2018: 11) report that precarious workers across Europe tend to be less unionised than others. During the recession, many employers did not need to offer permanent jobs and workers were obliged to accept less attractive terms and conditions, or face unemployment. Following the recession, the OECD (2014c) has expressed concerns regarding the slow progression of these contracts to more permanent status in many countries. As a result of labour market activation policies, job seekers may be obliged to take up low-paid insecure work. This has negative implications for workers, in the absence of adequate 'enabling' supports for labour market participation (Dukelow and Considine, 2017: 104). Bambra et al (2014) found an increased risk of workers across Europe, in precarious roles, self-reporting that their general health was 'not good'. The negative impact of low-paid insecure work on health, well-being and quality of life is evidenced by Eurofound (2015) and Broughton et al (2016) in the EU and by Pembroke (2018) in Ireland. In particular, precarious workers in the EU were found to be over twice as likely to report their mental well-being as poor (Eurofound, 2017a: 97). Reflecting this evidence, there is thus a risk that these workers may withdraw from the labour market due to poor health.

An example of weak employment laws in Ireland that have been exploited by employers to the detriment of workers was highlighted by an illustrative case in Chapter 6. Following a period in work, the respondent found that his social welfare claim was rejected and he was in need of assistance from a food bank. The respondent had been in 'false self-employment', where the legal arrangement was as a self-employed person but he was, in substance, an employee. According to the OECD (2000: 156), the term 'false self-employment' describes a worker who has become self-employed 'simply to reduce tax liabilities, or the employer's responsibilities'. A report on false self-employment in the construction industry indicates that it grew from 25 per cent of the workforce in 2006 to 38 per cent in 2015 (Wickham and Bobek, 2016). The benefits of false self-employment are heavily weighted in favour of the contractor, who is able to avoid providing full-time contracts, together with a range of employment benefits and associated protections required under employment law. The contractor can exploit this arrangement to cut labour costs, including tax and social insurance, and reduce staff administration such as accounting for wages and completing PAYE formalities. However, from the workers' perspective, the disadvantages include losing social insurance benefits (for example unemployment or illness/disability cover). Although the economic situation improved following the recessionary period post-2008, there is a risk that employers will continue to maintain the flexibility and cost savings of precarious workers. Uncertainty surrounding Brexit has raised anxiety about its impact on Ireland's economy and it has been suggested that this may be used by employers to justify measures that promote wage competitiveness, including false self-employment (Low-Pay Commission, 2016).

In-work poverty was a feature of the findings from this study. While research on poverty dynamics supports the view that paid employment is the most important route out of poverty, some people who transition from unemployment to work remain poor (Kemp, 2005). Ireland is characterised by low decommodification of labour, with weak bargaining and a deregulated employment market, pointing to a preponderance of low-paid work (Eurofound, 2017a). However, in-work poverty often arises from insufficient working hours, rather than low wages (Halleröd et al, 2015). The proportion of part-time workers in Ireland, defined as those who normally work less than 30 hours per week, was 20.6 per cent in 2019, higher than the OECD rate of 16.7 per cent (OECD, 2021). The problem of VLWI arises when working-age adults in a household work less than 20 per cent of their available time. Redmond (2016) revealed that in Ireland, 89 per cent of these households experienced problems in making ends meet in 2014. In the same year, Ireland had the highest proportion (21 per cent) of individuals living in VLWI households, compared to the EU average of 11 per cent (Redmond, 2016). Many of these household members were engaged in domestic and care duties (23 per cent in Ireland, compared to the EU15 average of 14.5 per cent). In Dublin, the National Economic and Social Council (NESC) (2018b) found that risk factors associated with VLWI include being a lone parent and having an illness or disability. In 2014, 20 per cent of households in Ireland with VLWI were lone parents, while 20 per cent of individuals in VLWI households were receiving a Disability Benefit.

For those working on low pay who have at least one child, the Government subsidises their income through WFP, although food bank users in this study, in receipt of WFP, still needed food aid. Although families supported by WFP increased significantly between 2012 and 2017, there is a requirement to work at least 38 hours per fortnight. This eligibility rule was a problem for respondents in this study who worked irregular hours, as they sometimes found it difficult to obtain sufficient work to meet this rule. A more flexible approach would be to track working hours for WFP over a longer period, say six months. This would take into account those working variable hours, such as seasonal work, who often do not have control over their working hours. While these measures help to address in-work poverty, they also benefit private businesses by lowering their labour costs (Collins and Murphy, 2016).

Koukiadaki and Katsaroumpas (2017) report that precarious employment is recognised as a widespread problem across the EU, and policy implications are under review. The Irish Government has introduced legislation which aims to improve the security and predictability of working hours for employees on insecure contracts and those working variable hours (DOEASP, 2018b). The Employment (Miscellaneous Provisions) Act 2018, which came into force in 2019, will address some of the problems identified in this section.

Conclusions

Pathways into and through food poverty for respondents were impacted by a range of policies and practices of government, employers and other relevant stakeholders. Food bank users who relied on social welfare found income protection inadequate to maintain a minimum standard of living. Respondents reported that serious financial challenges occurred as a result of interruptions in welfare payments, which arose from changes to their work patterns. These difficulties were exacerbated by a lack of responsiveness and flexibility of the social welfare system to support the needs of those for whom employment is precarious, that is, insecure work in low-paid sectors. Concerns about the impact of a reduction in income, due to welfare payment shortfalls, were an understandable deterrent to seeking paid work of this type, which was the most likely form of employment they would obtain. Other issues include the duration of some temporary welfare payments (for example, the Fuel Allowance), and persistent welfare traps. In addition, there were numerous problems with labour market activation practices and welfare conditionality.

Lack of social housing resulted in respondents having to rely on the relatively expensive private rental market. Food bank users experienced serious difficulties with the operation of housing allowances, where accommodation was found to be insecure and, in some cases, significant top-up rent payments had to be paid. The inability to access affordable housing occasionally gave rise to the experience of homelessness. Those with an illness or disability found the Disability Allowance inadequate, while they were burdened with a range of relatively high medical-related costs, not covered by social welfare. They experienced multiple barriers to labour market participation, including inadequate educational supports and lack of engagement by some employers in facilitating their requirements. Their difficulties were compounded by shortcomings in Ireland's healthcare system, including long waiting times for some essential treatments. Issues with the availability and affordability of childcare also presented a barrier to employment for low-income households with children, reflecting inadequate state investment in provision. A further driver of food poverty is insecure, temporary work in low-paid sectors, which is shown to have negative impacts on health and well-being. Precarious work is exacerbated by relatively weak employment protection in Ireland, which has facilitated arrangements such as false self-employment. In addition, respondents in receipt of the WFP found that it was inadequate.

8

Responses to food poverty

Introduction

This chapter reviews responses to food poverty in Ireland, including the Government's participation in the EU-wide FEAD and the United Nations' SDGs relating to food insecurity. It investigates the role of the voluntary sector, where food charity is delivered through food banks and other forms of emergency food aid. This leads to an assessment of the overall response in Ireland, in the context of the COVID-19 pandemic and both the growth and trends in food charity across Europe. Emerging developments in support models are also considered and the conclusion summarises the key messages.

Responses to food poverty in Ireland

Responses from state

In recent years, the state's response to food poverty has principally focused on the FEAD programme, which was set up by the EU in 2014 to support poverty alleviation measures undertaken by member countries. EU funding of over €3.8 billion, supplemented by national contributions, was made available to provide food and basic material assistance for the most deprived. In a further significant development, the United Nations' 2030 Agenda for Sustainable Development was launched in 2015, including a specific goal to end hunger and achieve food security (United Nations [UN], 2015).

FEAD has had a significant impact on the provision of food aid by facilitating voluntary sector involvement. The DSP is the designated managing authority for the operational programme in Ireland, which has a total value of €26.7m, including €4m from the Irish Exchequer (DSP, 2020b). The distribution of the fund is scheduled to end in 2022, when the EU will combine the current programme of food aid and material assistance with social inclusion measures. FEAD will then be incorporated into the European Social Fund Plus, which continues until 2027. Approximately 75 per cent of the current total FEAD funds are designated for the provision of food, with the remainder for basic material assistance (for example personal non-food items). The food is distributed through 154 charity organisations authorised by the DSP (as at May 2021), including charities with multiple approvals for different initiatives and locations – SVP (28), Barnardos (19) and Simon Community (4) (DSP, 2021a). Participating charities are required to report basic biographical information on users to DSP on a quarterly basis. In 2019, just over 195,000 people in Ireland received a total of 1,323 tonnes of food through the FEAD programme (DSP, 2020c).

FoodCloud, a not-for-profit social enterprise set up with the aim of addressing the problem of waste food, was chosen to coordinate the food element of the FEAD programme on behalf of the Government. A product list was prepared in consultation with participating charities, consisting of basic, non-perishable foods which are easy to transport and store. Following a public procurement process, supplies are sourced from the successful tenderers. FoodCloud stores the products at its warehouses in Dublin, Cork and Galway and subsequently organises collection by the approved charities that distribute the food. Participating charities have a credit allocation, which is monitored regularly against usage and helps the DSP to manage the overall drawdown of available funds.

In 2019, FoodCloud supplied 1,323 tonnes to charitable organisations through FEAD assistance and a further 482,722kg of surplus food, including meat, fish, dairy products and fresh fruit and vegetables. In 2020, FoodCloud distribution hubs supplied over 650 charities and community groups across Ireland with surplus food, which was not deemed suitable for sale in normal retail outlets (FoodCloud, 2021). Examples include items with incorrect or slightly damaged packaging, out of season goods, or goods that are approaching their use-by/sell-by date. FoodCloud makes a charge for surplus food, based on the weight of food supplied, which helps to defray the operational costs of running the three hubs. Surplus food is sourced by FoodCloud from its engagement with producers, manufacturers and wholesalers. Redistribution of surpluses results in savings for participating charities of approximately 90 per cent of the retail price of items supplied. Businesses also benefit through lower waste disposal costs. In addition, there is a positive environmental impact arising from reduced disposal of food waste sent to landfill, which reduces carbon emissions. In addition to providing redistributed food from its hubs, FoodCloud's smartphone app and notification system facilitates the distribution of fresh surplus food from businesses to local charities that can use it. Providing food aid using the FEAD programme gives participating charities the opportunity to offer other (non-food) assistance to those in need (European Commission, 2020). They may offer this directly at the location where the food aid is distributed, or make referrals to other services, for example, government-funded agencies in relation to housing, money advice or employment. However, in Ireland at the present time there is no specific requirement for participating charities to provide non-food assistance to users.

In 2015, the United Nations' 2030 Agenda for Sustainable Development included goals to address both poverty and food poverty. Goal 1 is to end poverty in all its forms everywhere, while Goal 2 sets out the target to 'end hunger, achieve food security and improved nutrition and promote sustainable agriculture' (UN, 2021a). This is elaborated in part 2.1, as follows: 'By 2030, end hunger and ensure access by all people, in particular the poor and people in vulnerable situations, including infants, to safe, nutritious and sufficient food all year round' (UN, 2021b). Following the establishment of these targets, the Government set out its plan to achieve specific SDGs for Ireland in the National Implementation Plan for 2018–20 (Department of Communications, Climate Action and Environment [DCCAE], 2018). The National Social Target for Poverty Reduction is to reduce the level of Consistent Poverty in Ireland to 2 per cent or below by 2025 (from 5.6 per cent in 2018). The Government also seeks to reduce the share of the total population which is At Risk of Poverty or Social Exclusion (AROPE) sufficiently to achieve a 'top five' ranking for Ireland in the EU. AROPE was estimated at 21.1 per cent in 2018 and this commitment would entail reducing the level to approximately 16.7 per cent, which the Government accepts is an ambitious target (Gov.ie, 2020b: 16).

While food poverty was acknowledged in a review of Ireland's SDGs (Government of Ireland, 2018b: 28), the corresponding action plan to address the issue principally relates to Ireland's aid programme for developing countries. Ireland's implementation and monitoring plan for Goal 2 focuses on helping developing countries to meet their own SDG goals. It proposes to achieve this through a range of international commitments, including foreign policy initiatives, international development and bilateral engagements. The Government's action plans thus appear to focus mainly on helping developing countries overcome hunger and food security, rather than seeking to address the problem in Ireland. This would explain the allocation of responsibility for SDG Goal 2 (zero hunger) 2.1 to the Department of Foreign Affairs. In addition, the plan refers to two national policies, 'One World, One Future' and 'The Global Island', which both relate to supporting less developed countries (DCCAE, 2018: 60). This contrasts with SDG target 2.2, which focuses on malnutrition, and is addressed by Ireland's action plan on obesity (Department of Health, 2016). By way of comparison, the approach adopted by Government in Ireland differs from the UK, which provides a critical assessment against Goal 2 targets. The UK goes further than acknowledging the issue of food poverty and considers causes and responses to the problem by both civil society and government (UK Parliament, 2019).

The UN monitors progress in relation to food poverty (Goal 2.1.2) using the Food Insecurity Experience Scale (FIES), as discussed in Chapter 4. This is designed to assess the 'prevalence of moderate or severe food insecurity in the population' (United Nations Food and Agriculture Organization

[UN FAO], 2021). In reporting the prevalence of food insecurity, which it describes as 'based on the FIES', the Central Statistics Office (CSO, 2021) uses SILC data. The composite measure of food poverty discussed in Chapter 4 is used, based on a lack of one or more of three food deprivation items. The UN SDG programme requires countries to publish disaggregated data, generally provided from official national sources, such as SILC. The use of SILC allows the data to be presented on a geographical basis, in order to set out regional differences in food poverty.

In 2020, the Government published the Roadmap for Social Inclusion 2020–2025, which acknowledges the problem of food poverty in Ireland (Gov.ie, 2020b). In the Roadmap, the Government expresses concern at its prevalence, reported as 7 per cent of the population in 2018 (2020b: 70). In its list of commitments under the plan (no. 61), the Government states that it will identify the drivers of food poverty through a cross-department initiative. It will then establish what actions are necessary to respond to the issues, with a target date of the second quarter of 2021 to deliver this plan. The Roadmap also sets out specific actions to address food poverty, which are focused on young children. These include a pilot meals programme in early learning and care settings and a review of the Hot School Meals Pilot Project (DSP, 2019). While noting the downward trend in food poverty since 2013, the Government considers that this can, at least partly, be attributed to Ireland's involvement in the EU FEAD programme, the widening of the school meals service, and initiatives such as 'Meals on Wheels'. However, as described in Chapter 4 (Figure 4.3), it is likely that the main reason was the overall reduction in the AROP level in Ireland over this period, which fell steadily as the economy continued to emerge from the last severe economic downturn. In the first quarter of 2021, the Minister of State at the DSP with responsibility for Community Development and Charities, announced the establishment of a Working Group to tackle the issue of food poverty, in accordance with the commitments in the Roadmap (DSP, 2021b).

Responses from voluntary sector

The provision of food aid in Ireland has largely been left to the voluntary sector, which has established a range of initiatives, including food banks, community cafes and hot meal services. This reflects the important role the voluntary sector plays in Ireland's mixed economy of welfare, often supplementing state provision (Fanning, 1999). For example, the SVP has been described as operating a 'shadow welfare state' through its welfare assistance (DSP, 1997: 31). A report published by the Charities Regulator in 2018 estimated that the total work of Ireland's charities had a value of at least €24 billion (Indecon, 2018).

While the voluntary sector has led charitable food provision in Ireland, the response has been fragmented and it is not possible to track the scale and reach of individual initiatives. This reflects the significant number of activities undertaken at a local level, often on a small scale and connected to community or church groups. Many of these responses rely on the FEAD programme, supplemented by supplies from local food drives or other initiatives. This pattern of responses contrasts with large European countries, where umbrella organisations, such as Tafel (Germany) and The Trussell Trust (UK), support networks of food banks and often play an advocacy role on a national scale. These organisations are noted for their active campaigning, which is rooted in experience gained across national networks and informs their engagement with policy makers. Their advocacy work provides a platform to promote awareness of food poverty in these countries, such as the 'Hunger Free Future' campaign by The Trussell Trust (2021). However, campaigns related to food poverty appear to be more effective in some countries than others, with Pfeiffer et al (2015) noting that the problem has a lower profile in Germany, than the UK.

The main focus of food charities is to offer short-term emergency assistance. For example, SVP, the largest voluntary charitable organisation in Ireland, provides short-term help with food, but its mission statement sets out its objective to promote self-sufficiency over the longer term (SVP, 2021b). It offers direct personal help based on the needs of the family or individual, with food-related assistance often provided in the form of supermarket vouchers. Although some charities have recently increased their focus on food poverty, there is a relatively small network of food banks in Ireland. In a food bank, a standard bag of food items is normally provided from a list of products, depending on household size. While some flexibility may be shown by food bank volunteers, this model may not always be able to cater for dietary requirements (for example, diabetes, coeliac) or family preferences (for example, culturally appropriate food).

In the Dublin area, SVP has established a small number of its own food banks, reflecting local initiatives rather than a national strategy. In addition to providing food aid directly, the East Region of SVP works closely with Crosscare (the social support agency of the Catholic Archdiocese of Dublin). The current network of five Crosscare community food banks in Dublin provides food parcels, based on referrals from SVP and other introductions. Crosscare provides premises, organises food procurement, prepares food parcels and distributes the food at its designated community food banks. Food supplies are sourced through the FEAD scheme and surplus food from membership of FoodCloud, topped up from their own food donations. Food parcels are also distributed by other charitable organisations in Dublin, sometimes in conjunction with the provision of hot meals. By way of example, the Capuchin Day Centre, run by the Franciscan Order from its city centre location, has a well-established food service, which was set up to help homeless people. It offers breakfast and lunch every day, with food parcels distributed on one day each week. The Centre is open to all in need of emergency food aid, without the requirement for a referral. In recent years, it has experienced significant growth in demand, with 381,000 meals and food parcels provided in 2018 (Capuchin Day Centre, 2021). The Centre also provides some clothing and personal hygiene products and can arrange basic healthcare, in conjunction with a medical charity.

In Cork, Ireland's second largest city, SVP is active in providing food aid across the city to individuals and families through its network of local groups. Feed Ireland, another national volunteer movement, was founded in 2017 as Feed Cork, a local initiative, to help address the problems of homelessness and food poverty (Feed Ireland, 2021). Sourcing food from FEAD and surpluses through FoodCloud, it provides a three-day emergency supply for households and also offers free counselling and other support services, with the assistance of trained volunteers. Feed Ireland has started to replicate its model in other towns, opening Feed Wexford food bank in the South East of Ireland. In the South West, Foodshare Kerry, a not-for-profit initiative between North & East Kerry Development and SVP, helps local charity groups provide food aid. It collects surplus food from commercial outlets, which it transports to a central depot where it is stored, sorted and graded, before being made available to charities for distribution in the Kerry region. Foodshare Kerry receives support from the Department of Rural and Community Development and Pobal through the Community Services Programme (Foodshare Kerry, 2021). In the Mid-West region of Ireland, the Mid-West Simon Community, established in 2006, is active in providing food aid, with a focus on alleviating the problem of homelessness. It operates four food banks, which participate in the FEAD programme, and the charity reported a three-fold increase in users across these locations between 2018 and 2020 (Raleigh, 2021).

The impact of the COVID-19 pandemic

As noted in Chapter 4, at the time of writing no national data are available regarding the impact of the COVID-19 pandemic on food poverty in Ireland. However, early evidence from food charities in Ireland points to a significant increase in households struggling with food poverty during the outbreak. When FoodCloud surveyed their charity participants in June 2020, 70 per cent reported an increase in demand, while a follow-up survey in January 2021 found requests for help had continued at a similar level. In particular, there was significantly higher demand from food banks, community centres, family resource centres and Meals on Wheels services. Charities such as SVP continued to provide help (including food vouchers) during the pandemic.

In order to assess the impact of COVID-19, several charities have carried out their own studies, which have also conveyed the increased demand for food aid during the pandemic. For example, the Mid-West Simon Community (Raleigh, 2021) and Barnardos children's charity (Barnardos, 2020) both reported strong demand for food support since the onset of COVID-19. Barnardos assisted over 21,000 children and families in 2019 with food parcels and hot meals (2020). Its research showed that 35 per cent of families with young children had to spend more on food, which reflected increased time spent at home during the pandemic. Parents also reported increased worry that their household would run out of food and, as a result, had restricted their own meals. However, despite this higher demand, the operation of some food banks during the pandemic was adversely affected by the shortage of volunteers, who were shielding at home, in line with public health advice.

In the UK, more wide-ranging research was carried out during the outbreak to assess responses to food poverty. For example, a comprehensive national study by Lambie-Mumford et al (2020) mapped and monitored interventions to address concerns regarding food access. The first part reviewed national level responses to improve food access for vulnerable people during COVID-19, while the second phase explored how the following four national responses worked in practice: i) school food (initiatives to replace food normally provided by schools when open); ii) emergency finance schemes; iii) emergency food (how food charities coped with challenges of providing food access); and iv) grocery box scheme (a weekly food supply for those shielding at home and not able to access food). Free school meals were replaced by alternatives, which included food parcels, supermarket vouchers and direct payments. However, in practice the complexity of different school arrangements (lockdowns/bubbles/groups isolating), which could vary at short notice, posed many challenges for ongoing provision of these alternative solutions. Although nationally funded emergency payments were available for those in financial hardship to buy food and other essentials, issues were raised in relation to barriers impeding access to these schemes. During the outbreak, the British Government relied heavily on food charities to supply emergency food and they were granted significant public funding of Stg£20 million. While food charities were able to operate at significantly higher levels of need, their systems were put under strain, exposing their limitations as a response to food poverty. Vulnerabilities cited in the study included the heavy reliance by food banks on volunteer workers, during a period when many were shielding, and the uncertain nature of food donation supply chains. These weaknesses, which were also experienced in Ireland, raise issues about the sustainability of some responses to food poverty.

European context

Food banking across the EU15

While it can be argued that charitable food banking in Europe is not yet normalised, as it has been in the US for several decades, research in different EU15 countries points to the significant development of food charities in the last decade (Lambie-Mumford and Silvasti, 2020). As indicated in Chapter 2, data on food bank users, usage levels and other aspects of food charity are regarded as a poor proxy for measuring the prevalence of food poverty. However, the growth of food charities supports the argument that there has been a rising demand for food aid. An indication of the scale of responses to food poverty across Europe may be obtained from the 24 members of FEBA. This non-profit representative body brings together food bank networks, which provide 4.2 million daily meals to 9.5 million people through more than 40,000 charitable organisations, with the help of 32,280, mostly volunteer, workers (FEBA, 2021). An important role carried out by FEBA is to raise awareness within the EU regarding the role of food banks in both reducing food poverty and food waste. Reflecting the recognition of the right to food in the Universal Declaration of Human Rights (1948), it also advocates at EU level in relation to the ethical and human rights dimension of food poverty. Some FEBA members have developed a significant range of operations and carry out their own advocacy work. By way of illustration, Tafel (which translates as 'dinner table') is an umbrella organisation for food banks in Germany, with 60,000 volunteers. Its network doubled from 2015 (480 branches) to 2020 (948 branches) and it currently operates over 2,000 food banks and pantries nationwide (Tafel, 2021a). The Tafel organisation provides regular food assistance to 1.65 million beneficiaries and sees the reduction of food waste as a key part of its mission. As in the UK, COVID-19 posed considerable operational challenges for Tafel food banks, given that 90 per cent of its 60,000 volunteer workers are older people. During the pandemic, many of these volunteers were shielding and 400 of the local Tafel food banks had to close temporarily due to a shortage of staff (Tafel, 2021b). In addition to the lack of volunteers, panic buying by the public at the start of the pandemic led to a sharp fall in donated food.

As in the case of FoodCloud, FEBA members redistribute food from FEAD, surpluses from the food supply chain and donated products. While difficult to assess, the provision of food charity in Ireland appears relatively low compared to other EU15 states, particularly for a problem affecting at least 300,000 people. By way of comparison, Northern Ireland, which has approximately 40 per cent of the population of the Republic of Ireland, had a network of 38 Trussell Trust food banks in 2019 (Trussell Trust, 2019), in addition to five SSM pilots (discussed later) and other smaller initiatives.

The coexistence of food deprivation with the problem of food wastage is acknowledged by Clause 14 of the EU FEAD Regulation No 223/2014 (EUR-Lex, 2021). Reflecting the importance conveyed by this EU food programme, many food charities in Europe regard using food surpluses that might otherwise go to waste as part of a dual mission, together with the provision of food aid. For example, the FEBA mission statement makes it clear that its role to help reduce hunger and malnutrition is closely linked to reducing food waste (FEBA, 2021). It foresees a changing context for redistributing food, given the increased importance of sustainability (FEBA, 2019). Its 2019 convention linked its activities with the UN SDGs, specifically the goal to prevent food waste. This target is set out in 12.3: 'By 2030, halve per capita global food waste at the retail and consumer levels and reduce food losses along production and supply chains, including post-harvest losses' (UN, 2021d). In addition to FEBA, other international organisations, including the Global FoodBanking Network (GFN, 2019) and the UN FAO, actively promote the role of food banks in reducing food wastage and protecting the environment, in addition to helping to alleviate food poverty.

Ireland's approach to food aid, through the FEAD programme and the role of FoodCloud, aligns closely with that of other FEBA members. For example, FoodCloud's primary goal is to 'reduce the environmental, social and economic impact of food waste' (FoodCloud, 2021). Across Europe, companies involved in the food business have found that food waste has become an important economic issue and increasingly seek to ensure that, where possible, surplus food is used by local charities. Some major retailers who donate surplus food also provide practical help (for example, fridges or transport) to charities so that food can be picked up, stored and distributed safely and efficiently (Pope, 2018). FoodCloud has developed innovative partnerships with charities involved in food waste prevention, with surplus foods contributed to their distribution hubs that would otherwise be wasted (FoodCloud, 2021). For example, volunteers organised by the Falling Fruit project collect apples from unpicked fruit trees (Falling Fruit Ireland, 2021) and donate the fresh fruit to charities that distribute the food. FoodCloud arrange to process the fruit into apple juice, a long-life product that can be distributed through their hubs (Times, 2020).

The use of surplus food as an important aspect of food aid has been portrayed as a positive development by food banking and other organisations. However, this is contested by significant advocacy work which argues that this development undermines the case to address the drivers of food poverty, as discussed in Chapter 7. Caraher and Fury (2017) recommend that separate solutions are sought for food waste and food poverty. While acknowledging the temporary relief provided by short-term food aid, they find a lack of evidence that the use of surplus food helps to resolve the problem of food poverty. Moreover, they have expressed concern that surplus food redistribution tends to depoliticise the issue, deflecting attention from the need for governments to address the underlying structural causes of food poverty.

Food poverty responses in Ireland: where next?

In some countries, food bank models have developed beyond the provision of emergency food parcels, with or without a referral. While the work of food charities in Ireland focuses on alleviating short-term emergencies, users often need ongoing support, as discussed in Chapter 5. In recognition of this need , many food charities in Ireland have already established, or plan to introduce a range of additional services, where users are encouraged (or in some cases required) to avail of help related to their situation. In the UK, these are sometimes referred to as 'food bank plus' models (Caraher and Furey, 2018).

As an illustration of this development in Ireland, Crosscare is currently reviewing its food banking programme. A representative from Crosscare advises that the next step to develop their community food bank model is the provision of food assistance, with users strongly encouraged to avail of wraparound support services. The proposed plan is that each user is introduced to an advocacy worker, who will undertake an initial assessment to identify why the need for food aid has arisen. Examples articulated to the author by respondents, as set out in Chapter 5, include not receiving their full social welfare entitlement , having issues in relation to migration status, financing substance abuse with household income, or not being able to manage on a low budget. Following an initial assessment, Crosscare aims to provide users with some support services directly, given that it already has expertise and experience through its Information and Advocacy Services unit and range of other services. For example, help in relation to housing, risk of homelessness, refugee status and social protection can be handled in-house. Referrals outside Crosscare would then be made for other services, such as MABS (Money Advice and Budgeting Service), in relation to guiding people through dealing with problem debt or other financial difficulties. At present, advocacy services are provided at one location and the proposed expansion of this service will depend on funding availability.

A further evolution of food bank models is the SSM, which makes food available at a large discount from normal retail prices to low-income users who are experiencing, or at risk of, food poverty. The environment is similar to a conventional supermarket, where users can choose freely and purchase items at the check-out. It contrasts with food banks, where there is little or no choice in food and the intention is to cater for short-term emergency needs. As FEAD products cannot be sold to consumers, SSMs primarily stock food surpluses that would not normally be acceptable in mainstream supermarkets. This may include, for example, blemished fruit and vegetables, mislabelled product, impaired packaging and excess stock (Saxena and Tornaghi, 2018). An SSM is generally accessed on a controlled basis by 'members', who are selected by using certain socio-economic or geographic criteria, in order to target those who are at risk of food poverty and need support. Other wraparound supporting social services are often provided, sometimes as a requirement for membership. Many SSMs have an environmental goal to reduce food waste by facilitating the redistribution of food surplus. In addition, there is normally a social goal, where users can participate in a range of programmes, such as healthy eating, family budgeting, benefits advice, debt counselling and training/employability skills.

SSMs have been in operation across several European countries since the 1980s (Holweg and Lienbacher, 2016). They have only been established in the UK since 2013 (Saxena and Tornaghi, 2018) and, at the time of writing, there are no SSMs in Ireland. However, Mid-West Simon Community commissioned the University of Limerick (UL) to undertake a study of social grocery stores (similar in principle to SSMs) (Mid-West Simon Community, 2021). Following this research, the charity is now seeking funding to set up the first store of this type in Ireland. The UL study included a review of the SSM model being piloted in five locations across Northern Ireland, where the initiative is being supported by public funds. This follows a Stg£1.65 million allocation by the UK Government to help reduce food poverty by 'improving access to affordable food through a network of community shops and social stores/supermarkets' (Department for Communities NI, 2018). The original pilot was extended to the end of March 2021, with the intention of rolling out SSMs more widely in Northern Ireland, although these plans were delayed by COVID-19. The Department for Communities NI issued a report card on the pilot programme up to March 2020, which reported that 1,119 members participated in the pilots and benefits reached 2,797 users, assuming a mean household size of 2.5. Based on a positive evaluation of the pilot, it is planned to continue the initiative, although this is subject to the availability of adequate funding. Operating SSMs would involve higher costs than food banks and require more complex supply logistics. This is likely to be a constraint on their wider establishment.

Conclusions

In the absence of sufficient government progress in tackling policy shortcomings, including those discussed in Chapter 7, a variety of relatively small-scale charitable initiatives have emerged in Ireland as a response to food poverty. However, this piecemeal provision of food aid is unlikely to have a significant impact in alleviating a problem that, according to official estimates, affects over 300,000 people, or 7 per cent of the population of Ireland. Moreover, a study of food banks in high-income countries found a lack of evidence that they help to reduce food poverty (Loopstra, 2018). It concluded that, even if they do succeed in some cases, food banks do not reach sufficiently large numbers of people who need food aid.

The FEAD programme and the availability of surplus food continue to have a significant impact on the landscape of food aid in Ireland. In recent years, supply-side factors have shaped responses to food poverty, greatly facilitating the provision of food aid. Assuming the continuation of food supply through the FEAD programme and the availability of food surpluses, the provision of food aid in Ireland is likely to continue at least at current levels. For many of those experiencing food poverty, this ongoing food aid provides a continuation of emergency short-term support for a problem with deeper roots. For this reason, food banks have been described as 'successful failures' (Caraher and Furey, 2018), reflecting opposing views on their merits. While they help to alleviate food poverty over the short term, they may also be seen as failures if they do nothing to address the underlying causes of the problem. There is a concern that this type of food aid takes pressure off the state to address the structural causes of food poverty, normalising temporary emergency help by food providers, which becomes an extension of the welfare state. Caraher and Furey (2018) argue that the further institutionalisation of food banks, as has happened in North America, would be a regressive development. This may occur if food banks and their related infrastructure become a permanent feature of the food aid landscape.

The interviews undertaken with food bank users conveyed that there are often multiple issues resulting in the need for assistance, as described in Chapter 5. Given concerns that food charities help to deal with the recipient's immediate problem, but not its underlying cause, it is encouraging that evolving models for food aid in Ireland are extending their scope to provide help beyond the provision of food aid. These include a range of support services tailored to the needs of the individual user and sometimes delivered at the location where food aid is provided. In this way, the response to food poverty is significantly enhanced, as it seeks to address the underlying problem. This may be particularly beneficial in cases where the user is introduced to a service with which they are not already aware, or may be unsure how to access.

Although food poverty has persisted in Ireland for many years, the relatively low level of responses targeted at the problem may, at least in part, be explained by the lack of public awareness of the issue. The variety of factors that may provide clues as to why food poverty has been largely hidden in Ireland include the low visibility of food banks in our towns and cities. As pointed out by Caraher and Furey (2018), food banks visible on the high street expose the need for them to the wider public. In addition, there is no umbrella organisation to help boost their profile and stimulate advocacy. In contrast to other countries, such as the UK, no charitable organisation in Ireland has announced plans to significantly expand their network of food aid. The lack of media coverage of food poverty, parliamentary reviews and an absence of high-profile campaigners also contribute to ensuring the problem remains largely hidden. However, despite the continuing low profile of food poverty in Ireland, there are signs of an increasing recognition of the problem at government level. The Government's latest Roadmap for Social Inclusion 2020–2025 (Gov.ie, 2020b) includes an acknowledgement of concern about the level of food poverty in Ireland and a commitment to address the problem.

The debate regarding food banks in the EU15 is increasingly linked to their contribution to reducing food waste. The Global FoodBanking Network (GFN, 2019) argues that food banks have an important role in reducing food wastage and protecting the environment, in addition to helping to alleviate food poverty. In Ireland, FoodCloud reports that businesses (farms, manufacturers and distributors) contribute surplus food to their distribution hubs that would otherwise be wasted (FoodCloud, 2021). As pointed out by Kessl et al (2020), the provision of food waste to those in need of food assistance is often presented as a win-win situation (2020: 59). However, while some consider it helps to address two important problems, namely food waste and food poverty, it may also obscure the underlying structural issues that lead to food poverty, as discussed in Chapter 7.

As in many other countries, COVID-19 has exacerbated the problem of food poverty in Ireland. Although not yet quantified by official statistics, evidence is provided by reports from food charities of a significant increase in demand for food aid during the COVID-19 restrictions. This demand put food charities under pressure, particularly as most rely heavily on volunteers. Given the higher risks of COVID-19 for older people, many charities found it difficult to maintain their food services during the outbreak, when demand was high. As restrictions ease, it is uncertain whether the increase in food poverty during the pandemic will be temporary, or a longer-term readjustment from the recent downward trajectory. However, the sustainability of some responses to food poverty in Ireland has been put in question by the COVID-19 outbreak, which has highlighted vulnerabilities, such as their heavy reliance on older volunteers.

Looking to the future development of charitable food provision, it is likely that there will be an increase in initiatives to provide non-food supports for recipients of food aid. Although users often face multiple and intractable problems, this approach is a positive development, particularly where services can be offered at the location where food aid is provided. SSMs, which have been piloted in Northern Ireland for the last three years and already operate in several other European countries, are likely to be the next initiative in the provision of food charity in Ireland. At the time of writing, Mid-West Simon Community (2021) is seeking funding to set up the first store of this type in Ireland. SSMs arguably provide a more dignified environment for those who need food aid, enabling users to choose their own food and make purchases at very low cost. In addition, a range of social supports and wraparound services are usually provided. However, SSMs involve higher set-up and running costs, compared with food banks, and the pilot programme in Northern Ireland has relied heavily on financial support from the UK Government. As in the case of food banks, the need to minimise the running costs of SSMs is likely to require heavy reliance on volunteers. Apart from the issue of costs, SSMs depend on food surpluses, which may be subject to uncertainty or unpredictability of supply (Saxena and Tornaghi, 2018). Overall, this is a topic that would merit further research, given the uncertainties about sustainability. In addition, given the dearth of existing research, it would be helpful to learn more about the user experience of SSMs, compared to other forms of food aid.

In conclusion, responses to food poverty by food charities in Ireland have shown a modest growth in recent years, although the current level and nature of responses is unlikely to have a material impact on the problem. Food charity appears relatively underdeveloped, in comparison with many other European countries, which is partly explained by the low profile of food poverty in Ireland, rather than its prevalence. The provision of food aid is largely driven by the availability of food through FEAD, with surplus food becoming increasingly significant. This aligns with developments across Europe, where many food banking organisations are promoting food banks as a win-win solution, which alleviates both food poverty and food waste. In Ireland, some positive steps have been made by food charities to innovate with non-food services and introduce models (for example, SSMs), designed to ease access to food and improve the experience for users.

9

Conclusions

Introduction

This concluding chapter summarises what has been learned about the concept of food poverty and its prevalence in Ireland. It considers what drives food poverty, in the light of the complex picture emerging from interviews with food bank users. Pathways into food poverty for respondents in this study were impacted by a range of policies and practices of government, employers and other relevant stakeholders, which have wide-ranging implications. Following an overview of responses to food poverty in a comparative European context, consideration is given to the implications of these findings for a range of social policies in Ireland, and the actions needed to address the issue effectively.

Understanding food poverty

One of the aims of this book is to improve understanding of the concept of food poverty. As pointed out by Lambie-Mumford (2017: 17), there is a lack of clarity and a risk of confusion with different terms in use, such as 'hunger' and 'food insecurity'. Underlying this ambiguity is the absence of agreed definitions, which gives rise to the use of different terminology. This results in inadequate assessments of the problem quantitatively, as the conceptualisation of food poverty affects measures to assess it. In order to address this shortcoming, the approach adopted in this work was to compare definitions of food poverty and food insecurity cited in the international literature. Four conceptualisations were chosen from different sources, principally from government departments and academics working on the topic. These definitions of food poverty, together with a further four definitions related to food insecurity, were broken down into their key elements (Chapter 2, Table 2.1) and their different aspects explored through interviews with food bank users. They include quantitative, qualitative, social and psychological dimensions.

An examination of the definitions of food poverty indicated that each one conveyed a quantitative dimension, reflecting a shortage of available food. In addition, each included a qualitative aspect, describing changes in food supplies and difficulties obtaining the desired variety of food or the preferred/required diet. These important aspects of food poverty were described clearly by respondents in interviews with food bank users (Chapter 6).

Two of the definitions indicated a social dimension, which is often framed in terms of acquiring food in socially acceptable ways, rather than having to resort to different forms of food aid, scavenging, begging or stealing. It also conveys that a core element of food poverty is exclusion from events involving food, for example being able to participate in a meal with family or friends. Although this important aspect of social inclusion is missing from two of the definitions of food poverty, it is a key theme that emerged from the interviews. Respondents highlighted the difficulty of participating in events and occasions which involved hospitality and the sharing of food with others. They also conveyed very clearly the stress associated with food poverty. This psychological aspect is characterised by the worry and uncertainty of having, or being able to access, sufficient food to provide for self and family. This element is absent in the definitions of food poverty, although uncertainty around access to food is included in each definition of food insecurity (see Table 2.1).

The qualitative data from the interviews highlights the importance of all four dimensions of food poverty: quantitative, qualitative, social and psychological. As no definition of food poverty covering all these aspects was identified, the following conceptualisation of food poverty is offered: *Food poverty exists when the ability to afford an adequate quality and quantity of food is limited or uncertain, and when acquiring it in socially acceptable ways is a problem. It has effects on social participation and psychological impact on those who experience it.* In line with the definitions of food poverty set out in Table 2.1, the new definition includes references to the quantitative and qualitative aspects of food poverty. However, it builds on them by including the social dimension, including the acquisition of food in socially acceptable ways and the impact on social participation. Both of these aspects were prominent in the qualitative strand of this study. In addition, the new definition refers to the psychological impact of food poverty, which was also an important theme in the interviews with food bank users.

It has been customary to use the term 'food poverty' in Europe, particularly in the UK, while the term 'food insecurity' is preferred in the US and Canada. However, it is now not uncommon for 'food poverty' and 'food insecurity' to be used interchangeably, and some researchers, based in Europe, favour the term 'food insecurity' (for example, Dowler and O'Connor, 2012 and Pfeiffer et al, 2015). The term 'food poverty' helps to convey that the issue is an *aspect* of poverty. By way of comparison, the term 'energy poverty' is used as another important dimension of poverty (Department of the Environment, Climate and Communications [DoECC], 2021).

The comparative data from EU-SILC and OECD used in Chapter 4 were based on a single deprivation indicator relating to food poverty (for example, unable to afford a meal with meat, or alternative, every second day). However, the qualitative data from interviews conveyed that food poverty is experienced at different levels. By way of illustration, the degree of severity can range from uncertainty about food supplies, through qualitative changes to diet and social effects (such as exclusion from participation in meals with family), to harsher consequences, including insufficient food and hunger. In order to adequately assess food poverty, one measure is therefore clearly not adequate. A series of questions specifically constructed to assess food poverty is needed, similar to the Food Insecurity Experience Scale (FIES) described in Chapter 4. The FIES is designed to measure the level of severity, classifying households ranging from having *low food security* to *very low food security*. Similar measures of severity would also significantly enhance the assessment of food poverty in EU-SILC. An appropriate way forward would be to incorporate a food poverty module in an existing survey, such as the European Social Survey or EU-SILC.

Survey questions in a food poverty module would need to be re-designed to more adequately measure food poverty. They should be calibrated to measure not only the graduated levels of food poverty according to an agreed scale, but to ensure that data on the quantitative, qualitative, social and psychological dimensions are captured. The survey could be based on the questions used by the US Department of Agriculture (USDA) (see Table 2.2 in Chapter 2), which have recently been included in the UK Family Resources Survey. This would have the advantage of achieving a close alignment of measures across the island of Ireland. However, none of the ten questions in this survey addresses the social aspects of food poverty, which have been conveyed strongly in this book. This is an omission that should be avoided in designing a survey for Ireland.

The prevalence of food poverty

In this book, the prevalence of food poverty in Ireland was assessed and compared with levels in other EU15 countries, using data from EU-SILC, OECD and the UN FAO. There was considerable variation in results, reflecting differences in survey questions and their timing. However, a composite indicator using three food-related deprivation indicators from the EU-SILC conveyed that approximately 7 per cent of the population in Ireland experienced food poverty in 2018. Trends in food poverty followed a 'crisis pattern', increasing from 2008 to a peak in 2013–14 and subsequently declining, as economic growth increased. However, a comparison with EU15 was not conclusive, as Ireland's relative position varied across the different sources of survey data. OECD and UN figures indicate that food poverty in Ireland is relatively high, while EU-SILC data suggests it is relatively low. As the latter is significantly different from the other data sources, it may understate the problem of food poverty, at least for Ireland. The situation highlights issues with survey data used for purposes for which they were not designed. Reliable and accurate measurement of food poverty is essential as a first step to assess the problem, as the current paucity of data has hindered progress in developing policy responses.

Following the onset of COVID-19, the available evidence suggests that recent progress in reducing food poverty has halted in many advanced countries. Ireland is no exception, although the extent of the increase is not yet clear as, at the time of writing, results from national surveys are awaited. It is reported that COVID-19 has disproportionately affected those least able to withstand the financial impact, including those working in low-paid jobs, renters and migrants (Byrne et al, 2020). The uneven impact has had particularly adverse consequences for vulnerable groups, who were already struggling before COVID-19 (SVP, 2021a). While the respondents in this study adopted a variety of coping strategies (such as requesting assistance from family and friends), research in the UK has shown that access to many supports was severely disrupted during the pandemic (Brewer and Patrick, 2021). In addition, core costs increased for many low-income families with children, due to school closures and other disruptions arising from COVID-19.

Using EU-SILC data from 2016, Chapter 4 investigated the socio-demographic characteristics of those experiencing food poverty in Ireland. Households at a relatively high risk of food poverty included lone parents with children, those renting at or below the market rate, the unemployed, ill/disabled and separated/divorced. All households with children were at a higher than average risk of food poverty. Food poverty was higher for lower socio-economic groups, compared with professional, clerical workers and self-employed and there were higher rates among those with lower levels of education. In relation to health, food poverty was higher for those reporting a relatively poorer health status, those with a chronic illness and those whose activities were restricted by their health condition. The risk of food poverty was also significantly higher for those in rented accommodation, particularly those living in social housing. Finally, the risk of food poverty was reported as higher in urban locations.

Pathways into and through food poverty

Interviews with food bank users revealed a complex picture, reflecting the multidimensionality of food poverty. While some respondents needed help to overcome temporary difficulties obtaining food, many conveyed longer-term food poverty, arising from a combination of factors, similar to those described as a 'toxic cocktail' by Daly and Kelly (2015: 41). This typically included low-paid work or no employment, because of ill health, disability or full-time caring responsibilities. In many cases, the situation was aggravated by accumulating high-cost debt from moneylenders. These respondents relied on the safety net of social welfare as their main source of income, but found that it was inadequate to cover their necessary weekly expenditure. In addition, issues with social transfers were frequently the trigger that resulted in the need for food aid. Examples provided by respondents included delays in payments due to adjustments, following changes in employment hours. These difficulties suggest a lack of responsiveness and flexibility in the support system that exacerbated their situation. For respondents in paid employment, low-pay, low work intensity and/or issues arising from the casualisation of the workforce, meant many were unable to earn enough money to meet essential needs. When these structural issues combined with the cost of housing, healthcare and the lack of affordable childcare, respondents experienced very serious challenges. For example, little money was left for food after paying rent, utilities and sometimes loan repayments. Even for those coping within their limited income, a relatively small additional expense for the family, often occurring unexpectedly, could give rise to a financial crisis and the need for food aid.

The interviews demonstrated that the impacts of living in food poverty manifest themselves in multiple ways. These include experiencing hunger and not being able to afford the right type of food to sustain good health. The experience of food poverty often involves significant stress, mostly driven by the struggle to survive on a low income and provide for families. While food aid was given free, there was evidence of the hidden cost to users in terms of its emotional impact, including shame and embarrassment. Definitions of food poverty tend to overlook these important aspects of the experience of food poverty. The findings of this study also demonstrate how food poverty is interwoven with other aspects of poverty, including energy poverty and social exclusion.

Respondents used a range of coping mechanisms to try to make ends meet. They struggled with difficult decisions regarding how best to prioritise their limited resources. It was necessary to make hard choices between maintaining rent payments, ensuring adequate heating or light, meeting essential medical costs or providing food for themselves and their family. Respondents ranked rent and utility costs ahead of expenditure on food. As a result, many families had insufficient money to spend on food, which severely restricted their food choices. This raises concern about the quantity and quality of food being consumed. Children were always regarded as a priority and parents found that providing for them was a particular strain on special occasions, such as Christmas. Social networks provided a key resource for many, although in some cases these were limited, as friends and family members were also experiencing financial difficulties. Some respondents turned to high-cost loans from moneylenders to provide temporary financial relief, although they found that this usually exacerbated their difficulties over the longer term. Other respondents resorted to desperate measures, with one divulging that he stole to get money to feed his children.

Drivers of food poverty: policy and practice implications

The findings from interviews with food bank users conveyed that their pathways into and through food poverty were impacted by a range of policies and practices of government, employers and other relevant stakeholders. Respondents who relied on social welfare found that income protection was inadequate to maintain a minimum standard of living. This deficit was exacerbated when interruptions in welfare payments arose, as a result of changes in the working patterns of respondents undertaking non-standard, precarious employment. These difficulties resulted from a lack of flexibility and responsiveness in the delivery of services to support the needs of these social welfare recipients. Other issues included the duration of some temporary welfare payments, persistent welfare traps and problems with labour market activation practices.

Housing costs were also a serious concern for many respondents, reflecting government policies that have resulted in a significant shortfall of available social housing. Respondents who had to rely on the relatively expensive private rental market found this type of accommodation insecure and encountered serious problems with housing allowances. Some respondents had experienced homelessness, as they had not been able to access affordable housing. Those with an illness/disability found the Disability Allowance inadequate and had difficulties affording relatively high out-of-pocket medical-related expenses not covered by social welfare. They experienced multiple barriers to labour market participation, while their difficulties were exacerbated by shortcomings in Ireland's healthcare service, including long waiting times for treatment in the health system. Issues with the availability and, in particular, the affordability of childcare also presented a barrier to employment for low-income households with children, reflecting inadequate state investment in provision. A significant driver of food poverty arises from insecure, temporary work in low-paid sectors, and such employment is shown to have negative impacts on health and well-being. Precarious work is exacerbated by relatively weak employment protection in Ireland. This has facilitated arrangements which disadvantage workers, such as false self-employment, where legally a person is self-employed but is, de facto, an employee. In addition, respondents found that the WFP, a social welfare subsidy for low-paid employees with children, was inadequate. Respondents often reported multiple challenges, such as housing problems, coupled with a disability and the inability to afford the cost of childcare.

The implications of these findings for policy and practice are wide-ranging. Some policy drivers represent structural issues of international concern, such as the casualisation of work. Supranational bodies, including the EU, are continuing to monitor and investigate these developments, which have a global impact. Other areas, such as access to affordable housing and healthcare, also present complex challenges in many countries. However, Ireland has its own set of structural issues that are of particular concern and there are specific areas where policy reforms and improved practices could improve the lives for those experiencing food poverty. Given the importance of adequate accommodation conveyed by respondents in the study, further measures to increase the availability of social housing are required. An improvement in the responsiveness of welfare services would ensure that those with non-standard work patterns receive entitlements promptly. Another area for consideration would be the elimination of poverty traps. An example is the 'three-day rule', which applies to those in part-time employment and restricts eligibility for a welfare payment to those not working more than three days per week. This issue has increased in importance, as a greater proportion of the workforce is in part-time employment, with variable hours. A possible option to resolve the problem would be to base Jobseeker's Benefit payments on hours worked, rather than days in employment.

Responses

The voluntary sector, which has historically played an important role in Ireland's mixed economy of welfare, dominates the distribution of food aid. Responses to food poverty may be characterised as piecemeal in nature, with a wide range of relatively small-scale initiatives. Given the localised nature of responses and absence of umbrella organisations that collate and publish national data, it is difficult to assess the overall reach and impact of assistance provided. However, the current level of responses is unlikely to reach a significant proportion of those experiencing food poverty. While demand for food aid increased significantly during COVID-19, some food charities found it difficult to maintain their services during the outbreak. This reflected a reduction in the availability of volunteers, many of whom were shielding, in line with government restrictions. However, the supply of food aid was sustained during COVID-19, as it is underpinned for the larger food charities by Ireland's participation in the EU's FEAD initiative. The redistribution of food surpluses has also become important and supports Ireland's SDG to prevent food waste.

Respondents in this study conveyed that assistance with food comes at a cost, in terms of the shame and embarrassment for many users. In addition, many are unable to access a food bank, given transportation difficulties and the limited number in Ireland. However, some positive steps have been made by food charities to innovate with non-food services and consider new initiatives, such as SSMs. While this model is designed to provide choice and ease access to food, research is needed in relation to the user experience, given membership restrictions and other differences in comparison with using a mainstream food store.

In this book, it is argued that the state's social safety net should be sufficient to ensure that income assistance replaces the need for the third sector's growing involvement in the provision of food aid. Given that the Government has set Ireland's SDG goals to significantly reduce poverty levels, acting now on food poverty would send a clear signal of serious intent to meet these targets. In Ireland, while charities play an important role in society, no organisation has led responses to food poverty, and the issue has remained hidden from view for most citizens. The nature of responses to food poverty in Ireland contrasts with coordinated campaigns led by national organisations that are prevalent in some European countries. For example, in the UK the significant growth in food banking has been led by The Trussell Trust, which has helped to draw public attention to the problem (Loopstra, 2018). The lack of similar coordinated responses in Ireland may at least partly explain why food poverty has been largely hidden. FoodCloud, which operates on a national scale in Ireland, is well positioned to play an increasingly important role to promote awareness of food poverty, as well as food surpluses. In addition, it has international experience and participates as the only member from Ireland in FEBA.

Responses to food poverty in Ireland appear relatively low compared to many other European countries, which is partly explained by its lack of profile, rather than its prevalence. In addition, it is not possible to discern the extent of food charity and its impact on alleviating food poverty, as much of the work takes place discreetly at a local level and there is a lack of available data. For example, SVP volunteers carry out personal visiting in people's homes on a confidential basis and may provide supermarket vouchers, referral to a food bank or other practical assistance towards day-to-day essentials. Overall, the structure of food aid provision, through FEAD and the increasing use of surplus food, aligns with developments across Europe. In common with trends across the EU15, the provision of food aid by charities in Ireland is increasingly driven by surplus food donated by food-processing entities or food retailers. The collection and redistribution of these surpluses has become integral to the operations of food charities and is facilitated in Ireland by FoodCloud. The model used may be compared with Denmark, which has a similar population to Ireland. The Danish Food Bank works with a large number of food companies that donate surpluses, which are then delivered by volunteers to social organisations who distribute the food (Danish Food Bank, 2021).

While there is a limited number of food banks in Ireland, there is an increasing awareness of the need to avoid food waste, one of many environmental issues related to sustainable development. Food banking organisations in many countries argue that they have an important role in reducing food wastage and protecting the environment, in addition to helping to alleviate food poverty (Global FoodBanking Network [GFN], 2019). Although this role of food banks is sometimes presented as a win-win solution, in the UK it has been criticised in a letter signed by 58 leading academics and campaigners as '"left over" food for "left behind" people' (*Guardian*, 2019). Those concerned about the further institutionalisation of charitable food aid in Europe point to countries such as the US and Canada. Their experience demonstrates that the normalisation of food banks does not solve the problem of food poverty, as it does not address its root causes. De Schutter, the UN Special Rapporteur on the Right to Food, has endorsed this viewpoint in a lecture in the UK, arguing that: 'foodbanks, however, are a testimony to the failure of public authorities to deliver on the right to food and should be neither a permanent feature nor a substitute for more robust social programs' (2013: 9).

Conclusions

This book contributes to an understanding of an issue that has remained hidden for too long in Ireland and is a serious concern for health and well-being. Although food poverty has been largely overlooked in Ireland, it is a significant problem that affects over 7 per cent of the population. Based on the high demand for food aid during COVID-19, the prevalence of food poverty increased significantly during the outbreak. The limited information available indicates that vulnerable groups, already at high risk of food poverty, were disproportionately affected. Given the low awareness and understanding of the problem, the daily struggle for many of those interviewed in this study to provide food for their families and themselves is hidden from public view. This study has enabled respondents affected by food poverty to voice their experiences and demonstrate how seriously it impacts on many low-income households. The qualitative research revealed that respondents who turned to food aid for assistance have very difficult lives, including the daily struggle of coping on a low income, often combined with ill health and onerous caring responsibilities. Some respondents relayed a sense of personal failure and blamed themselves for having to resort to a food bank, in order to feed their families. However, the findings of this study demonstrate that various policies and practices of government, employers and other relevant stakeholders contribute to food poverty.

While it is difficult to discern the future evolution of food banks and other forms of food aid, the limited level of current responses to food poverty in

Ireland has little impact on alleviating the problem. However, rather than expanding food charity that fails to tackle the structural causes, food poverty needs to be addressed with further investment in Ireland's anti-poverty infrastructure. An important first step is to establish an official definition and methodology to obtain adequate data, as discussed in this book. In the Government's Roadmap for Social Inclusion 2020–2025 (Gov.ie, 2020b), it has set challenging poverty reduction targets, which align with SDG Goal 1 to eradicate poverty by 2030. The Government has established a target to reduce consistent poverty to 2 per cent or less by 2025 (from 5.6 per cent in 2018) and make Ireland one of the most socially inclusive countries in the EU. As a separate initiative, it has committed to move the wages floor to a living wage during the Government's lifetime (Gov.ie, 2021). While these are positive measures, the Government has other competing expenditure priorities. These include the challenges of housing and health, where policy shortcomings have exacerbated the problem of food poverty. It is encouraging that the Roadmap has acknowledged the issue of food poverty and the Government has indicated that it will identify mitigating actions. The Government has a formal strategy to combat energy poverty (DoECC, 2021) and now needs to commit to anti-poverty measures to address food poverty. Much progress can be made through the introduction of a living wage, income security and a responsive, adequately funded welfare system. Following publication of the recent Roadmap, it is hoped that this book will go some way to inform the preparation of a set of policy responses to address the root causes of food poverty in Ireland.

APPENDIX 1

Secondary analysis of survey data

This study used secondary data to examine the prevalence of food poverty across Europe. An outline of the data sources used on food poverty (Survey of Income and Living Conditions and OECD) and food insecurity (UN FAO) is briefly summarised in the following sections.

European Union – Survey of Income and Living Conditions

The main source of data on food poverty in Europe is the EU-SILC, which enables annual monitoring of poverty and deprivation. EU-SILC is a voluntary, household survey carried out annually across the EU since 2003. It provides a large representative sample of different types of households, with data on 5,219 households (incorporating 13,186 individuals) available in the 2016 survey. It captures demographic, socio-economic and health data, which enables the relationship between food poverty and a range of characteristics to be explored. The two-stage sample design ensures proportionate representation of different population density strata groups, from cities to rural areas (Central Statistics Office [CSO], 2015). It is the official source of data in Ireland on both household and individual income, coupled with living conditions, and provides key national poverty indicators. The EU SILC 2006–18 datasets for Ireland were obtained from the Irish Social Science Data Archive.

There are limitations in using EU-SILC data to assess food poverty. Because it is a household survey, it may not capture deprivation at an individual level within households. The sample does not include some vulnerable groups, such as the homeless, Travellers or asylum seekers in institutional settings, who may be at a relatively high risk of food poverty. In addition, EU-SILC is based on a common framework, rather than a common survey, which allows flexibility at national level and results in different food poverty questions across countries. Ireland's SILC questionnaire includes four topics that relate to food poverty:

- Unable to afford a meal with meat, chicken, fish (or vegetarian equivalent) every second day.
- Unable to afford a roast joint (or its equivalent) once a week.

- Unable to afford to have a substantial meal one day in the last fortnight.
- Unable to afford to have family or friends for a drink or meal once a month.

A search of EU-SILC questionnaires across the EU15 indicates that these questions are not generally included by other countries. Although the question 'unable to afford to have family or friends for a drink or meal once a month' is included in seven of the national surveys, these data are not transmitted to Eurostat and thus are not available from its scientific use files. No other EU15 country, apart from Ireland, includes a question regarding the affordability of a cultural norm, which is having a weekly roast joint, although it is suggested that this is somewhat outdated (Carney and Maître, 2012: 11). In addition, the current EU-SILC questions relating to food poverty do not facilitate an assessment of the severity of deprivation. For example, the experience of food poverty ranges in degrees from uncertainty of food access, through to being able to afford food of only poor nutritional value and, in a worse case, being hungry with no food to eat.

An analysis of food poverty in Ireland was undertaken, using the four food-related items from EU-SILC in Ireland. Absolute levels and trends over time were considered. A composite measure to assess food poverty was introduced, using three of the aforementioned questions. Food poverty, using this composite measure, was assessed by determining the population reporting deprivation in one or more of the three items. The question referring to 'drink' was excluded from this composite, as it arguably extends the measurement to wider issues than those involving food. However, as explained in Chapter 4, this approach effectively ignores an important aspect of social inclusion, where the level of deprivation is comparatively high. The characteristics of respondents reporting food poverty (based on the composite indicator) were then explored in more detail, using the 2016 survey results. This aligned with the timescale of interviews carried out in the qualitative research strand of this study.

In order to locate Ireland's position in a European context, a comparative analysis between Ireland and other member States between 2006 and 2018 was undertaken. The analysis was based on the one food poverty question that is asked consistently in surveys across all EU27 countries: the inability to afford a meal with meat, chicken, fish (or vegetarian equivalent) every second day. The data files were obtained from Eurostat, which confirmed that it receives data for only this one food-related question.

Organisation for Economic Co-operation and Development

In 2014, the OECD published a biennial review of social indicators, which included data on food poverty collected by Gallup World Poll. Sample sizes varied between approximately 1,000 and 4,000, depending on country (OECD, 2014b: 136). The results of the survey were averaged over two-year periods (2006/07 and 2011/12), in order to minimise fluctuations from year to year. The food-related question asked was 'have there been times in the past 12 months when you did not have enough money to buy food that you or your family needed?'

United Nations Food and Agricultural Organization

The UN FAO developed the Food Insecurity Experience Scale (FIES), in order to establish the level of food insecurity according to its severity, as illustrated in Figure A.1.

The survey involved asking respondents food-related questions across a spectrum of increasing food insecurity (see Table A.1). In Ireland, approximately 1,000 people were interviewed by phone for the survey.

Table A.1: Food Insecurity Experience Scale survey questions

Question	During the last 12 months was there a time when....
1	...you were worried you would not have enough food to eat because of a lack of money or other resources?
2	...you were unable to eat healthy and nutritious food because of a lack of money or other resources?
3	...you ate only a few kinds of food because of a lack of money or other resources?
4	...you had to skip a meal because there was not enough money or other resources to get food?
5	...you ate less than you thought you should because of a lack of money or other resources?
6	...your household ran out of food because of a lack of money or other resources?
7	...you went without eating for a whole day because there was not enough or other resources for food?
8	...you went without eating for a whole day because of a lack of money or other resources?

The threshold of moderate food insecurity was set at the item 'ate less than thought you should' (Question 5), while severe food insecurity was set at the severity level 'did not eat for a whole day' (Question 8) (UN FAO, 2016b).

Figure A.1: Food insecurity severity levels: the Food Insecurity Experience Scale (FIES)

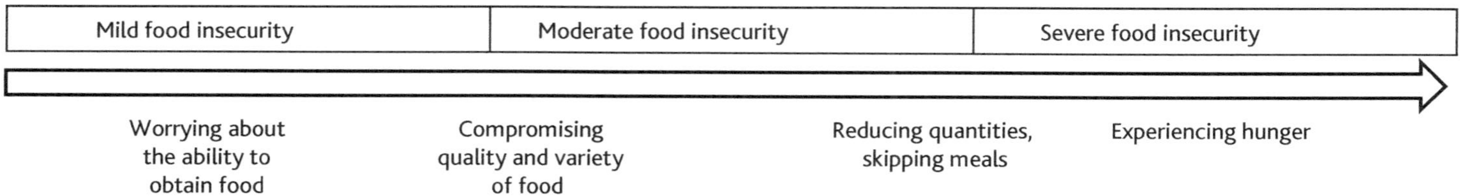

Source: Prepared by author, based on UN FAO (2016b: 4)

APPENDIX 2

Interview methodology

This Appendix provides background on the qualitative research, which included semi-structured interviews with food bank users. It considers data collection, sampling, data analysis and ethical issues related to this work.

Data collection

Semi-structured interviews provide an effective method to ascertain the reasons and motivations for attitudes and opinions (Keats, 2000: 72). The interviews were used to gather data on different themes related to the experience of food poverty. Open questions were designed to allow the respondents freedom in their responses, while providing adaptability, so that responses could be developed and clarified, as necessary (Keats, 2000: 35).

Interview topics included why users needed food assistance, their experience of food poverty and how they envisaged their situation might be improved. Different pathways into food poverty were identified, by enquiring why respondents needed food aid. The study investigated how each participant managed financial hardship and overcame daily challenges in their lives. While the interviews probed the resilience of respondents, they also explored the limitations of this strength, by asking about critical pressure points and stressful events. Participants described a range of situations, including special occasions (such as Christmas) and the stress caused by uncertainty of food access. The study also investigated issues related to social exclusion, social relationships and the role of social supports provided by family, friends and community. As an important part of users' experiences, it also explored the shame, stigma and humiliation that may be associated with asking for food aid. The interviews also sought to understand how respondents felt their situation could be improved, so that they would not need to seek food aid.

All the interviews were recorded with the approval of respondents. The accurately preserved personal stories gave voice to the experience of food poverty. The recordings also ensured that the data were available for external scrutiny or re-analysis, as required.

Sampling

In order to identify a sample of suitable respondents, contact was initiated with a number of food charities, including providers of hot meals and food parcels. Crosscare, a charity which provides food aid at five food banks in the Dublin area, facilitated semi-structured, confidential interviews at their premises. A total of 42 interviews were arranged with users of food aid during visits to food bank locations at Dun Laoghaire (Boylan Centre), Dundrum (Methodist Church), Tallaght (Community Outreach Centre, St Thomas the Apostle) and Darndale (New Life Centre). Over 90 per cent of those approached consented to an interview. Although some users expressed initial concerns regarding confidentiality, they agreed to continue, having received assurances that all participants would remain anonymous. The sample obtained using the aforementioned approach generated the characteristics as set out in Table A.2.

The profile of respondents broadly corresponds to the composition of families AROP in Ireland at the time of the interviews (CSO, 2017b). However, further insights may be obtained by investigating the experience of those using other types of food aid, such as food vouchers, hot meals or soup runs.

Data analysis

Familiarisation with the data was enhanced by the author's transcription of the interview recordings. Although this was a lengthy process, as pointed out by Bryman (2008: 453), it was found to be beneficial. Analysis was undertaken concurrent with data collection, as recommended by Miles et al (2014: 70). The interweaving of data collection and ongoing analysis helped the author to reflect on any gaps or blind spots in the interviews that could be improved in subsequent interviews, leading to enhanced data collection. In order to provide structure to the investigation and draw out the experience of food poverty across the range of areas that it impacts, a thematic approach to data gathering was adopted. Some 'pre-coding' (Layder, 1998) of transcripts was carried out, by highlighting rich or striking quotes by participants, which served as illustrative examples. Different approaches to first-cycle coding were considered, with reference to Saldana's 'The Coding Manual for Qualitative Researchers' (Saldana, 2013). NVivo software was used to organise and analyse the interview data. Initially, material was gathered into nodes, which are containers for coding, facilitating the gathering of related material in the same place, to review emerging patterns. As explained by Miles et al (2014: 277), an understanding of the data was obtained by noting recurring patterns and themes and making comparisons between responses that may highlight contrasts or reinforce similarities. For example, a node for hunger was set up and references to hunger in the interview transcripts were allocated to this code. Additional sub-nodes were added, such as 'going to bed hungry',

Table A.2: Sample characteristics

Type	Number
Household composition	
Two-parent	16
Lone parent	20
Single	6
Number of children in each family type	
Two-parent households – 2 children or less	8
Two-parent households – more than 2 children	7
Lone-parent households – 2 children or less	13
Lone-parent households – more than 2 children	8
Families with at least one adult in employment	
Full-time employment	4
Part-time employment	6
Unemployed	32
Receiving social protection	
Jobseeker's Allowance	14
Disability Allowance	16
Carers Allowance	5
Back to Work Enterprise Allowance (BTWEA)	1
Supplementary Welfare Allowance	1
Working Family Payment (WFP)	2
None	3
Interviewee Male*	14
Interviewee Female*	30
Total	42

Note: * Two interviews involved both partners

'money for food runs out' and 'parents going without eating, in order to feed children', in order to collate the data relating to these aspects of hunger, as described by respondents.

The subsequent write-up of the interview data was based on exploration of relevant themes and the output of the literature review. It was structured around an investigation of pathways 'into', 'through' and 'out of' food poverty. NVivo facilitated organisation of the data, including when further issues and variations emerged from the analysis of the interview outputs.

Ethics

Full ethical approval for the study was obtained from University College Dublin and its Code of Good Practice in Research (2010) was adhered to in all respects. Food bank users and the staff/volunteers at each food bank were supportive of the research, particularly when the purpose was made clear. The study conformed with all areas of ethical concern, including the right to privacy, informed consent and the fundamental principle to do no harm. In accordance with the principal of informed consent, the participants were provided with as much information as they needed to make an informed decision concerning their participation. At the outset, all respondents signed a consent form and, before the interview commenced, provided approval for the recording.

Although Hammersley and Traianou (2012: 57) argue that there is a risk of harm in any research activity, from the beginning this research was designed and carried out in a manner to minimise harm to anyone involved. As part of this approach, contingency arrangements were made for referral to a professional counsellor, should support be needed. In some cases, respondents became emotional as they described the difficulties of their unrelenting daily struggles. However, they strongly wished to tell their stories and complete their interviews.

Data handling complied with the Data Protection Acts 1988 and 2003, together with UCD Data Protection policy and procedures (www.ucd.ie/dataprotection). Controls over access to information relating to individual interviewees included the use of identifier codes on data files, with participants and their identifier codes stored securely in a separate location. A minimal amount of biographical data was requested from participants, as these were useful in providing context to respondents' answers (Bryman, 2008: 442). Pseudonyms were used in order to ensure that the identity of participants would remain anonymous.

References

ACOSS (Australian Council of Social Service) (2012) *Poverty in Australia.* Strawberry Hills, NSW: Australian Council of Social Services.

Adamson, P. (2008) *The Childcare Transition: A League Table of Early Childhood Education and Care in Economically Advanced Countries, Report Card 8.* Florence: UNICEF Innocenti Research Centre.

Alkire, S. (2007) 'The Missing Dimensions of Poverty Data: Introduction to the Special Issue', *Oxford Development Studies*, 35(4), 347–59.

All-Party Parliamentary Inquiry (2014) *Feeding Britain.* Available at: https://feedingbritain.org/wp-content/uploads/2019/01/feeding_britain_report_2014-2.pdf

Anderson, S.A. (1990) 'Core Indicators of Nutritional Status for Difficult-to-Sample Populations', *Journal of Nutrition*, 120, 1559–99.

Andress, H. and Lohmann, H. (2008) 'Introduction: The Working Poor in Europe', in H. Andress and H. Lohmann (eds) *The Working Poor in Europe: Employment, Poverty and Globalisation.* Cheltenham: Edward Elgar.

Ashton, R., Middleton, J. and Lang, T. (2014) 'Open Letter to Prime Minister David Cameron on Food Poverty in the UK', *The Lancet*, 383(9929), 1631.

Atkinson, A. (1983) *The Economics of Inequality. Second Edition.* Oxford: Oxford University Press.

Atkinson, A., Cantillon, B., Marlier, E. and Nolan, B. (2002) *Social Indicators: The EU and Social Inclusion.* Oxford: Oxford University Press.

Australian Bureau of Statistics (2017) *4363.0 - National Health Survey 2014–2015: Questionnaire [Internet].* Canberra (AUST). Available at: www.abs.gov.au/ausstats/abs@.nsf/Lookup/by%20Subject/~2014-15~Main%20Features~Users'%20Guide~1

Bambra, C. (2006) 'Decommodification and the Worlds of Welfare Revisited', *Journal of European Social Policy*, 16(1), 73–80.

Bambra, C., Lunau, T., Van der Wel, K., Eikemo, T. and Dragano, N. (2014) 'Work, Health, and Welfare: The Association between Working Conditions, Welfare States, and Self-reported General Health in Europe', *International Journal of Health Services*, 44(1), 113–36.

Barker, M., Lawrence, W., Woadden, J., Crozier, S. and Skinner, T. (2008) 'Women of Lower Educational Attainment Have Lower Food Involvement and Eat Less Fruit and Vegetables', *Appetite*, 50, 464–8.

Barnardos (2020) *Barnardos.* Available at: www.barnardos.ie/

Barrett, C. (2010) 'Measuring Food Insecurity', *Science*, 327, 825–8.

Barry, F. and Welsum, D. (2005) 'Services FDI and Offshoring into Ireland', paper given at the *OECD Directorate for Science, Technology and Industry Panel Session on Offshoring*, France, 9–10 June. Paris: OECD.

Beacom, E., Furey, S., Hollywood, L.E. and Humphreys, P. (2020) 'Stakeholder-informed Consideration for a Food Poverty Definition', *British Food Journal*, 11 September.

Beirne, K., Doorley, K., Regan, M. Roantree, B. and Tuda, D. (2020) *The Potential Costs and Distributional Effect of COVID-19 Related Unemployment in Ireland*. Available at: www.esri.ie/publications/the-potential-costs-and-distributional-effect-of-covid-19-related-unemployment-in

Björnberg, A. and Phang, A. (2019) 'Euro Health Consumer Index 2018 Report', *Health Consumer Powerhouse*. Available at: https://healthpowerhouse.com/media/EHCI-2018/EHCI-2018-report.pdf

Böhnke, P. (2008) 'Are the Poor Socially Integrated? The Link between Poverty and Social Support in Different Welfare Regimes', *Journal of European Social Policy*, 18(2), 133–50.

Boland, T. and Griffin, R. (2015) *The Sociology of Unemployment*. Manchester: Manchester University Press.

Bonoli, G. (1997) 'Classifying Welfare States: A Two-dimensional Approach', *Journal of Social Policy*, 26(3).

Bonoli, G. (2007) 'Time Matters: Post-industrialisation, New Social Risks and Welfare State Adaptation in Advanced Industrial Democracies', *Comparative Political Studies*, 40(5), 495–520.

Booth, C. (1892) *Pauperism, a Picture; And the Endowment of Old Age, an Argument*. London: MacMillan.

Booth, S. (2014) 'Food Banks in Australia: Discouraging the Right to Food', in G. Riches and T. Silvasti (eds) *First World Hunger Revisited: Food Charity or the Right to Food?*. Basingstoke: Palgrave Macmillan.

Bowpitt, G. (2000) 'Poverty and its Early Critics: The Search for a Value Free Definition of the Problem', in J. Bradshaw and R. Sainsbury (eds) *Getting the Measure of Poverty: The Early Legacy of Seebohm Rowntree*. Aldershot: Ashgate Publishing.

Bowyer, S., Caraher, M., Eilbert, K. and Carr-Hill, R. (2009) 'Shopping for Food: Lessons from a London Borough', *British Food Journal*, 111(5), 452–74.

Bradshaw, J., Kemp, P., Baldwin, S. and Rowe, A. (2004) *The Drivers of Social Exclusion*. London: Office of the Deputy Prime Minister.

Brewer, M. and Patrick, R. (2021) 'Pandemic Pressures. Why Families on a Low Income are Spending More During Covid-19'. *Resolution Foundation*. Available at: www.resolutionfoundation.org/publications/pandemic-pressures/

Broughton, A., Green, M., Rickard, C., Swift, S., Eichhorst, W., Tobsch, V. and Tros, F. (2016) *Precarious Employment in Europe: Patterns, Trends and Policy Strategies*. Brussels: European Parliament.

Broughton, M., Janssen, P., Hertzman, C., Innis, S. and Frankish, C. (2006) 'Predictors and Outcomes of Household Food Insecurity Among Inner City Families with Preschool Children in Vancouver', *Revue Canadienne de Sante Publique*, 97(3).

Bryman, A. (2008) *Social Research Methods. Third Edition*. Oxford: Oxford University Press.

Burchi, F. and De Muro, P. (2012) *A Human Development and Capability Approach to Food Security: Conceptual Framework and Informational Basis. Working Paper 2012–009*. United Nations Development Programme. Available at: www.undp.org/content/dam/rba/docs/Working%20Papers/Capability%20Approach%20Food%20Security.pdf

Byrne, S., Coates, D., Keenan, E. and McIndoe-Calder, T. (2020) 'The Initial Impacts of the COVID-19 Pandemic on Ireland's Labour Market', *Economic Letters*, 2020(4). Dublin: Central Bank of Ireland.

Callan, T. and Nolan, B. (1991) 'Concepts of Poverty and the Poverty Line', *Journal of Economic Surveys*, 5, 243–61.

Callan, T., Nolan, B. and Whelan, C. (1993) 'Resources, Deprivation and the Measurement of Poverty', *Journal of Social Policy*, 22(2), 141–72.

Cantillon, B., Van Mechelen, N., Pintelon, O. and Van den Heede, A. (2014) 'Social Redistribution, Poverty and the Adequacy of Social Protection', in B. Cantillon and F. Vandenbroucke (eds) *Reconciling Work and Poverty Reduction: How Successful are European Welfare States?*. Oxford: Oxford University Press.

Cantillon, S. (2000) 'Equality in Economic and Other Dimensions', in J. O'Hagan (ed) *The Economy of Ireland; Poverty and Performance of a European Region*. Dublin: Gill & Macmillan.

Cappellari, L. and Jenkins, S. (2007) 'Summarizing Multiple Deprivation Indicators', in J. Micklewright (ed) *Inequality and Poverty Re-Examined*. Oxford: Oxford University Press.

Capuchin Day Centre (2021) *The Capuchin Day Centre*. Available at: www.capuchindaycentre.ie/Capuchin_Day_Centre_2013/Capuchin_Day_Centre_-_Services.html

Caraher, M. and Furey, S. (2017) 'Is it Appropriate to Use Surplus Food to Feed People in Hunger? Short-term Band-Aid to More Deep Rooted Problems of Poverty'. *Food Research Collaboration Policy Brief. 26 January*. Available at: https://foodresearch.org.uk/download/11839

Caraher, M. and Furey, S. (2018) *The Economics of Emergency Food Aid Provision. A Financial, Social and Cultural Perspective*. Cham: Palgrave Pivot.

Caraher, M., Lloyd, S., Lawton, J., Singh, G., Horsley, K. and Mussa, F. (2010) 'A Tale of Two Cities: A Study of Access to Food, Lessons for Public Health Practice', *Health Education Journal*, 69(2), 200–10.

Care Association in Partnership with Caring for Carers Ireland and Care Alliance Ireland (2008) *Listen to Carers: Report on a Nationwide Carer Consultation.* Available at: https://familycarers.ie/media/1420/listening-to-carers-2008.pdf

Carletto, C., Zezza, A. and Banerjee, R. (2013) 'Towards Better Measurement of Household Food Security: Harmonizing Indicators and the Role of Household Surveys', *Global Food Security*, 2, 30–40.

Carney, C. and Maître, B. (2012) *Constructing a Food Poverty Index for Ireland using the Survey on Income and Living Conditions. Social Inclusion Technical Paper No. 3.* Dublin: DOEASP.

Castles, F. (2010) 'The English-Speaking Countries', in F. Castles, S. Leibfried, J. Lewis, H. Obinger and C. Pierson (eds) *The Oxford Handbook of the Welfare State.* UK: Oxford.

Castles, F. and Ferrera, M. (1996) 'Home Ownership and the Welfare State: Is Southern Europe Different?', *Southern European Society and Politics*, 1(2).

Castles, F. and Mitchell, D. (1993) 'Worlds of Welfare and Families of Nations', in F. Castles (ed) *Families of Nations. Patterns of Public Policy in Western Democracies.* Aldershot: Dartmouth Publishing.

Center on Budget and Policy Priorities (2021) *A Quick Guide to SNAP Eligibility and Benefits.* Available at: https://www.cbpp.org/sites/default/files/atoms/files/11-18-08fa.pdf

Church, J., Jackson, J., Jackson, V., Kershaw, A., Lillistone, C., Manners, A., Mill, N., Sharp D., Shipsey, C. and Short, M. (2001) *Office for National Statistics. Social Trends 31.* London: HMSO.

Chzhen, Y. and Bradshaw, J. (2012) 'Lone Parents, Poverty and Policy in the European Union', *Journal of European Social Policy*, 22(5), 487–506.

Citizens's Information (2018a) *Claiming for a Child Dependant.* Available at: http://www.citizensinformation.ie/en/social_welfare/irish_social_welfare_system/claiming_a_social_welfare_payment/claiming_and_increase_in_your_payment_for_a_child_dependant.html.

Citizens Information (2018b) *Medical Card Means Test.* Available at: www.citizensinformation.ie/en/health/medical_cards_and_gp_visit_cards/medical_card_means_test_under_70s.html

Citizens Information (2020) *Minimum Rates of Pay.* Available at: www.citizensinformation.ie/en/employment/employment_rights_and_conditions/pay_and_employment/pay_inc_min_wage.html

Citizens Information (2021a) *Jobseeker's Allowance.* Available at: www.citizensinformation.ie/en/social_welfare/social_welfare_payments/unemployed_people/jobseekers_allowance.html

Citizens Information (2021b) *Jobseeker's Benefit.* Available at: https://www.citizensinformation.ie/en/social_welfare/social_welfare_payments/unemployed_people/jobseekers_benefit.html)

Clúid (2021) *About Clúid.* Available at: www.cluid.ie/about-us/

Coakley, A. (2001) 'Healthy Eating: Food and Diet in Low Income Households', *Administration*, 49(3), 87–103.

Coakley, A. (2004) 'Poverty and Insecurity', in B. Fanning, P. Kennedy, G. Kiely and S. Quinn (eds) *Theorising Irish Social Policy*. Dublin: UCD Press.

Coates, D., Anand, P. and Norris, M. (2013) 'Housing and Quality of Life for Migrant Communities in Western Europe: A Capabilities Approach', *Journal on Migration and Human Security*, 1(4), 163–209.

Coleman-Jensen, A., Gregory, C. and Singh, A. (2014) *Household Food Security in the United States in 2013. Economic Research Report No. 173*. Washington: US Department of Agriculture.

Coleman-Jensen, A., Nord, M. and Singh, A. (2013) *Household Food Security in the United States in 2012. Economic Research Report No. 155. September 2013*. Washington: US Department of Agriculture.

Coleman-Jensen, A., Rabbitt, M., Gregory, C. and Singh, A. (2017) *Household Food Security in the United States in 2016. Economic Research Report No. 237*. Washington: US Department of Agriculture.

Coleman-Jensen, A., Rabbitt, M., Gregory, C. and Singh A. (2020) *Household Food Security in the United States in 2019, ERR-275*. Washington: US Department of Agriculture.

Collins, M. (2015) 'Earnings and Low Pay in the Republic of Ireland: A Profile and Some Policy Issues', *NERI Working Paper*, 2015/No. 29. Dublin: NERI.

Collins, M. and Murphy, M. (2016) 'Activation: Solving Unemployment or Supporting a Low-Pay Economy?', in M. Murphy and F. Dukelow (eds) *The Irish Welfare State in the Twenty-First Century*. London: Palgrave Macmillan.

Commission on the Relief of the Sick and Destitute Poor (1927) *Report of Commission on the Relief of the Sick and Destitute Poor*. Dublin: Stationery Office.

Commission on Social Welfare (1986) *Report of the Commission on Social Welfare*. Dublin: Stationery Office.

Cooper, N. and Dumpleton, S. (2013) *Walking the Breadline: The Scandal of Food Poverty in 21st Century Britain*. Oxford: Oxfam, p 3. Available at: http://policy-practice.oxfam.org.uk/publications/walking-the-breadline-the-scandal-of-food-poverty-in-21st-century-britain-292978

Cooper, N., Purcell, S. and Jackson, R. (2014) *Below the Breadline. The Relentless Rise in Food Poverty in Britain*. Available at: www.trusselltrust.org/resources/documents/foodbank/6323_Below_the_Breadline_web.pdf

Cousins, M. (2005) *Explaining the Irish Welfare State: An Historical, Comparative and Political Analysis*. New York: Edwin Mellen Press.

Cousins, M. (2016) '*The Irish Social Protection System: Change in Comparative Context*', in M. Murphy and F. Dukelow (eds) *The Irish Welfare State in the Twenty-First Century*. London: Palgrave Macmillan.

CSO (Central Statistics Office) (2010) *National Disability Survey 2006, Volume 2*. Dublin: Stationery Office.

CSO (Central Statistics Office) (2012) *Household Budget Survey 2009–2010 First Results*. Cork: CSO.

CSO (Central Statistics Office) (2015) *SILC Background Notes*. Available at: www.cso.ie/en/silc/methodology/

CSO (Central Statistics Office) (2016) *Percentage of Population with a Medical Card by Age Group, 2007 and 2016. Figure 4.1*. Available at: https://data.gov.ie/dataset/figure-41-percentage-of-population-with-a-medical-card-by-age-group-2007-and-2016 www.cso.ie/en/releasesandpublications/er/silc/surveyonincomeandlivingconditions2016/

CSO (Central Statistics Office) (2017) *Statistical Yearbook of Ireland 2015*. Available at: www.cso.ie/en/releasesandpublications/ep/p-syi/statisticalyearbookofireland2015/people/labourmarket/

CSO (Central Statistics Office) (2018a) *Survey on Income & Living Conditions*. Available at: www.cso.ie/en/aboutus/takingpartinasurvey/surveysofhouseholdsindividuals/surveyonincomelivingconditions/

CSO (Central Statistics Office) (2018b) *Household Budget Survey 2015–2016*. Available at: www.cso.ie/en/releasesandpublications/ep/p-hbs/hbs20152016/hexp/

CSO (Central Statistics Office) (2020a) *Survey on Income and Living Conditions (SILC) 2019. Poverty and Deprivation*. Available at: www.cso.ie/en/releasesandpublications/ep/p-silc/surveyonincomeandlivingconditionssilc2019/povertyanddeprivation/

CSO (Central Statistics Office) (2020b) *Consumer Price Index*. Available at: www.cso.ie/en/statistics/prices/consumerpriceindex/

CSO (Central Statistics Office) (2020c) *Comparative Price Levels for Food, Beverages and Tobacco 2018*. Available at: www.cso.ie/en/releasesandpublications/ep/p-cpl/comparativepricelevelsforfoodbeveragesandtobacco2018/food/

CSO (Central Statistics Office) (2021) *Ireland's UN SDGs 2019: Report on Indicators for Goal 2 Zero Hunger*. Available at: www.cso.ie/en/releasesandpublications/ep/p-sdg2/irelandsunsdgs2019-reportonindicatorsforgoal2zerohunger/hunger/

Cummins, S., Pettricrew, M. and Sparks, L. (2005) 'Large Scale Food Retail Provision Alone May Not Have A Substantial Impact on Diet', *British Medical Journal*, 330(26), 683–4.

Curry, J. (2011) *Irish Social Services. Fifth Edition*. Dublin: IPA.

Dáil Éireann Debate (2016) *Medical Card Administration*. 911(1). Written Answer No. 672.

Dáil Éireann Debate (2018) *Food Poverty*. Available at: www.oireachtas.ie/en/debates/question/2018-05-03/3/#pq-answers-3

Daly, M. and Kelly, G. (2015) *Families and Poverty: Everyday Life on a Low Income*. Bristol: Policy Press.

Daly, M. and Lewis, J. (2000) 'The Concept of Social Care and the Analysis of Contemporary Welfare States', *British Journal of Sociology*, 51(2), 281–99.

Daly, M. and Leonard, M. (2002) *Against all Odds. Family Life on a Low Income in Ireland*. Dublin: IPA.

Daly, M. and Yeates, N. (2003) 'Common Origins, Different paths: Adaptation and Change in Social Security in Britain and Ireland', *Policy & Politics*, 31(1), 85–97.

Danish Food Bank (2021) *Danish Food Bank*. Available at: https://download.delfi.com/download/Cases/Case_F%C3%B8devareBanken_EN.pdf

Darmon, I. and Perez, C. (2010) '"Conduct of Conduct" or the Shaping of Adequate Dispositions? Labour Market and Career Guidance in four European Countries', *Critical Social Policy*, 31(1), 77–101.

Davis, B. and Tarasuk, V. (1994) 'Hunger in Canada', *Agriculture and Human Values*, 11(4), 50–7.

Davis, O. and Baumberg Geiger, B. (2017) 'Did Food Insecurity Rise Across Europe after the 2008 Crisis? An Analysis Across Welfare Regimes', *Social Policy and Society*, 16(3), 343–60.

DCCAE (Department of Communications, Climate Action and Environment) (2018) *The Sustainable Development Goals National Implementation Plan 2018–2020*. Available at: https://assets.gov.ie/19344/32f9bdd2aae2464caae37760edd1da04.pdf

DoECC (Department of the Environment, Climate and Communications) (2021) *Strategy to Combat Energy Poverty*. Available at: www.gov.ie/en/publication/14e2b-strategy-to-combat-energy-poverty/

De Schutter, O. (2013) 'The Right to Food in Times of Crisis', in *Freedom from Hunger: Realising the Right to Food in the UK, Just Fair Report*. London: Just Fair, p 9.

Department for Communities NI (2018) *Social Supermarkets Pilot Programme*. Available at: www.communities-ni.gov.uk/sites/default/files/publications/communities/social-supermarkets-pilot-programme-screening.pdf

Department of Health (2016) *A Healthy Weight for Ireland: Obesity Policy and Action Plan 2016–2025*. Dublin: Stationery Office.

Department of Health UK (2005) *Choosing a Better Diet: A Food and Health Action Plan*. London: Department of Health Publications.

Department of Social and Family Affairs (2007) *The National Action Plan for Social Inclusion 2007–2016*. Dublin: Stationery Office.

Derrickson, J., Sakai, J. and Anderson, J. (2001) 'Interpretations of the "Balanced Meal" Household Food Security Indicator', *Journal of Nutrition Education*, 33(3), 155–60.

Dibsdall, L., Lambert, N., Bobbin, R. and Frewer, L. (2003) 'Low-Income Consumers' Attitudes and Behaviours Towards Access, Affordability and Motivation to Eat Fruit and Vegetables', *Public Health Nutrition*, 6(2), 159–68.

DOEASP (Department of Employment Affairs and Social Protection) (2018a) *Poverty Indicators*. Available at: www.welfare.ie/en/Pages/Poverty-Indicators.aspx

DOEASP (Department of Employment Affairs and Social Protection) (2018b) *Legislation to Improve the Security and Predictability of Working Hours for Employees*. Available at: https://www.gov.ie/en/speech/a2a3cc-legislation-to-improve-the-security-predictability-of-working-hours-/?referrer=https://www.welfare.ie/en/pressoffice/Pages/pr180518.aspx

Dowler, E. (1998) 'Food Poverty and Food Policy', *IDS Bulletin*, 29(1).

Dowler, E. (2003) 'Food and Poverty: Insights from the UK', *Development Policy Review*, 21(5–6), 569–80.

Dowler, E. and Dobson, B. (1997) 'Nutrition and Poverty in Europe: An Overview', *Proceedings of the Nutrition Society*, 56(5), 51–62.

Dowler, E. and Lambie-Mumford, H. (2015) 'How Can Households Eat in Austerity? Challenges for Social Policy in the UK', *Social Policy and Society*, 14(3), 417–28.

Dowler, E. and Leather, S. (2000) '"Spare Some Change for a Bite to Eat?" From Primary Poverty to Social Exclusion: The Role of Nutrition and Food', in J. Bradshaw and R. Sainsbury (eds) *Experiencing Poverty.*. Aldershot: Ashgate, pp 200–18

Dowler, E. and O'Connor, D. (2012) 'Rights Based Approaches to Addressing Food Poverty and Food Insecurity in Ireland and the UK', *Social Science & Medicine*, 74(1), 44–51.

Downing, E., Kennedy, S. and Fell, M. (2014). *Food Banks and Food Poverty. House of Commons Library. Standard Note: SN0665*. Available at: http://researchbriefings.parliament.uk/ResearchBriefing/Summary/SN06657#fullreport

Doyal, L. and Gough, I. (1991) *A Theory of Human Need*. Basingstoke: MacMillan.

Drèze, J. and Sen, A. (1989) *Hunger and Public Action*. Oxford: Clarendon Press.

Drudy, P.J. (2016) *'The Housing Problem and the Case for Rent Regulation in the Private Rented Sector', Submission to the Committee on Housing and Homelessness by P.J. Drudy*. Available at: https://data.oireachtas.ie/ie/oireachtas/committee/dail/32/committee_on_housing_and_homelessness/submissions/2016/2016-05-10_submission-p-j-drudy_en.pdf

DSP (Department of Social Protection) (1997*) Supportive Voluntary Activity: A Green Paper on the Community and Voluntary Sector and its Relationship with the State*. Dublin: Stationery Office.

DSP (Department of Social Protection) (2010) *Report on the Desirability and Feasibility of Introducing a Single Social Assistance Payment for People of Working Age*. Dublin: DSP.

DSP (Department of Social Protection) (2015) *Statistical Information on Social Welfare Services 2014*. Dublin: DOESP.

DSP (Department of Social Protection) (2016a) *Statement of Strategy*. Dublin: DOESP.

DSP (Department of Social Protection) (2016b) *Updated National Action Plan for Social Inclusion 2015–2017*. Available at: www.welfare.ie/en/downloads/Updated%20National%20Action%20Plan%20For%20Social%20Inclusion%202015-2017.pdf

DSP (Department of Social Protection) (2019) *36 Schools Selected for Hot School Meals Pilot Project*. Available at: www.gov.ie/en/press-release/0ff9f0-36-schools-selected-for-hot-school-meals-pilot-project/#

DSP (Department of Social Protection) (2020a) *Habitual Residence Condition (HRC1)*. Available at: www.gov.ie/en/publication/170e70-habitual-residence-condition/

DSP (Department of Social Protection) (2020b) *FEAD: The Fund for European Aid to the Most Deprived*. Available at: www.gov.ie/en/publication/f68e91-fead-the-fund-for-european-aid-to-the-most-deprived/

DSP (Department of Social Protection) (2020c) *FEAD 2019 Annual Implementation Report*. Available at: www.gov.ie/pdf/?file=https://assets.gov.ie/99825/914b142e-0c18-40a9-9ef6-f754e595faf9.pdf#page=null

DSP (Department of Social Protection) (2020d) *Roadmap for Social Inclusion 2020–2025*. Available at: https://www.gov.ie/en/press-release/0b2e3d-minister-doherty-publishes-roadmap-for-social-inclusion-2020-2025/

DSP (Department of Social Protection) (2021a) *List of Charities in Receipt of FEAD Food Product Support*. Available at: www.gov.ie/en/publication/f68e91-fead-the-fund-for-european-aid-to-the-most-deprived/

DSP (Department of Social Protection) (2021b) *Minister O'Brien Announces New Working Group on Food Poverty*. Available at: www.gov.ie/en/press-release/4f450-minister-obrien-announces-new-working-group-on-food-poverty/

Dublin City Council (2021) *Rental Accommodation Scheme*. Available at: www.dublincity.ie/residential

Dukelow, F. and Considine, M. (2014) 'Outlier or Model of Austerity in Europe? The Case of Irish Social Protection Reform', *Social Policy and Administration*, 48, 413–29.

Dukelow, F. and Considine, M. (2017) *Irish Social Policy. A Critical Introduction*. Bristol: Policy Press.

Dukelow, F. and Murphy, M. (2016) 'Welfare States: How They Change and Why', in M. Murphy and F. Dukelow (eds) *The Irish Welfare State in the Twenty-First Century*. London: Palgrave Macmillan.

DWP (Department of Works and Pensions) (2021) *Family Resources Survey: Financial Year 2019 to 2020*. Available at: www.gov.uk/government/statistics/family-resources-survey-financial-year-2019-to-2020/family-resources-survey-financial-year-2019-to-2020#household-food-security-1

Earner-Byrne, L. (2017) *Letters of the Catholic Poor. Poverty in Independent Ireland, 1920–1940*. Cambridge: Cambridge University Press.

Economist Intelligence Unit (2021) *Global Food Security Index*. Available at: https://foodsecurityindex.eiu.com/Index

EIGE (European Institute of Gender Equality) (2016) *Poverty, Gender and Lone Parents in the EU*. Available at: https://eige.europa.eu/publications/poverty-gender-and-lone-parents-eu

Electric Ireland (2018) *Is the Price of Electricity more Expensive with a Pay As You Go Meter?*. Available at: www.electricireland.ie/residential/help/pay-as-you-go/is-the-price-of-electricity-more-expensive-with-a-pay-as-you-go-meter

Elliott, V. (2021) 'Food Deserts Threaten Health of Poor and Old', *Electric Ireland*. Available at: https://www.electricireland.ie/residential/help/pay-as-you-go/is-the-price-of-electricity-more-expensive-with-a-pay-as-you-go-meter

Englander, D. and O'Day, R. (1995) *Retrieved Riches: Social Investigation in Britain, 1840–1914*. New York: Scholars' Press.

Esping Anderson, G. (1990) *The Three Worlds of Welfare Capitalism*. Cambridge and Princeton: Polity and Princeton University Press.

EUR-Lex (2021) *Regulation (EU) No 223/2014 of the European Parliament and of the Council of 11 March 2014 on the Fund for European Aid to the Most Deprived*. Available at: https://eur-lex.europa.eu/legal-content/EN/TXT/?uri=celex%3A32014R0223

Eurofound (2015) *Sixth European Working Conditions Survey: Overview Report*. Luxembourg: Publications Office of the European Union.

Eurofound (2017a) *Sixth European Working Conditions Survey: Overview Report (2017 update)*. Luxembourg: Publications Office of the European Union.

Eurofound (2017b) *In-work Poverty in the EU*. Luxembourg: Publications Office of the European Union.

Eurofound (2020) *Living, Working and COVID-19 Dataset*. Luxembourg: Publications Office of the European Union. Available at: http://eurofound.link/covid19data

Eurofound (2021) *COVID-19: Implications for Employment and Working Life, COVID-19 series*. Luxembourg: Publications Office of the European Union.

European Commission (1985) 'On Specific Community Action to Combat Poverty' (Council Decision of 19 December 1984), 85/8/EEC', *Official Journal of the EEC*, 2, 24.

European Commission (2011a) *Employment and Social Developments in Europe 2011*. Luxembourg: Publications Office of the European Communities.

European Commission (2011b) *Economic Adjustment Programme for Ireland, Autumn 2011 Review*. Brussels: European Commission.

European Commission (2012) *Economic Adjustment Programme for Ireland, Winter 2011 Review*. Brussels: European Commission.

European Commission (2014) *Employment and Social Developments in Europe 2014*. European Commission, Directorate-General for Employment, Social Affairs and Inclusion. Luxembourg: Publications Office of the European Union.

European Commission (2020) *Fund for European Aid to the Most Deprived (FEAD). Key Facts and Figures*. Available at: https://ec.europa.eu/social/main.jsp?catId=1089#:~:text=The%20Fund%20for%20European%20Aid,e.g.%20shoes%2C%20soap%20and%20shampoo

Eurostat (2018a) *Expenditure on Means-Tested Social Protection Benefits, 2015*. Available at: http://ec.europa.eu/eurostat/statistics-explained/index.php/File:Expenditure_on_means-tested_social_protection_benefits,_2015_(%25_of_total_expenditure_on_social_protection_benefits)_SPS17.png

Eurostat (2018b) *Database*. Available at: https://ec.europa.eu/eurostat/data/database?node_code=tespm030

Eurostat (2021) *Income Poverty Statistics*. Available at: https://ec.europa.eu/eurostat/statistics-explained/index.php?title=Income_poverty_statistics&oldid=440992#:~:text=The%20at%2Drisk%2Dof%2D,population%20above%20the%20poverty%20threshold

Fahey, T. (1998) 'The Catholic Church and Social Policy', in S. Healy and B. Reynolds (eds) *Social Policy in Ireland: Principles, Practice and Problems*. Dublin: Oak Tree Press.

Fahey, T., Kielthy, T. and Polek, E. (2012) *Family Relationships and Family Well-Being: A Study of the Families of Nine Year-Olds in Ireland*. Dublin: Family Support Agency.

Falling Fruit Ireland (2021) *Falling Fruit Ireland*. Available at: www.fallingfruit.ie/

Fanning, B. (1999) 'The Mixed Economy of Welfare', in G. Kiely, A. O'Donnell, P. Kennedy and S. Quinn (eds) *Irish Social Policy in Context*. Dublin: UCD Press.

Faughnan, P. and Byrne, A. (1998) *The Dublin City Food Bank*. Dublin: Crosscare.

FEBA (European Food Banks Federation) (2019) *FEBA Annual Convention 2019. Towards the Next Decade, Together*. Available at: https://annualconvention2019.eurofoodbank.org/

FEBA (European Food Banks Federation) (2020) *FEBA Annual Forum on Food Aid and Social Inclusion*. Available at: https://lp.eurofoodbank.org/annual-forum-2020/

FEBA (Federation of European Food Banks) (2021) *Our Mission, Impact and Values*. Available at: https://www.eurofoodbank.org/our-mission-impact-values/

Feed Ireland (2021) *Feed Ireland Food Banks*. Available at: www.feedcork.com/projects

Feichtinger, E. (1997) 'Looking Beyond Nutrients: Towards a More Holistic View of Poverty and Food', in B. Kohler, E. Feichtinger, E. Barlosius and E. Dowler (eds) *Poverty and Food in Welfare Societies*. Berlin: Edition Sigma.

Finnerty, J., O'Connell, C. and O'Sullivan, S. (2016) 'Social Housing Policy and Provision: A Changing Regime?', in M. Murphy and F. Dukelow (eds) *The Irish Welfare State in the Twenty-First Century*. London: Palgrave Macmillan.

Fisher, G. (1992) 'The Development and History of the Poverty Thresholds', *Social Security Bulletin*, 55(4), Winter 1992, 3–14.

Fisher, G. (2008) 'Remembering Mollie Orshansky: The Developer of the Poverty Thresholds', *Social Security Bulletin*, 68(3).

Focus Ireland (2021) *About Homelessness*. Available at: www.focusireland.ie/resource-hub/about-homelessness/#:~:text=How%20many%20people%20are%20homeless,monthly%20figures%20started%20being%20published

FoodCloud (2021) *FoodCloud*. Available at: https://food.cloud/

Foodshare Kerry (2021) *Foodshare Kerry*. Available at: http://fsk.ie/

Food Standards Agency Wales (2003) *Food and Well Being*. Cardiff: Food Standards Agency Wales. Available at: www.aber.ac.uk/en/media/departmental/sell/pdf/wellbeinghealth/Food-and-Wellbeing-2003.pdf

Friel, S. and Conlon, C. (2004) *Food Poverty and Policy*. Dublin: Combat Poverty Agency.

Friel, S., Walsh, O. and McCarthy, D. (2006) 'The Irony of a Rich Country: Issues of Financial Access to and Availability of Healthy Food in the Republic of Ireland', *Journal of Epidemiology and Community Health*, 60, 1013–19.

FSA (Food Standards Agency in Northern Ireland) (2007) *Homelessness and Food Poverty*. Available at: https://webarchive.nationalarchives.gov.uk/20120409182459/http://www.food.gov.uk/northernireland/researchni/ninutritionhomeless

FSA (Food Standards Agency in Northern Ireland) (2021) *The Cost of a Healthy Food Basket in Northern Ireland in 2020*. Available at: www.food.gov.uk/research/research-projects/the-cost-of-a-healthy-food-basket-in-northern-ireland-in-2020

Furey, S., McLaughlin, C., Beacom, E., Quinn, U. and Surgenor, D. (2019) 'What Predicts Food Insecurity? An Online Survey', *The Lancet*, 394(Special Issue S41).

Gannon, B. and Nolan, B. (2006) *The Dynamics of Disability and Social Inclusion*. Dublin: The Equality Authority.

Garthwaite, K. (2016) *Hunger Pains, Life Inside Foodbank Britain*. Bristol: Policy Press.

GFN (Global FoodBanking Network) (2019) *Toward Zero Hunger. Food Banks as a Green Solution to Hunger*. Available at: www.foodbanking.org/wp-content/uploads/2019/03/GFN_WasteNot.pdf

Gibney, E. et al (2020) *The National COVID-19 Food Study*. Dublin: University College Dublin, Institute of Food and Health.

Ginsburg, N. (2001) 'Globalization and the Liberal Welfare States', in R. Sykes, B. Palier and P. Prior (eds) *Globalization and European Welfare States: Challenges and Change*. Basingstoke: Palgrave, pp 173–91.

Gordon, D. (2006) 'The Concept and Measurement of Poverty', in C. Pantazis, D. Gordon and R. Levitas (eds) *Poverty and Social Exclusion in Britain. The Millennium Survey*. Bristol: Policy Press.

Government of Ireland (1997) *National Anti-Poverty Strategy*. Dublin: Stationery Office.

Government of Ireland (1999) *National Childcare Strategy. Report of the Partnership 2000 Expert Working Group on Childcare*. Dublin: Stationery Office.

Government of Ireland. Joint Committee on Enterprise and Small Business (2005) *Grocery Prices*. Available at: www.oireachtas.ie/ga/debates/debate/joint_committee_on_enterprise_and_small_business/2005-02-23/3/

Government of Ireland (2018a) *Comprehensive Employment Strategy for People with Disabilities 2015–2024*. Available at: www.justice.ie/en/JELR/Comprehensive%20Employment%20Strategy%20for%20People%20with%20Disabilities%20-%20FINAL.pdf/Files/Comprehensive%20Employment%20Strategy%20for%20People%20with%20Disabilities%20-%20FINAL.pdf

Government of Ireland (2018b) *Ireland: Voluntary National Review 2018: Report on the Implementation of the 2030 Agenda to the UN High-level Political Forum on Sustainable Development*. Available at: https://sustainabledevelopment.un.org/content/documents/19382Ireland_Voluntary_National_Review_2018.pdf

Gov.ie (2020a) *FEAD: The Fund for European Aid to the Most Deprived*. Available at: www.gov.ie/en/publication/f68e91-fead-the-fund-for-european-aid-to-the-most-deprived/#what-is-fead

Gov.ie (2020b) *Roadmap for Social Inclusion 2020–2025*. Available at: https://assets.gov.ie/46557/bf7011904ede4562b925f98b15c4f1b5.pdf

Gov.ie (2021) *Work on Progressing to Living Wage to Formally Begin: Tánaiste*. Press Release, 15 April. Available at: www.gov.ie/en/press-release/c8e08-work-on-progressing-to-living-wage-to-formally-begin-tanaiste/

Greater London Authority (2013) *A Zero Hunger City. Tackling Food Poverty in London*. London: Greater London Authority.

Green, R., Henri, T., Campbell, J. and Greaves, B. (2014) *Putting Food on the Table. Understanding Food Poverty: Exploring Food Bank Use in Lewisham*. London: Goldsmiths, University of London.

Guardian, The (2019) *Food Banks are No Solution to Poverty*. 24 March 24. Available at: www.theguardian.com/society/2019/mar/24/food-banks-are-no-solution-to-poverty

Halleröd, B., Ekbrand, H. and Bengtsson, M. (2015) 'In-work Poverty and Labour Market Trajectories: Poverty Risks Among the Working Population in 22 European Countries', *Journal of European Social Policy*, 25(5), 473–88.

Hammersley, M. and Traianou, A. (2012) *Ethics in Qualitative Research: Controversies and Contexts*. London: Sage.

Hansard (2013) *Food: Food Banks*. House of Lords, 2 July. Available at: https://publications.parliament.uk/pa/ld201314/ldhansrd/text/130702-0001.htm

Harrington, J., Fitzgerald, A., Layte, R., Lutomski, J., Molcho, M. and Perry, I. (2011) 'Sociodemographic, Health and Lifestyle Predictors of Poor Diets', *Public Health Nutrition*, 14(12), 2166–75.

Healy, A. (2019) 'Measuring Food Poverty in Ireland: The Importance of Including Exclusion', *Irish Journal of Sociology*, 27(2), 105–27.

Hemerijck, A. (2013) *Changing Welfare States*. Oxford: Oxford University Press.

Hick, R. (2012) 'The Capability Approach: Insights for a New Poverty Focus', *Journal of Social Policy*, 41(2).

Hick, R. (2016) 'Material Poverty and Multiple Deprivation in Britain: The Distinctiveness of Multidimensional Assessment', *Journal of Public Policy*, 36(2), 277–308.

Hick, R. (2018) 'Enter the Troika: The Politics of Social Security during Ireland's Bailout', *Journal of Social Policy*, 47(1).

Hick, R. and Lanau, A. (2018) 'Moving In and Out of In-work Poverty in the UK: An Analysis of Transitions, Trajectories and Trigger Events', *Journal of Social Policy*. Available at: www.cambridge.org/core/journals/journal-of-social-policy/article/moving-in-and-out-of-inwork-poverty-in-the-uk-an-analysis-of-transitions-trajectories-and-trigger-events/4B9A7F2F57BD23A5106328C3D72BE994

Hickey, C. and Downey, D. (2003) *Hungry for Change: Social Exclusion, Food Poverty and Homelessness in Dublin*. Dublin: Focus Ireland.

Hirsch, D. (2015) *A Minimum Income Standard for the UK in 2015*. York: Joseph Rowntree Foundation.

Holweg, C. and Lienbacher, E. (2016) *Social Supermarkets in Europe: Investigations from a Retailing Perspective in Selected European Countries*. Vienna: Institute for Retailing and Marketing.

Holweg, C., Lienbacher, E. and Zinn, W. (2010) 'Social Supermarkets: A New Challenge in Supply Chain Management and Sustainability', *Supply Chain Forum: International Journal*, 11(4) 50–8.

Horemans, J. and Marx, I. (2013) 'Should We Care About Part-time Work from a Poverty Perspective? An Analysis of the EU-15 Countries', in M. Koch and M. Fritz (eds) *Non-Standard Employment in Europe: Paradigms. Prevalence and Policy Responses*. Houndmills: Palgrave Macmillan, pp 169–89.

Hossain, N., Byrne, B., Campbell, A., Harrison, E., McKinley, B. and Shah, P. (2011) *The Impact of the Global Economic Downturn on Communities and Poverty in the UK*. York: Joseph Rowntree Foundation. Available at: www.jrf.org.uk/sites/files/jrf/experiences-of-economic-downturn-full.pdf

House of Commons Environment, Food and Rural Affairs Committee (2015) *Food Security: Demand, Consumption and Waste. Sixth Report of Session 2014–15*. London: The Stationery Office.

Housing Agency (2017) *Summary of Social Housing Assessments. 2017 Key Findings*. Available at: www.housing.gov.ie/sites/default/files/publications/files/sha_summary_2017.pdf

Housing Agency (2021) *Summary of Social Housing Assessments 2020 Key Findings*. Available at: www.housingagency.ie/news-events/housing-agency-welcomes-reduction-number-households-social-housing-waiting-list

HSE (Health Service Executive) (2014) *Report of the Expert Panel on Medical Need for Medical Card Eligibility*. Available at: www.hse.ie/eng/services/publications/corporate/expertpanelmedicalneed.pdf

HSE (Health Service Executive) (2016) *Discretionary Hardship Arrangements*. Available at: www.hse.ie/eng/staff/pcrs/circulars/pharmacy/discretionary%20hardship%20arrangements.pdf

Hutto, N., Waldfogel, J., Kaushal, N. and Garfinkel, I. (2011) 'Improving the Measurement of Poverty', *Social Service Review*, 85(1), 39–74.

Indecon (2018) *Registered Irish Charities Social and Economic Impact Report*. Available at: www.charitiesregulator.ie

INIS (Irish Naturalisation and Immigration Services) (2017) *Permission, Stamps & Conditions. Department of Justice and Equality*. Available at: www.inis.gov.ie/en/INIS/Pages/registration-stamps

Inza-Bartolomé, A. and San-Epifanio, L. (2020) 'Food Aid in Post-Crisis Spain', in H. Lambie-Mumford and T. Silvasti (eds) *The Rise of Food Charity in Europe*. Bristol: Policy Press.

Irish Congress of Trade Unions (2015) *False Economy. The Growth of 'Bogus Self-Employment' in the Construction Industry*. Available at: https://www.ictu.ie/publications/false-economy-growth-bogus-self-employment-construction

Jenkins, S. and Micklewright, J. (2007) 'New Directions in the Analysis of Poverty', in S. Jenkins and J. Micklewright (eds) *Inequality and Poverty Re-Examined*. Oxford: Oxford University Press.

Joseph, K. and Sumption, J. (1979) *Equality*. London: John Murray.

Kearney, J., McCartney, D., McCarthy, S., Bourke, S., Knox, B. and Barton, M. (2008) *Food and Nutrient Intake and Attitudes among Disadvantaged Groups on the Island of Ireland: Summary Report*. Safefood.

Keats, D. (2000) *Interviewing: A Practical Guide for Students and Professionals*. Buckingham: Open University Press.

Kemp, P. (2005) 'Escape Routes from Poverty', *Benefits*, 13(3), 173–8.

Kempson, E. (1996) *Life on a Low Income*. York: Joseph Rowntree Foundation.

Kennedy, F. (2001) *Cottage to Crèche: Family Change in Ireland*. Dublin: IPA.

Kennedy, P. (2013) *Key Themes in Social Policy*. London: Routledge.

Kessl, F., Lorenz, S. and Schoneville, H. (2020) 'Social Exclusion and Food Assistance in Germany', in H. Lambie-Mumford and T. Silvasti (eds) *The Rise of Food Charity in Europe*. Bristol: Policy Press.

Kingdon, G. and Knight, J. (2006) 'Subjective Well-Being Poverty versus Income Poverty and Capabilities Poverty?', *Journal of Development Studies*, 42(7), 1199–224.

Kirkpatrick, S. and Tarusuk, V. (2011) 'Housing Circumstances are Associated with Household Food Access among Low-income Urban Families', *J Urban Health*, 88(2), 284–96.

Kiss, M. (2017) *The Future of Work in the EU. Briefing April 2017*. Brussels: European Parliamentary Research Service.

Kneafsey, M., Dowler, E., Lambie-Mumford, H., Inman, I. and Collier, R. (2013) 'Consumers and Food Security: Uncertain or Empowered?', *Journal of Rural Studies*, 29, 101–02.

Kore, J. (2014) 'Hunger and Food Aid in Estonia: A Local Authority and Family Obligation', in G. Riches and T. Silvasti (eds) *First World Hunger Revisited: Food Charity or the Right to Food?*. Basingstoke: Palgrave MacMillan.

Kotz, N. (1969) *Let Them Eat Promises: The Politics of Hunger in America*. New Jersey: Prentice-Hall.

Koukiadaki, A. and Katsaroumpas, I. (2017) *Temporary Contracts, Precarious Employment, Employees' Fundamental Rights and EU Employment Law*. Brussels: European Parliament.

Lambie-Mumford, H. (2013) '"Every Town Should Have One": Emergency Food Banking in the UK', *Journal of Social Policy*, 42(1), 73–89.

Lambie-Mumford, H. (2017) *Hungry Britain. The Rise of Food Charity*. Bristol: Policy Press.

Lambie-Mumford, H. and Dowler, E. (2014) 'Rising Use of "Food Aid" in the United Kingdom', *British Food Journal*, 116(9), 1418–25.

Lambie-Mumford, H. and Silvasti, T. (eds) (2020) *The Rise of Food Charity in Europe*. Bristol: Policy Press.

Lambie-Mumford, H., Loopstra, R. and Gordon, K. (2020) *Mapping Responses to Risk of Rising Food Insecurity during the COVID-19 Crisis across the UK, Food Vulnerability during COVID-19, Phase 1 Report March–July 2020* (Sheffield: SPERI, 2020). Available at: http://speri.dept.shef.ac.uk/wp-content/uploads/2020/08/Food-Vulnerability-During-COVID-19-first-project-report.pdf

Lambie-Mumford, H., Crossley, D., Jensen, E., Verbeke, M. and Dowler, E. (2014) *Household Food Security in the UK: A Review of Food Aid, Food Ethics Council*. Warwick: University of Warwick. Available at: www.foodethicscouncil.org/uploads/publications/2014%20Household%20food%20insecurity%20in%20the%20UK.pdf

Lang, T. (1997) 'Dividing up the Cake: Food as Social Exclusion', in A. Walker and C. Walker (eds) *Britain Divided*. London: Child Poverty Action Group Ltd.

Lawrence, W., Keyte, J. and Tinati, T. (2012) 'A Mixed-Methods Investigation to Explore How Women Living in Disadvantaged Areas might be Supported to Improve their Diets', *Journal of Health Psychology*, 17(6), 785–98.

Layder, D. (1998) *Sociological Practice: Linking Theory and Social Research*. London: Sage.

Layte, R., Nolan, B. and Whelan, C. (2000) 'Targeting Poverty', *Journal of Social Policy*, 29(4), 553–75.

Layte, R., Nolan, B. and Whelan, C. (2004) 'Explaining Poverty Trends in Ireland during the Boom', *The Irish Banking Review: Quarterly Review*, 2, 2–13. Available at: www.esri.ie/pubs/JACB200409.pdf

Layte, R., Harrington, J., Sexton, E., Perry, I., Cullinan, J. and Lyons, S. (2011) 'Irish Exceptionalism? Local Food Environments and Dietary Quality', *Journal of Epidemiology and Community Health*, 65(10), 881–8.

Lenhart, N. and Read, M. (1989) 'Demographic Profile and Nutrient Intake Assessment of Individuals Using Emergency Food Programs', *Journal of the American Dietetic Association*, 89(9).

Lister, R. (2004) *Poverty*. Cambridge: Polity Press.

Living Wage (2020) *Living Wage 2020*. Available at: www.livingwage.ie/

Livingstone, N. (2015) 'The Hunger Games: Food Poverty and Politics in the UK', *Capital & Class*, 39(2), 188–95.

Lockie, S. and Pietsch, J. (2012) *Food Security: What are the Real Issues for Australia?*. Canberra: National Institute of Rural and Regional Australia, University of Australia.

Lohmann, H. and Marx, I. (2008) 'The Different Faces of In-Work Poverty across Welfare State Regimes', in H. Andress and H. Lohmann (eds) *The Working Poor in Europe: Employment, Poverty and Globalisation*. Cheltenham: Edward Elgar.

Loopstra, R. (2018) 'Interventions to Address Household Food Insecurity in High-income Countries', *Proceedings of the Nutrition Society*, 77(3), 270–81.

Loopstra, R. and Tarasuk, V. (2015) 'Food Bank Usage Is a Poor Indicator of Food Insecurity: Insights from Canada', *Social Policy and Society*, 14(3), 443–55.

Loopstra, R., Fledderjohann, J., Reeves, A. and Stuckler, D. (2017) 'The Impact of Welfare Benefit Sanctioning on Food Insecurity: A Dynamic Cross-area Study of Food Bank Usage in the UK', *Journal of Social Policy*, 47(3), 437–57.

Loopstra, R., Reeves, A., McKee, M. and Stuckler, D. (2016) 'Food Insecurity and Social Protection in Europe: Quasi-natural Experiment of Europe's Great Recessions 2004–2012', *Preventive Medicine*, 89: 44–50.

Loopstra, R., Reeves, A., Taylor-Robinson, A., Barr, B., McKee, M. and Stuckler, D. (2015) 'Austerity, Sanctions, and the Rise of Food Banks in the UK', *BMJ*, 350: h1775.

Low-Pay Commission (2016) *Recommendations for the National Minimum Wage, LPC No 2*. Dublin: LPC.

Lynch, K. (2010) 'From a Neo-Liberal to an Egalitarian State: Imagining a Different Future', *TASC Annual Lecture*, Royal Irish Academy, Dublin, 17 June. Available at: http://researchrepository.ucd.ie/handle/10197/2468

Mack, J. and Lansley, S. (1985) *Poor Britain*. London: Allen & Unwin.

Mack, J. and Lansley, S. (2015) *Breadline Britain. The Rise of Mass Poverty*. London: Oneworld Publications.

MacMahon, B. and McEvoy, O. (2018) *Stories of Struggle: Experiences of Living Below the Minimum Essential Standard of Living*. Dublin: Vincentian Partnership for Social Justice.

MacMahon, B., Carey, J. and Stokes, A. (2006) *Minimum Essential Budgets for Six Households*. Dublin: Vincentian Partnership for Social Justice.

MacMahon, B., Thornton, R. and Moloney, N. (2016) *Minimum Essential Standard of Living 2016. Update Report*. Dublin: Vincentian Partnership for Social Justice.

MacMahon, B., Thornton, R. and Moloney, N. (2017) *Minimum Essential Standard of Living 2017. Update Report*. Dublin: Vincentian Partnership for Social Justice.

Maître, B., Nolan, B. and Whelan, C. (2006) *Reconfiguring the Measurement of Deprivation and Consistent Poverty in Ireland. Policy Research Series number 58*. Dublin: ESRI.

Marlier, E., Atkinson, A., Cantillon, B. and Nolan, B. (2007) *The EU and Social Inclusion. Facing the Challenges*. Bristol: The Policy Press.

Marx, I. and Nolan, B. (2014) 'In-work Poverty', in B. Cantillon and F. Vandenbroucke (eds) *Reconciling Work and Poverty Reduction: How Successful are European Welfare States?*. Oxford: Oxford University Press.

McCashin, A. (2015) 'A Long Hello to Beveridge': Social Security in the Republic of Ireland, 1981–2007. Unpublished PhD Thesis. Trinity College Dublin.

McKechnie, R., Turrell, G., Giskes, K. and Gallegos, D. (2018) 'Single-item Measure of Food Insecurity Used in the National Health Survey May Underestimate Prevalence in Australia', *Australian and New Zealand Journal of Public Health*, 42, 389–95. Available at: https://doi.org/10.1111/1753-6405.12812

McKenzie, H. and McKay, J. (2017) 'Food as a Discretionary Item: The Impact of Welfare Payment Changes on Low-income Single Mother's Food Choices and Strategies', *Journal of Poverty and Social Justice*, 25(1), 35–48.

McIntosh, W. (1996) *Sociologies of Food and Nutrition*. New York: Plenum Press.

McKay, F.H., Haines, B.C. and Dunn, M. (2019) 'Measuring and Understanding Food Insecurity in Australia: A Systematic Review', *International Journal of Environmental Research and Public Health*, 16(3), 476. Available at: https://doi.org/10.3390/ijerph16030476

McKenzie, J. (1970) 'Poverty: Food and Nutrition Indices', in P. Townsend (ed) *The Concept of Poverty: Working Papers on Methods of Investigation and Life-Styles of the Poor in Different Countries*. London: Heinemann.

McManus, A. (2003) 'Social Security and Disability', in S. Quin and B. Redmond (eds) *Disability and Social Policy in Ireland*. Dublin: UCD Press.

Menton, C. (2007) *An Investigation of the Measurement of Poverty in Ireland*. Dublin: IPA.

Mid-West Simon Community (2021) *Social Grocery Final Report*. Available at: www.midwestsimon.ie/social-grocery-final-report/

Miewald, C. and Ostry, A. (2014) 'A Warm Meal and a Bed: Intersections of Housing and Food Security in Vancouver's Downtown Eastside', *Housing Studies*, 29(6), 709–29.

Miles, M., Huberman, A. and Saldaña, J. (2014) *Qualitative Data Analysis. A Methods Sourcebook*. London: Sage.

Miller, I. (2013) *Addressing Food Poverty in Ireland: Historical Perspectives*. Available at: www.historyandpolicy.org/policy-papers/papers/addressing-food-poverty-in-ireland-historical-perspectives

Minas, C., Jacobson, D., Antoniou, E. and McMullan, C. (2014) 'Welfare Regime, Welfare Pillar and Southern Europe', *Journal of European Social Policy*, 24(2), 135–49.

Morel, N., Palier, B. and Palme, J. (2012) 'Beyond the Welfare State as We Knew It?', in N. Morel, B. Palier and J. Palme (eds) *Towards a Social Investment Welfare State?: Ideas, Policies and Challenges*. Bristol, UK: Bristol University Press, pp 1–30.

Murphy, M. (2012) 'Interests, Institutions and Ideas: Explaining Irish Social Security Policy', *Policy & Politics*, 40(3), 347–65.

Murray, A., McGinnity, F. and Russell, H. (2016) 'Inequalities in Access to Early Care and Education in Ireland', in J. Williams, E. Nixon, E. Smyth and D. Watson (eds) *Cherishing All the Children Equally?*. Cork: Oak Tree Press.

Mwatsama, M. and Stewart, L. (2005) 'Food Poverty and Health Briefing Statement', *Faculty of Public Health of the Royal College of Physicians in the United Kingdom*. London: Faculty of Public Health.

National Audit Office (NAO) (2016) *Benefit Sanctions. Report by the Comptroller and Auditor General*. London: NAO. Available at: www.nao.org.uk/wp-content/uploads/2016/11/Benefit-sanctions.pdf

National Childcare Scheme (2021) Available at: https://www.ncs.gov.ie/en/

National Economic and Social Council (NESC) (2018a) *Moving from Welfare to Work: Low Work Intensity Households and the Quality of Supportive Services*. Dublin: NESC.

National Economic and Social Council (NESC) (2018b) *Social Insurance and the Welfare System: Towards a Sustainable Developmental Welfare State*. Dublin: NESC.

National Research Council (2005) *Measuring Food Insecurity and Hunger: Phase 1 Report. Panel to Review U.S Department of Agriculture's Measurement of Food Insecurity and Hunger*. Washington: National Academies Press. Available at: www.nap.edu/catalog/11227.html

Nelson, M., Erens, B., Bates, B., Church, S. and Boshier, T. (2007) *Low Income Diet and Nutrition Survey*. London: The Stationery Office.

NERI (Nevin Economic Research Institute) (2014) *Quarterly Economic Facts: Autumn 2014*. Available at: www.nerinstitute.net/research/quarterly-economic-facts-autumn-2014/

NESC (National Economic and Social Council) (2005) *The Developmental Welfare State*. Dublin: NESC.

Nolan, B. and Whelan, C. (1996) *Resources, Deprivation and Poverty*. Oxford: Clarendon Press.

Nolan, B. and Whelan, C. (2007) 'On the Multidimensionality of Poverty and Social Exclusion', in S. Jenkins and J. Micklewright (eds) *Inequality and Poverty Re-Examined*. Oxford: Oxford University Press.

Nolan, B. and Whelan, C. (2011) *Poverty and Deprivation in Europe*. Oxford: Oxford University Press.

Nord, M. (2012) 'How Much Does the Supplemental Nutrition Assistance Program Alleviate Food Insecurity? Evidence from Recent Programme Leavers', *Public Health Nutrition*, 15(5), 811–17.

Norris, M. and Byrne, M. (2017) 'A Tale of Two Busts (and a Boom): Irish Social Housing before and after the Global Financial Crisis', *Critical Housing Analysis*, 4(2), 19–28.

Norris, M. and Byrne, M. (2018) 'Housing Market (In)stability and Social Rented Housing: Comparing Austria and Ireland during the Global Financial Crisis', *Journal of Housing and the Built Environment*, 33, 227–45.

Nugent, C. (2018) 'A Time-Series Analysis of Precarious Work in the Elementary Professions in Ireland', *Psycho-sociological Issues in Human Resource Management*, 6(1), 7–37.

Ó Cinnéide, S. (1972) *The Extent of Poverty in Ireland. Paper presented to the Conference on Poverty, Kilkenny, November 1971, Social Studies*, 1(4), 397.

O'Connell, P., McCoy, S. and Clancy, D. (2006) 'Who went to College? Socio-economic Inequality in Entry to Higher Education in the Republic of Ireland in 2004', *Higher Education Quarterly*, 60(4), October, 312–32.

O'Connor, D. (2018) 'Food Poverty and the Policy Context in Ireland', in P. Beresford and S. Carr (eds) *Social Policy First Hand. An International Introduction to Participatory Welfare*. Bristol: Policy Press.

O'Connor, D., Cantillon, S. and Walsh, J. (2008) 'Rights Based Approaches to Food Poverty in Ireland', *Research Working Paper Series 11/01*. Dublin: Combat Poverty Agency.

O'Flaherty, A. (2020) '7,156 Applicants on Council Housing Waiting List', *Echo.ie*. 16 November. Available at: https://www.echo.ie/7-156-applicants-on-council-housing-waiting-list/

Ó Riain, S. (2017) 'Ireland's Low Learning Trap', *Administration*, 65(4), 31–8.

O'Sullivan, M. and Royle, T. (2014) 'Everything and Nothing Changes: Fast-food Employers and the Threat to Minimum Wage Regulation in Ireland', *Economic and Industrial Democracy*, 35(1), 27–47.

OECD (Organisation for Economic Co-operation and Development) (2000) *OECD Employment Outlook: June 2000*. Paris: OECD.

OECD (Organisation for Economic Co-operation and Development) (2014a) *Social Expenditure Update. Social Spending is Falling in Some Countries, but in Many Others it Remains at Historically High Levels*. Paris: OECD.

OECD (Organisation for Economic Co-operation and Development) (2014b) *Society at a Glance 2014. OECD Social Indicators*. Paris: OECD Publishing.

OECD (Organisation for Economic Co-operation and Development) (2014c) *Employment Outlook 2014*. Paris: OECD.

OECD (Organisation for Economic Co-operation and Development) (2014d) *OECD Family Database Charts PF3.4.B and PF3.4.C*. Available at: www.oecd.org/els/family/database.htm

OECD (Organisation for Economic Co-operation and Development) (2017) *Earnings and Wages. Wage Levels (Indicator)*. Available at: www.oecd-ilibrary.org/employment/wage-levels/indicator/english_0a1c27bc-en

OECD (Organisation for Economic Co-operation and Development) (2018) *OECD Indicators of Employment Protection*. Available at: www.oecd.org/els/emp/oecdindicatorsofemploymentprotection.htm

OECD (Organisation for Economic Co-operation and Development) (2019a) *PF3.1: Public Spending on Childcare and Early Education*. Available at: www.oecd.org/els/soc/PF3_1_Public_spending_on_childcare_and_early_education.pdf

OECD (Organisation for Economic Co-operation and Development) (2019b) *Workers on Low Pay. OECD Earnings Distribution Database*. Available at: https://pbs.twimg.com/media/EBwdiueX4AAYPNl?format=png&name=4096x4096

OECD (Organisation for Economic Co-operation and Development) (2019c) *OECD Employment Outlook 2019, The Future of Work*. OECDiLibrary. Paris: OECD Publishing.

OECD (Organisation for Economic Co-operation and Development) (2021) *Part-time Employment Rate*. Available at: https://data.oecd.org/emp/part-time-employment-rate.htm

Orshansky, M. (1959) 'Low-Cost Food Plans: New Regional Estimates. Research and Statistics Note No. 28'. U.S. Department of Health, Education, and Welfare, Social Security Administration, Division of Program Research.

Orshansky, M. (1965) *Counting the Poor: Another Look at the Poverty Profile, Social Security Bulletin*. Available at: www.ssa.gov/policy/docs/ssb/v28n1/v28n1p3.pdf

Palier, B. and Martin, C. (2007) 'From "a Frozen Landscape" to Structural Reforms: The Sequential Transformation of Bismarckian Welfare Systems', *Social Policy & Administration*, 41, 535–54.

Pembroke, S. (2018) *Precarious Work, Precarious Lives: How Policy Can Create More Security*. Dublin: TASC.

Pembroke, S., Wickham, J. and Bobek, A. (2017) *The Nature and Extent of Precarious Work in Ireland*. Dublin: TASC.

Pérez de Armiño, K. (2014) 'Erosion of Rights, Uncritical Solidarity and Food Banks in Spain', in G. Riches and T. Silvasti (eds) *First World Hunger Revisited: Food Charity or the Right to Food?*. Basingstoke: Palgrave Macmillan.

Pfeiffer, S., Ritter, T. and Hirseland, A. (2011) 'Hunger and Nutritional Poverty in Germany: Quantitative and Qualitative Empirical Insights', *Critical Public Health*, 21(4), 417–28.

Pfeiffer, S., Ritter, T. and Oestreicher, E. (2015) 'Food Insecurity in German Households: Qualitative and Quantitative Data on Coping, Poverty Consumerism and Alimentary Participation', *Social Policy & Society*, 14(3), 483–95.

Pierson, P. (2011) *The Welfare State over the Very Long Run*, ZeS-Working Paper, 02/2011. Bremen: Zentrium for Sozialpolitik.

Poole, D. and Parker, A.J. (1990) *Effects on Retailing of an Ageing Population*. Dublin: Centre for Retail Studies.

Pope, C. (2018) *The Battle Against Food Waste*. The Irish Times. 22 March 22. Available at: www.irishtimes.com/news/environment/the-battle-against-food-waste-1.3425288

Poppendieck, J. (1998) *Sweet Charity? Emergency Food and the End of Entitlement*. New York: Viking.

Powell, M. and Barrientos, A. (2004) 'Welfare Regimes and the Welfare Mix', *European Journal of Political Research*, 43, 83–105.

Purdy, J., McFarlane, G., Harvey, H., Rugkasa, J. and Willis, K. (2007) *Food Poverty and Policy in Northern Ireland*. Belfast: Public Health Alliance.

Radimer, K. (2002) 'Measurement of Household Food Security in the USA and Other Industrialised Countries', *Public Health Nutrition*, 5(6A), 859–64.

Radimer, K., Olson, C. and Campbell, C. (1990) 'Development of Indicators to Assess Hunger', *Journal of Nutrition*, 120, 1544–8.

Radimer, K., Olson, C., Greene, J., Campbell, C. and Habicht, J. (1992) 'Understanding Hunger and Developing Indicators to Assess it in Women and Children', *Journal of Nutrition Education*, 24(1), S36–45.

Raleigh, D. (2021) *Sharp Rise in Numbers Availing of Food Bank Services during COVID-19 Lockdown*. Available at: www.limerickpost.ie/2021/05/24/sharp-rise-in-numbers-availing-of-food-bank-services-during-covid-19-lockdown/

Ravaillon, M. (1992) *Poverty Comparisons: A Guide to Concepts and Methods*. LSMS Working Paper Number 88. Washington: The World Bank.

Redmond, P. (2016) *Very Low Work Intensity in Ireland and the EU*. Publicpolicy.ie. Available at: http://www.publicpolicyarchive.ie/wp-content/uploads/Redmond2016-v1.pdf

Rein, M. (1970) 'Problems in the Definition and Measurement of Poverty', in P. Townsend (ed) *The Concept of Poverty: Working Papers on Methods of Investigation and Life-Styles of the Poor in Different Countries*. London: Heinemann.

Renobales, M.D., San-Epifanio, L.E. and Molina, F. (2015) 'Social Supermarkets: A Dignifying Tool against Food Insecurity for People at Socio-Economic Risk', in M.D. Renobales and L.E. San-Epifanio (eds) *Envisioning a Future Without Food Waste and Food Poverty*. Bilbao: Wageningen, pp 285–90.

Riches, G. (1997) 'Hunger, Food Security and Welfare Policies: Issues and Debates in First World Societies', *Proceedings of the Nutrition Society*, 56(1a): 63–74.

Riches, G. (2002) 'Food Banks and Food Security: Welfare Reform, Human Rights and Social Policy: Lessons from Canada?', *Social Policy and Administration*, 36(6), 648–63.

Riches, G. and Silvasti, T. (2014) 'Hunger in the Rich World: Food Aid and Right to Food Perspectives', in G. Riches and T. Silvasti (eds) *First World Hunger Revisited*. London: Palgrave Macmillan.

Riches, G. and Tarasuk, V. (2014) 'Canada: Thirty Years of Food Charity and Public Policy Neglect', in G. Riches and T. Silvasti (eds) *First World Hunger Revisited*. London: Palgrave Macmillan.

Ringen, S. (1988) 'Direct and Indirect Measures of Poverty', *Journal of Social Policy*, 17(3), 351–65.

Robinson, S., Crozier, S. and Borland, S. (2004) 'Impact of Educational Attainment on the Quality of Young Women's Diets', *European Journal of Clinical Nutrition*, 58, 1174–80.

Rowntree, B.S. (1901) *Poverty: A Study of Town Life*. London: Macmillan.

Rowntree, B.S. (1937) *The Human Needs of Labour*. London: Longmans Green.

RTB (Residential Tenancies Board) (2018) *Rent Index 2018. Quarter 2.* Cork: ESRI.

Russell, H., McGinnity, F., Fahey, E. and Kenny, O. (2018) *Maternal Employment and the Cost of Childcare in Ireland. Research Series Number 73.* Dublin: ESRI.

Safefood (2011) *Food on a Low Income.* Available at: https://www.safefood.net/getmedia/b40137ee-815d-43dd-8f30-cbfdb08edd07/Full-report---Food-on-a-low-income.aspx?ext=.pdf

Safefood (2019) *What is the Cost of a Healthy Food Basket in the Republic of Ireland in 2018?.* Available at: www.budgeting.ie/download/pdf/vpsj__safefood_-_food_basket_research_-_report_roi_-_2018.pdf

Saint-Arnaud, S. and Bernard, P. (2003) 'Convergence or Resilience? A Hierarchical Cluster Analysis of the Welfare Regimes in Advanced Countries', *Current Sociology*, 51(5), 499–527.

Saint Ville, A., Po, J.Y., Sen, A., Bui, A. and Melgar-Quiñonez, H. (2019) 'Food Security and the Food Insecurity Experience Scale (FIES): Ensuring Progress by 2030', *Food Security*, 11, 483–91.

Saldaña, J. (2013) *The Coding Manual for Qualitative Researchers.* London: Sage Publications.

Saunders, P. (2012) 'Inequality and Poverty', in F. Castles, S. Leibfried, J. Lewis, H. Obinger and C. Pierson (eds) *The Oxford Handbook of the Welfare State.* Oxford: Oxford University Press.

Saxena, L.P. and Tornaghi, C. (2018) *The Emergence of Social Supermarkets in Britain: Food poverty, Food waste and Austerity Retail. Research Report. Centre for Agroecology, Water and Resilience.* Coventry: Coventry University.

Schoukens, P. and Barrio, A. (2017) 'The Changing Concept of Work: When does Typical Work become Atypical?', *European Labour Law Journal*, 8(4), 306–32.

Scruggs, L. and Allan, J. (2006) Welfare-state Decommodification in 18 OECD Countries: A Replication and Revision, *Journal of European Social Policy*, 16(1), 55–72.

Sen, A. (1983) 'Poor, Relatively Speaking', *Oxford Economic Papers*, 35, 153.

Sen, A. (1984) *Resources, Values and Development.* Oxford: Blackwell.

Shin, Y. and Ylä-Anttila, T. (2018) 'New Social Risk Groups, Industrial Relations Regimes and Union Membership', *Journal of European Social Policy*, 28(3), 242–54.

Silvasti, T. (2015) 'Food Aid: Normalising the Abnormal in Finland', *Social Policy & Society*, 14(3), 471–82.

Silvasti, T. and Karjalainen, J. (2014) 'Hunger in a Nordic Welfare State: Finland', in G. Riches and T. Silvasti (eds) *First World Hunger Revisited: Food Charity or the Right to Food?.* Basingstoke: Palgrave MacMillan.

Silvasti, T. and Tikka, V. (2020) 'New Frames for Food Charity in Finland,' in H. Lambie-Mumford and T. Silvasti (eds) *The Rise of Food Charity in Europe*. Bristol: Policy Press.

Simon Community (2018) *Locked Out of the Market XI. The Gap between Rent Supplement/HAP Limits and Market Rents*. Available at: https://galwaysimon.ie/wp-content/uploads/2020/10/Locked-Out-of-the-Market-XI-August-2018.pdf

Smeeding, T. (2016) 'Poverty Measurement', in D. Brady and L. Burton (eds) *The Oxford Handbook of the Social Science of Poverty*. Oxford: Oxford University Press.

Smith, M., Rabbitt, M. and Coleman- Jensen, A. (2017) 'Who Are the World's Food Insecure? New Evidence from the Food and Agriculture Organization's Food Insecurity Experience Scale', *World Development*, 93, 402–12.

Snell, C., Lambie-Mumford, H. and Thomson, H. (2018) 'Is there Evidence of Households Making a Heat or Eat Trade Off in the UK?', *Journal of Poverty and Social Justice*, 26(2), 225–43.

Social Exclusion Unit (2003) *Making the Connections: Transport and Social Exclusion. Interim findings from the Social Exclusion Unit*. London: Office of the Deputy Prime Minister, p 2.

Solar, O. and Irwin, A. (2010) *A Conceptual Framework for Action on the Social Determinants of Health. Social Determinants of Health Discussion Paper 2 (Policy and Practice)*. Geneva: World Health Organisation.

Sosenko, F., Livingstone, N. and Fitzpatrick, S. (2013) *Overview of Food Aid Provision in Scotland*, Heriot-Watt University. Edinburgh: The Scottish Government.

Sosenko, F., Littlewood, M., Bramley, G., Fitzpatrick, S., Blenkinsopp, J. and Wood, J. (2019) *State of Hunger. A Study of Poverty and Food Insecurity in the UK*. The Trussell Trust. Available at: www.stateofhunger.org/wp-content/uploads/2019/11/State-of-Hunger-Report-November2019-Digital.pdf

Spicker, P. (1990) 'Charles Booth: The Examination of Poverty', *Social Policy and Administration*, 24(1), 21–38.

Spicker, P., Leguizamón, S. and Gordon, D. (2007) *Poverty: An International Glossary. Second Edition*. London: Zed Books.

Spannagel, D. (2013) *In-work Poverty in Europe: Extent, Structure and Causal Mechanisms*, COPE Research Paper, Combating Poverty in Europe. Oldenburg, Germany.

Stabile, D. (2008) *The Living Wage: Lessons from the History of Economic Thought*. Cheltenham: Edward Elgar Publishing.

Standing, G. (2012) 'The Precariat: From Denizens to Citizens?', *Polity*, 44(4).

Standing, G. (2016) *The Precariat: The New Dangerous Class*. London: Bloomsbury Publishing.

Statistica (2019) *Distribution of Population with a Medical Card in Ireland from 2006 to 2018*. Available at: www.statista.com/statistics/660763/medical-card-scheme-ireland/

Stephens, M. and Leishman, C. (2017) 'Housing and Poverty: A Longitudinal Analysis', *Housing Studies*, 32(8), 1039–61.

Steptoe, A., Pollard, T.M. and Wardle, J. (1995) 'Development of a Measure of the Motives Underlying the Selection of Food: The Food Choice Questionnaire', *Appetite*, 25(3), 267–84.

Stigler, G. (1954) 'Schumpeter's History of Economic Analysis', *Journal of Political Economy*, 62.

SVP (Society of St Vincent de Paul) (2014) *Planning for the Right Kind of Recovery*. Dublin: SVP. Available at: www.svp.ie/getattachment/9003412e-ca8d-4efd-a83c-316cef5800a1/Pre-Budget-Submission-2015-Planning-for-the-right.aspx

SVP (Society of St Vincent de Paul) (2021a) *Cutting Back and Falling Behind Red C Report March 2021*. Available at: www.svp.ie/news-media/submissions/poverty-in-ireland/cutting-back-and-falling-behind-red-c-report-march.aspx

SVP (Society of St Vincent de Paul) (2021b) *Mission Statement*. Available at: www.svp.ie/about-us/mission-statement.aspx

Tafel (2021a) *Tafel Deutschland*. Available at: www.tafel.de/english-information/

Tafel (2021b) *Overcoming the Crisis Together*. Available at: https://www.tafel.de/fileadmin/media/Themen/Coronavirus/2020-12-04_Corona-Wirkungsbroschuere_EN_web.pdf

Taylor-Robinson, D., Rougeaux, E., Harrison, D., Whitehead, M., Barr, B. and Pearce, A. (2013) 'The Rise of Food Poverty in the UK', *British Medical Journal*, 347, f7157.

Threshold (2014) *Threshold Submission: Supplementary Welfare Allowance. Review of Maximum Rent Limits to Department of Social Protection*. Dublin: Threshold. Available at: www.threshold.ie/download/pdf/threshold_submission_to_review_of_rent_supplement_limits_july_2014.pdf

Times, The (2020) *Find the Gleaning of Life*. 13 December. Available at: www.thetimes.co.uk/static/audi-living-progress-technology/?region=ie

Townsend, P. (1979) *Poverty in the United Kingdom*. Harmondsworth: Penguin.

Townsend, P. (1985) 'A Sociological Approach to the Measurement of Poverty: A Rejoinder to Professor Amartya Sen', *Oxford Economic Papers*, 37, 659.

Townsend, P. (1993) *The International Analysis of Poverty*. London: Harvester Wheatsheaf.

Trussell Trust (2019) *Northern Ireland Food Banks Fear for Busiest Summer Ever*. Available at: www.trusselltrust.org/2019/06/27/northern-ireland-food-banks-fear-busiest-summer-ever/#:~:text=There%20are%2038%20food%20bank,Trust's%20network%20in%20Northern%20Ireland

Trussell Trust (2020a) *End of Year Stats*. Available at: www.trusselltrust.org/news-and-blog/latest-stats/end-year-stats/

Trussell Trust (2020b) *Primary Reasons for Referral to Trussell Trust Food Banks in 2019–20*. Available at: www.trusselltrust.org/news-and-blog/latest-stats/end-year-stats/

Trussell Trust (2021) *Hunger Free Future*. Available at: www.trusselltrust.org/hunger-free-future/

UK Parliament (2019) *Sustainable Development Goals in the UK Follow Up: Hunger, Malnutrition and Food Insecurity in the UK*. House of Commons Environmental Audit Committee. Available at: https://publications.parliament.uk/pa/cm201719/cmselect/cmenvaud/1491/1491.pdf

UK Parliament (2021) *Food Insecurity Exposed by COVID-19*. Available at: https://old.parliament.uk/business/committees/committees-a-z/commons-select/environment-food-and-rural-affairs-committee/news-parliament-2017/covid-19-and-food-supply-report-published-19-21/

UKSSD (UK Stakeholders for Sustainable Development) (2018) *Measuring Up. How the UK is performing on the UN Sustainable Development Goals*. Available at: https://sdgtoolkit.org/wp-content/uploads/2018/10/UKSSD-Measuring-up.pdf

UN (United Nations) (2015) *Resolution adopted by the General Assembly on 25 September 2015. A/RES/70/1. Transforming our World: The 2030 Agenda for Sustainable Development*. Available at: https://sdgs.un.org/2030agenda

UN (United Nations) (2019) *Sustainable Development Goals*. Available at: www.un.org/sustainabledevelopment/hunger/

UN (United Nations) (2021a) *UN Department of Economic and Social Affairs. Sustainable Development*. Available at: https://sdgs.un.org/goals

UN (United Nations Human Rights) (2021b) *International Covenant on Economic, Social and Cultural Rights*. Available at: www.ohchr.org/EN/ProfessionalInterest/Pages/CESCR.aspx

UN (United Nations Human Rights) (2021c) *OHCHR and the Right to Food*. Available at: www.ohchr.org/En/Issues/ESCR/Pages/food.aspx

UN (United Nations) (2021d) *Envision2030 Goal 2: Zero Hunger*. Available at: www.un.org/development/desa/disabilities/envision2030-goal2.html

UN FAO (United Nations Food and Agriculture Organization) (2016a) *Methods for Estimating Comparable Rates of Food Insecurity Experienced by Adults Throughout the World*. Rome: FAO.

UN FAO (United Nations Food and Agriculture Organization) (2016b) *The Food Insecurity Experience Scale*. Available at: www.fao.org/3/a-bl354e.pdf

UN FAO (United Nations Food and Agriculture Organization) (2018) *FAO Food Price Index*. Rome: Food and Agricultural Organisation of the United Nations. [Online]. Available at: www.fao.org/worldfoodsituation/foodpricesindex/en/

UN FAO (United Nations Food and Agriculture Organization) (2020) *The State of Food Security and Nutrition in the World. Transforming Food Systems for Affordable Healthy Diets*. Rome: FAO.

UN FAO (United Nations Food and Agriculture Organization) (2021) *Sustainable Development Goals*. Available at: www.fao.org/sustainable-development-goals/indicators/212/en/

USDA (United States Department of Agriculture) (2015) *Commemorating 20 Years of U.S. Food Security Measurement*. Available at: www.ers.usda.gov/amber-waves/2015/october/commemorating-20-years-of-us-food-security-measurement/

USDA Food and Nutrition Service (2021) *Supplemental Nutrition Assistance Program (SNAP). SNAP Eligibility*. Available at: www.fns.usda.gov/snap/eligibility#What are the SNAP income limits?

US Department of Health and Human Services (2018) *Poverty Thresholds and Poverty Guidelines*. Available at: https://aspe.hhs.gov/frequently-asked-questions-related-poverty-guidelines-and-poverty

Viebrock, E. and Clasen, J. (2009) 'Flexicurity and Welfare Reform: A Review', *Socio-Economic Review*, 7, 305–31.

Walker, R. (2014) *The Shame of Poverty*. Oxford: Oxford University Press.

Wang, J. and Van Vliet, O. (2016) 'Social Assistance and Minimum Income Benefits: Benefit Levels, Replacement Rates and Policies across 26 OECD countries, 1990–2009', *European Journal of Social Security*, 18(4).

Wanless, D. (2002) *Securing our Future Health: Taking a Long-Term View. Final Report*. London: HM Treasury.

Watson, D. and Maître, B. (2013) *Social Transfers and Poverty Alleviation in Ireland*. Dublin: Economic and Social Research Institute.

Watson, D., Banks, J. and Lyons, S. (2015) *Educational and Employment Experiences of People with a Disability in Ireland: An Analysis of the National Disability Survey*. Dublin: National Disability Authority.

Watson, D., Maître, B. and Whelan, C. (2012) *Work and Poverty in Ireland: An Analysis of the CSO Survey on Income and Living Conditions 2004–2010, Social Inclusion Report No. 3*. Dublin: Department of Social Protection.

Watson, D., Maître, B., Whelan, C. and Russell, H. (2016) *Social Risk and Social Class Patterns in Poverty and Quality of Life in Ireland: An Analysis of the CSO Survey on Income and Living Conditions, 2004 to 2013, Social Inclusion Report No. 6*. Dublin: Department of Social Protection and the Economic and Social Research Institute.

Watson, D., Maître, B., Grotti, R. and Whelan, C. (2018) *Poverty Dynamics of Social Risk Groups in the EU: An Analysis of the EU Statistics on Income and Living Conditions, 2005 to 2014*. Dublin: ESRI.

Wayand, O. (1970) *The Measurement of Poverty* (No. 19). Canada: Department of National Health and Welfare.

Wickham, J. and Bobek, A. (2016) *Bogus Self-Employment in the Construction Industry*. Available at: www.tasc.ie/download/pdf/bogus_selfemploymentfinal.pdf

Williamson, D. and Reutter, L. (1999) 'Defining and Measuring Poverty: Implications for the Health of Canadians', *Health Promotion International*, 14(4), 355–64.

Wills, W. (2011) 'Introduction to Food: Representations and Meanings', *Sociological Research Online*, 16(2), 16.

World Food Summit (1996) *Food Security. Policy Brief. June 2006. Issue 2.* Available at: www.fao.org/fileadmin/templates/faoitaly/documents/pdf/pdf_Food_Security_Cocept_Note.pdf

Wren, M. and Connolly, S. (2016) *Challenges in Achieving Universal Healthcare in Ireland*. Dublin: ESRI.

Wrigley, N. (2002) '"Food Deserts" in British Cities: Policy Context and Research Priorities', *Urban Studies*, 39(11), 2029–40.

Wunderlich, G. and Norwood, J. (2006) *Food Insecurity and Hunger in the United States: An Assessment of the Measure. Panel to Review U.S Department of Agriculture's Measurement of Food Insecurity and Hunger, Committee on National Statistics, National Research Council*. Washington: National Academies Press.

Zappone, K. (2018) *High Childcare Costs Linked to Lower Employment among Mothers. Response to Findings*. Available at: www.esri.ie/news/high-childcare-costs-linked-to-lower-employment-among-mothers/

Zimmerman, C. (1932) 'Ernst Engel's Law of Expenditures for Food', *The Quarterly Journal of Economics*, 47(1), 78–101.

Index

S